With Heart and Hand

A Manual for Women in God's Service

Beneth Jones and Bobbie Yearick

D1403515

 BOB JONES UNIVERSITY PRESS
Greenville, South Carolina 29614

Library of Congress Cataloging-in-Publication Data:

Jones, Beneth Peters, date.
    With heart and hand : a manual for women in God's service /
Beneth Jones and Bobbie Yearick.
        p.   cm.
    ISBN 0-89084-641-3
    1. Women in church work—Protestant churches. 2. Clergymen's
wives. I. Yearick, Bobbie, date.   II. Title.
    BV4415.J57   1992
    248.8 ' 92 ' 082—dc20   92-24757
                                                            CIP

NOTE:
The fact that materials produced by other publishers are referred to in this volume does not constitute an endorsement by Bob Jones University Press of the content or theological position of materials produced by such publishers. The position of Bob Jones University Press, and the University itself, is well known. Any references and ancillary materials are listed as an aid to the student or the teacher and in an attempt to maintain the accepted academic standards of the publishing industry.

All Scripture used throughout the book is from the King James Version unless otherwise indicated. Italicized portions indicate emphases by the authors.

With Heart and Hand
A Manual for Women in God's Service

Beneth Jones and Bobbie Yearick

Edited by Carolyn Cooper and Rebecca Moore
Graphics by Roger Bruckner and Brian Johnson

© 1992 Bob Jones University Press
Greenville, South Carolina 29614

ISBN 0-89084-641-3

20   19   18   17   16   15   14   13   12   11   10   9   8   7   6

Table of Contents

The Maidservant's Hazards

Preface

The simple life has disappeared in America. Pressures are evident everywhere, and stress has become a national characteristic. As uncomplicated living fades, Christian ministry faces ever greater challenges. The church is experiencing intense, complex spiritual warfare. The struggle may leave church shingles unmarked, but it batters ministry personnel. The urgency of the times and pleas from ministry women have motivated our writing this book.

Because we are addressing both married and unmarried women, terminology has proved cumbersome. To simplify the matter, therefore, the term *Maidservants* is often used.

Throughout the book we try to emphasize that effective Christian service is not just a matter of doing. Our doing must consistently reflect and rise from a *being* that is well pleasing to our heavenly Father: hence the title, **With Heart and Hand.** In these spiritually dark days, it is evident there is much work for our hands; ceaseless, expansive activity of hands, however, can amount to "wood, hay, and stubble" if our hearts are not constantly open to the working of God's hands.

Our intention in writing this book is not to entertain you.

It is not to feed you intellectual or emotional froth.

It is not to make you feel a failure.

Instead, our burden is to *help you*—by presenting scriptural and practical materials in as many areas as possible to strengthen you in spirit, mind, and heart.

We pray God will use this book to minister to you who are so important to His great cause. We write . . .

Sincerely in His love—and ours,
Beneth Jones and Bobbie Yearick

The
Maidservant
Herself

Chapter 1

Who Is This Woman?

So—you are or hope to be a preacher's wife/full-time Christian servant. What tremendous opportunity, privilege, and responsibility await you! In the pages that follow we will consider many facets of this high and holy calling. But it is appropriate to begin by focusing upon you, upon the *self* you bring to service.

Your Call

Is there a need for a calling into ministry? Do you *feel* called? If you are single, you doubtless do have that sure sense of direct calling from the Lord. But there are some who say that a wife of a full-time Christian servant also must have a personal, "feelable" call. Bible principle says otherwise: the wife of a God-called *man* is herself called—as she submits to her husband's leadership. Feelings have little or nothing to do with the matter.

Perhaps your question concerning the call to ministry is not "whether" but "*why*—why me?" We women tend to focus on our flaws, failures, weaknesses, inadequacies. We consider them barriers to service. Scripture contradicts that self-denigration in II Corinthians 4:7: "But we have this treasure in *earthen vessels,* that the excellency of the power may be of God, and not of us." Our very inadequacies give God the opportunity to demonstrate and derive glory from His all-sufficiency! If we will listen beyond the sound of our knocking knees, we can hear the Lord's still, small voice assuring us, "Faithful is he that calleth you, who also will do it" (I Thess. 5:24).

In our humanity, each of us at times may struggle with doubts. But *serious* and *chronic* doubts about the call to service spring from one of two sources: lack of salvation or presence of sin.

Salvation? Could that be a need in the life of a woman in full-time Christian service? Yes. It is easy to adopt the outward marks of believership without ever having known the inward cleansing of Christ's blood. Not long ago a Christian periodical printed a story about a woman who had been a ministry wife for *eighteen years* before she at last realized she had never been saved. And yes, this was a fundamentalist, Bible-believing church. The Lord Jesus Himself sounded a solemn warning when He said, "Not every one that saith unto me, Lord, Lord, shall enter into the kingdom of heaven" (Matt. 7:21). The Apostle Paul, addressing those who claimed to be Christians, urged, "Examine yourselves, whether ye be in the faith" (II Cor. 13:5). We must each be sure that we have personally appropriated God's free gift of salvation. The steps are these:

A—*Acknowledging* that we are sinners and deserve punishment in hell
B—*Being sorry for,* confessing, and forsaking our sins
C—*Claiming* the cleansing from sin possible only through the vicarious, substitutionary death of Jesus Christ on the cross of Calvary

God's Word makes salvation clearly understandable in the following passages:

Romans 3:10-12	II Corinthians 5:21
Romans 3:23	Galatians 2:16
Romans 6:23	Ephesians 2:8-9
Romans 10:9-10, 13	Colossians 1:21-22
Romans 5:1	Colossians 2:13-14
Romans 8:1	

We do not want you to *doubt* your salvation; we want you *to be sure* of it. Assurance is not a matter of feeling but a recognition of fact. It is a God-stated fact that "whosoever shall call upon the name of the Lord shall be saved" (Rom. 10:13). If you have sincerely called upon Jesus Christ to cleanse you from your sins by His blood, then He has done so. Otherwise, God is a liar.

The second reason for consistently doubting a call to service is unconfessed sin. The psalmist said, "If I regard iniquity in my heart, the Lord will not hear me" (Ps. 66:18). God does not expect a flawless vessel for His service; He does demand a *clean* one. We must daily confess our specific sins to the Lord (agree with God that they *are* sins), repent of them, and through His forgiveness keep our hearts pure before Him. We frail humans need daily to undergo the spiritual renovation the psalmist craves in Psalm 51:10: "Create in me a clean heart, O God, and renew a right spirit within me."

The Christian life is not the frivolous thing some claim it to be. It presents us with a strong challenge: "But as he which hath called you is holy, so be ye holy in all manner of conversation [life]; Because it is written, Be ye holy; for I am holy" (I Pet. 1:15-16). Holiness as sanctification—a special setting-apart *unto the Lord*—is God's desire for His servants. Although every believer should possess holiness, we to whom God entrusts spiritual leadership have a special responsibility to do so.

Please settle the matter of your call right now, dear Maidservant. Take care of whatever heart work needs to be done. Then move forward—rejoicing in God's promises and resisting Satan's promptings.

Your Qualifications

Do you question your qualifications for ministry? Satan uses two weapons in this attack: your unrealistic concept of a ministry woman and your unhealthy concept of self.

If a Polly Perfection towers in our subconscious, the inability to measure up haunts us. The truth is, of course, that Polly doesn't exist apart from our imagination, and *nobody* could attain the standard of perfection she represents. But Satan never tires of using those "green withs" (Judges 16:7) to bind us and hinder our service for God.

The way we feel about ourselves influences our actions and our attitudes. Knowing that, the Devil plays upon feminine tendencies toward introspection and self-denigration, orchestrating feelings of inadequacy. He has some favorite tunes to pluck upon those strings.

Background

To the Maidservant with a blighted personal or family history, Satan hisses, "Just who do you think you are? You really came from the pits; how can *you* be in full-time Christian service?" Don't listen to him! Instead, go to the Word of God. Neither Ruth nor Rahab could point with pride to her past; yet the Lord recorded their service for time and eternity.

Perhaps youthful memories center on rejection, and you struggle against feelings of worthlessness. Read the Bible account of Joseph, a supreme example of rejection and mistreatment—but also of incalculable usefulness as he committed himself and his hurts to God.

You may wrestle with the memory of specific sins. Satan not only rattles skeletons but also runs 3-D pictures from the past. Blank out those sights and sounds with reassuring verses such as Psalm 103:12; Isaiah 44:22; Micah 7:18-19; and Joel 2:25.

That which is forgiven is *forgotten* by God; He doesn't want yesterday's sin to hinder today's service. In refusing to let the Devil use your past against you, you enable God to *use it positively* in ministry. How? He will bring along your pathway people you can help in a special way *because of your own experiences.* Our loving Lord delights to give "beauty for ashes" (Isa. 61:3).

Personality

Most of us at one time or another wonder whether we have the personality for Christian work. But just what type really meets the "requirements"? God uses all kinds of personalities in His service. He prepares and fits individuals for specific places and types of ministry. While we should accept and use our basic personality types, we also need to evaluate honestly and eliminate any personality "porcupine quills." Those spiky qualities that irritate others are not God's fault; they're ours. Among them are a whining manner, overaggressiveness, and a cutting tongue.

Education

Do you feel inadequate because of limited formal education? Don't. In the first place, there are some Ph.D.'s who lack the common sense to get out of a rain shower. Second, you can trust the Lord to make possible the training needed for the job He asks you to do. Educational opportunities should, of course, be grasped when offered. If, however, the doors of formal schooling did not open to you, why continue to stand outside them to cry or complain? Learning is not restricted to high school and college. Experience educates. An important part of real education—a part easily acquired—is knowing where to go for the information you need.

Biblical Knowledge

Must a full-time Christian servant be a walking Bible concordance? She should have enough knowledge of Scripture to help needy hearts; but a *living* familiarity with God's Word outweighs any theological studies. Faithfulness in applying the Word to your own life will show God faithful in supplying Scripture passages for the help of others.

Natural Abilities

Few ministry women look upon all aspects of service as "their thing" by natural inclination or talent. For example, most preachers' wives are not the never-meet-a-stranger, gregarious type; yet, obviously, they must constantly be meeting people. Does their lack of "type" mean they are unfit for ministry? Actually, it indicates the opposite. A natural lack is an opportunity for the *supernatural* to be demonstrated. When a Maidservant knows she is inadequate for a task, she relies all the more upon the Lord. His all-sufficiency becomes both prop and praise. It is in our "unfit" points that we learn to say with the Apostle Paul, "When I am weak, then am I strong" (II Cor. 12:10).

Some feelings of inadequacy are artificial—self-inflicted by our comparing ourselves with someone else. Either we measure ourselves against some nonexistent ideal, or we compare ourselves with a flesh-and-blood person who seems to shine in areas in which we barely flicker. But "comparisons are odious," as we have heard. They are also harmful and foolish. Paul warned the Corinthians against the error of those who "measuring themselves by themselves, and comparing themselves among themselves, are not wise" (II Cor. 10:12). Comparisons bind us with excuses, feelings of inferiority, and fear.

An Honest Evaluation

If God cared enough to design you right down to the finest details (Ps. 139), you should at least care enough to recognize the uniqueness that He created. Think about yourself—a vessel created for God's use—in the following areas.

Emotional stability/maturity. What do small emotional blows do to you? What about big ones? Do you maintain a fairly consistent emotional plane from day to day, or do you swing wildly between highs and lows? Is there a particular emotional pattern discernibly connected with your menstrual cycle? What about *control* of your emotions? Are you master of them, or are they of you?

Personality. What is your basic personality type? There are several distinct personality profiles and combinations of them. Each has strong and weak points. Knowing something of your general type can not only enhance understanding of yourself but also give clues to why other personality types interact with you as they do.

Appearance. What does the way you look say to those around you? Appearance is a strong indicator of character, and it inspires either positive or negative reactions in others. Cleanliness and care are musts for the ministry woman.

Leadership ability. Are you able to lead, when necessary, without either cringing self-denigration or dictatorial self-assertion?

Social conduct. Are you at ease in social situations at various cultural, educational, and professional levels? Does your knowledge and practice of etiquette serve you well?

Mental ability. Do you recognize and accept the level of mentality God has given you, neither writing yourself off as "dumb" nor priding yourself with intellectual superiority? Do you provide yourself meaningful mental exercise with thought-provoking reading?

Marriage. How would you classify your husband-wife relationship? Is it excellent, mediocre, or poor? Are you constantly working to build your marriage? Or do you assume it will survive on its own momentum?

If you are a single Maidservant, are you at peace in your heart about your singleness? Do you honestly and wholeheartedly believe that God's plan for you is loving and just?

Undertake your evaluation honestly. Neither give yourself unearned credit nor withhold recognition of worth. You certainly may choose whatever form you'd like for your self-scrutiny. But whatever the form, begin by listing your *best attribute* in each category. (Yes, we are trying to offset your natural tendency to downgrade yourself!)

No one need ever see your analysis. You can tear it up and throw it in "File 13" if you want. First, though, look it over carefully. Think about it. Pray about it. As you recognize your positives and negatives, you can claim God's help to utilize the former and shore up the latter.

Your goal is that "ultimate attitude" toward yourself that is God's view. Reaching it requires four steps:

1. Recognize God's specific, special creation of your unique self: "Thy hands have made me and fashioned me: give me understanding, that I may learn thy commandments" (Ps. 119:73).
2. Rejoice in the wisdom and sufficiency of the One whom you serve: "Thou art my servant; I have chosen thee and not cast thee away. Fear thou not for I am with thee. Be not dismayed for I am thy God. I will strengthen thee, yea I will help thee, yea I will uphold thee with the right hand of my righteousness" (Isa. 41:9-10).
3. Respond to the obligation of being a "worker together with God." Pinpoint those things that detract from your co-laboring with God and prevent your best performance. Tackle the adjustments joyfully, claiming this encouragement: "Take away the dross from the silver, and there shall come forth a vessel for the finer" (Prov. 25:4).
4. Rededicate yourself to God, relinquishing the controls of your life to Him who "is able to keep you from falling, and to present you faultless before the presence of his glory with exceeding joy, . . . the only wise God our Saviour, [to whom] be glory and majesty, dominion and power, both now and ever" (Jude 24-25).

Chapter 2

The Secret Saint

A woman's Christian service can be no more effective than her private devotional life. We have been given a heavenly task. If we try to do it with earthly resources, we will only fail and bring discredit to the Lord. No wonder the Devil untiringly tries to destroy our private times with God.

First Peter 1:13-16 states the results of a vital devotional life: "Wherefore gird up the loins of your mind; be sober, and hope to the end for the grace that is to be brought unto you at the revelation of Jesus Christ. As obedient children, not fashioning yourselves according to the former lusts in your ignorance: But as he which hath called you is holy, so be ye holy in all manner of conversation." Here we may find six "S" elements to enable our lives and service:

Gird up tells us to seek and nurture **strength.**
Be sober urges us to **sobriety** (moral alertness).
Hope to the end indicates **steadfastness.**
Obedient recommends **submissiveness.**
Resisting enjoins to **spotlessness.**
Be ye holy challenges to **sanctification.**

Strength, sobriety, steadfastness, submissiveness, spotlessness, sanctification—these are the evidences of our readiness for service. Only as we **daily** ingest spiritual vitamins through Bible study and prayer can we attain this standard.

Bible Study

Authenticity of the Bible

Our Christian faith is no ethereal concoction; it is rooted in the Bible—God's own Word. It is no wonder that Satan makes varied, vicious, and constant attacks upon scriptural authenticity, not only in the world at large but also at the personal, private level. He never wearies of whispering, "*Hath* God said?" The Lord Himself has responded for us: "Heaven and earth shall pass away, but my words shall not pass away" (Matt. 24:35). Paul underscores this truth in his words to Timothy: "All scripture is given by inspiration of God, and is profitable for doctrine, for reproof, for correction, for instruction in righteousness" (II Tim. 3:16). That eternally settled Word of God, the Bible, is our text for the ministry God has given us. It must be *taken in* before it can be *lived out* or *given out* effectively.

Attitude Toward the Bible

We are to have a hunger, a thirst, a consuming love for the blessed Book that would cause us to exclaim with the psalmist, "Oh, how I love thy law!" and "How sweet are thy words unto my taste!" Without daily intake from the Bible, we become weak, incapable of rendering the service to which we are called. With this intake, we acquire the necessary enablement and full preparedness of the mature Christian servant, "perfect [mature], throughly furnished unto all good works" (II Tim. 3:17).

Approach to Bible Study

The Bible is not a self-help, fill-in-the-blanks textbook. It does not mean merely what *we want it to mean*. God's Word specifically warns against "private interpretation." Instead, we are given a teacher to help us understand the Word: the Holy Spirit.

But the Comforter, which is the Holy Ghost, whom the Father will send in my name, he shall teach you all things, and bring all things to your remembrance, whatsoever I have said unto you (John 14:26).

But God hath revealed them unto us by his Spirit; for the Spirit searcheth all things, yea, the deep things of God. For what man knoweth the things of a man, save the spirit of man which is in him? even so the things of God knoweth no man, but the Spirit of God. Now we have received, not the spirit of the world, but the spirit which is of God; that we might know the things that are freely given to us of God (I Cor. 2:10-12).

Rather than being haphazard, we should apply a firm approach to Bible study. That comes from recognizing our personal need, determining to be faithful, and setting a specific time for daily Bible reading.

There are practical points to consider for establishing and maintaining a viable daily devotional period. First, *determine the place*. It should be reasonably apart from busyness, the comings and goings of the household. The Bible calls it "the closet," a place of privacy and concentration.

Second, *choose the time of day* that is best for you. Some state unequivocally that one time is superior to all others. They do not realize that they are insisting on what is best for *them*. Your schedule and indeed your whole physical and emotional makeup may legislate against that artificially prescribed "best" time. Choose whatever segment of the day offers the least interruption and allows the greatest alertness and responsiveness.

Bible reading itself needs to have a concrete, manageable format. It is not enough just to let the Bible fall open haphazardly in "eenie-meenie-minie-moe" style.

No matter how earnestly we plan for daily devotions, we must ultimately *work the plan*. Go to the appointed place, at the chosen time, to follow your established reading plan. Do it faithfully, every day. We are creatures of habit; we can make habit work *for* instead of *against* our spiritual growth.

Personal devotions are exactly that: personal. Tailor your devotions to fit your individual life. It may take some time to devise a plan that fits precisely yet leaves freedom for adjustment. Our lives, our very selves, are not stagnant; they fluctuate. Sometimes your usual Bible study may leave you "dry." That's the time to vary your pattern, to approach from a different direction, as it were. For instance, perhaps you've enjoyed a read-through-the-Bible plan for more than a year. But then comes a period when your reading stirs you neither mentally nor spiritually. Change!

Drop the read-through approach. Begin a study of a single character, a word, a book, a theme.

A reducible-expandable provision in your reading plan also is helpful, since days so seldom produce identical demands. God of course knows and understands exactly where we are emotionally and spiritually. He can just as powerfully give encouragement from a single verse as from ten chapters read in tandem. This provision in no way excuses skipping or skimping Bible reading; it simply allows for reasonable flexibility for ever-varied days. The important thing is that we genuinely seek blessing and instruction each time we open the Word. The psalmist prayed to this purpose when he said, ''Open thou mine eyes, that I may behold wondrous things out of thy law'' (Ps. 119:18).

There are women who like to brag of the hours they spend in Bible reading—to the exclusion of other responsibilities. Such women have things topsy-turvy; their touted spiritual superiority masks pride and laziness. The Bible is a **living** Book; God intends that it be used to fit us for daily living.

Sometimes the day's schedule is not the problem: our feelings are. Some days we simply don't *feel* like reading the Bible. We grump inwardly with ''I'm too tired'' or ''I'm not 'with it' today'' or ''I can't seem to get anything out of it anyway'' or ''I'm just not in the mood.'' Do our grumps and grumblings excuse us from our appointment? No. Let's face it: feelings fluctuate crazily. If we relegate Bible reading to the days we feel like reading, our spiritual selves will wither. We must go to the Word daily, regardless of feelings. In fact, we most need the Word when we *least* feel like reading it.

Daily Bible reading and study will not have the needed impact if our focus is incorrect. First, we must focus upon the Word itself. Simple as that sounds, it is not always simple to maintain. The outstanding diverters of proper focus are study helps. A study Bible, Bible dictionary, commentary, handbook, or Bible atlas, while useful, can impair our taste for the undiluted milk of the Word. Any ready-made ''formula'' is necessarily diluted, inadequate for our needs.

Second, proper Bible study focuses on the Lord Jesus Christ. The written Word becomes a telescope to reveal the Living Word, the Word made flesh. It is *His Person* we are to know, to love, to cling to, to reflect. Pitifully, there are any number of Christians (even Christian leaders) across America who can quote reams of Scripture but whose attitudes, words, and lives reflect little or nothing of the Living Word.

Biblical knowledge should be *personalized* knowledge. It is, after all, God's personal, intimate communication with us. One way to personalize biblical knowledge is to mark pertinent passages. You may choose underlining, highlighting, starring, or some other method. A *color-coded* system makes it especially easy to locate verses according to subject. The following is the color key for Beneth's Bible:

Red—salvation
Blue—prophecy and promises
Green—the Godhead
Yellow—Christian living
Orange—sin and Satan
Pink—women and family

Bobbie, too, uses color coding, but she makes different color-subject assignments.

Whether helping you find a passage for your own edification or directing you to a verse for counseling others, your chosen marking formula will guide you to the needed portions of the Word.

When we come upon a section of Scripture that speaks to us in a special way, we think, "This is wonderful; I'll never forget the blessing of this passage and its application for today!" But we do forget—very quickly. Keeping a **spiritual diary** crystallizes our thinking. It is also a wonderful way to store up blessing for later read-throughs when we feel discouraged, dry, or desperate. A spiritual diary is both personal and private. It need not be an example of flawless penmanship or journalistic skill. It is, in essence, a heart talking to itself about how God has talked to it.

Just as our study of the written Word is to reveal the Living Word, so our own handwritten response/interpretation/application is only a means to an end: an encourager to life integration. The Bible is not a museum piece to be studied with detached, analytical interest. It is God's tool for changing us, for shaping us into conformity to the Lord Jesus Christ.

The essential ingredient for filling a life with the Living Word is to fill heart and mind with the written Word. Satan delights to see us close our Bibles and our spiritual diaries, leaving the message within closed covers. God, on the other hand, is delighted when we are not content to read thoughtlessly. He urges us, in the words of Paul, "Meditate upon these things; give thyself wholly to them; that thy profiting may appear to all" (I Tim. 4:15).

Meditation is the key to extending Bible intake beyond actual clock time. Scripture meditation is not difficult. Choose a verse (or two) from your day's Bible reading. Memorize it or write it on a card to keep with you throughout the day. Let your mind *circulate* through the passage—asking questions that delve into meaning, examining nuances by emphasizing various words, illustrating truths by your own experience, and thinking of similar or complementary passages.

Meditation for the believer is not done in a pretzeled squat with a beatific facial expression. It takes place while the body is occupied with those myriad duties that fill our days but leave our minds free. Meditation goes beyond memorization: it channels God's Word from the mind to the heart, where it can influence our attitudes and actions. The psalmist understood the importance of meditation when he wrote, "Thy word have I hid in mine heart, that I might not sin against thee" (Ps. 119:11). Likewise Solomon, in his warning to the young, said, "Keep thy heart with all diligence; for out of it are the issues of life" (Prov. 4:23).

Bible study is half of the Maidservant's ongoing conversation with God: the listening half. The more we attend to the instruction of the written Word and see revealed in it the Living Word, the more we will be driven to practice the second half of our spiritual conversation.

Prayer

Here is the other half of the living spiritual relationship: talking to our heavenly Father. Of all believers, we Maidservants should be leaders in the principles and practice of prayer. But to the question "Do you pray enough?" few could answer yes. By and large we are a prayerless people. The anemic condition of fundamentalist churches proclaims the sad fact that we have substituted formulas, programs, and principles for prayer. One study showed that the average preacher spends less than seven minutes per day in prayer!

Preparation for Prayer

We dash into, and out of, prayer times so breathlessly that the thought of *preparing* for prayer seems strange. These preliminary steps would increase our prayers' effectiveness:

1. Be certain of salvation (Rom. 10:13).
2. Search out any unconfessed sin (Ps. 51:10).
3. Prepare the heart by reading the Word (Rom. 10:17).
4. Genuinely desire to please God (Heb. 11:6).
5. Reverence God's holiness and righteousness (Matt. 6:14-15).

The Power of Prayer

We have lost sight of prayer's potency: in prayer we enter the very presence of the GOD WHO IS. Despite puny challenges to His existence and His Being, the great I AM broods eternally, unchangingly, over all. His eye is in every place, beholding the evil and the good. All that we know, all that exists, was created by Him and continues only as He allows. If we could grasp even in the smallest degree what God's existence really means, our prayer lives would be more active and our self-sufficient lives closer to retirement.

God not only exists; He rewards. Throughout the Bible that fact is stated and illustrated. Rather than being aloof from His creation, God maintains constant interest in it. He says to us now as clearly as to Jeremiah in his day, "Call unto me, and I will answer thee, and shew thee great and mighty things, which thou knowest not" (Jer. 33:3).

The power tapped by prayer is **limitless power.** There are no impossibles with our heavenly Father. Despite that fact, we choose to bumble along in our own strength, grope via our scant wisdom, and stand helpless before minor obstacles.

The Price of Prayer

Whatever our excuses for prayerlessness, the real reason is simple: **prayer costs.** It means sacrifice. She who desires effectiveness in prayer must be ready to sacrifice herself, her worldly reputation (after all, prayer isn't a *spotlight,* but a *closet* thing), her time and energy, her feelings, and her will. Real prayer is labor—agonizing labor—and so rare in our day as to be almost nonexistent. How different we, and the world, would be were we pray-ers!

Persons of Prayer

The Bible is filled with examples of praying believers. Just a passing mention of some should encourage our personal prayer efforts.

Daniel and Nehemiah demonstrate patriotic prayers. The New Testament tells us to pray for those in authority over us. The psalmist reminds us that the leader's heart is as a river in God's hand, which He directs according to His will.

The prayer of the prodigal son shows tremendous change in heart attitude. His first petition, "give me," is selfish; his latter, "make me," indicates submission.

Virtually every prayer recorded in God's Word can instruct and inspire. Who can fail to be taught and encouraged by the prayers of Hannah, of the publican, of the Apostle Paul? God doesn't stop with giving us examples of those who prayed. The Lord Jesus gave a pattern prayer in answer to a disciple's request, "Lord, teach us to pray" (Luke 11:1-4). Careful study of that pattern yields rich insights into prayer. The Lord Himself practiced His teaching on prayer. Even a cursory look at the earthly ministry of Jesus shows that what He talked about, He did: He who was Himself God was the **most prayerful of men.**

Principles of Prayer

As we go to God in prayer, we should recognize that He has the resources to supply our every need: physical, material, spiritual, and social. If we feel poorly supplied, in most instances it is because we have not prayed. We have not because we ask not (James 4:2).

Prayer is not without its problems. For instance, the answer may be delayed; it may be difficult, not what we had in mind; or there may be only silence in response to our petitions. When facing such question marks, the believer ultimately must come to the place where he *lets God be God,* trusting his Father's omniscience and love.

Prayer is basically of three types: adoration, intercession, and petition. Most of us major on the latter and skimp on (or skip) the former two.

There is no prescribed, set posture for prayer. The Bible shows individuals praying in a variety of body positions: kneeling, lying prostrate, standing, sitting, walking, and bowing. It is thrilling to realize that we can pray *any*time, *any*where, *every*where.

Practicalities for Prayer

We Maidservants may feel frustrated by the fact that so many prayer requests come to us. Those within our immediate circle of ministry and those outside it seem to be always saying, "Please pray for . . ." The request for prayer support or intercession is a precious demonstration of trust as people share their hearts' burdens and rely upon our joining their prayer efforts. But soon the cry comes, "How can I possibly remember and take time to pray for all the prayer needs?"

The answer is to join practical organizational and scheduling skills to spiritual endeavor. Your prayer plan, like your Bible-reading plan, should be individually tailored. The following suggestions may prove helpful.

Prayer cards. Include one name per card. List specific prayer needs. Record dates the person was prayed for.

Lists. Keep one for preachers and their wives, one for evangelistic couples, one for missionaries, one for the unsaved, one for wayward believers.

Prayer bulletins. Start with the one from your own ministry.

Missionary notebook. Include a map, a prayer card, a photograph, and the latest letter from each missionary work.

Church directory. Bobbie and Dave take Hampton Park Baptist's directory with them on driving trips, praying through the directory as they travel.

Assigned days. Prayer requests can be grouped and assigned to specific days of the week.

> Monday—family
> Tuesday—friends
> Wednesday—church
> Thursday—missions
> Friday—unsaved
> Saturday—local, state, and national leaders
> Sunday—special requests

Assigned times. Rather than grouping and distributing prayer requests among the days of the week, you may prefer to compartmentalize according to the clock:

Morning—family
Noon—missions and ministries
Evening—the unsaved
Bedtime—special requests

The above suggestions are only that. They simply illustrate various methods for achieving effectiveness in prayer.

A final note: consider *letting people know when they are being remembered in your prayers.* This does not mean, necessarily, sending a personal note each time. It might be a matter of writing once to each missionary on your list to say, ''I want you to know that I pray specifically for you and your ministry on/at _____.'' Or send the prayer card with that person's name and the times/dates prayed for over a certain period. What an encouragement it is for any one of us to learn that someone really is praying! We blood-cleansed believers have the immeasurable privilege of constant communication with the God of all eternity as we stand before Him clothed in the robes of Christ's righteousness.

Bible study and prayer—these form the foundation and superstructure of our Christian life and ministry. Without them we stand upon, and extend to others, **nothing.**

Chapter 3

Hale and Hearty

Guarding the physical health of herself and her family, if she is married, is an important part of a ministry woman's stewardship responsibility. These earthly bodies are only clay; their neglect or mistreatment lessens effective service for the Lord.

It may be more difficult for the single ministry woman to monitor her nutrition rightly than for the married woman: she has no family for whose health she's responsible; her daily schedule may be less structured because of her independent activities; mealtimes' opportunity for relaxed conversation is not a factor; cooking meals for one may seem unnecessary effort; the temptation to eat on the run while doing something "constructive" may be strong. Although those may seem legitimate excuses on the human level, they do not circumvent our assignment as temple caretakers.

Nutrition

Food Necessities

A sensible diet promotes good health. Healthful food intake is less a matter of bounty than it is of balance. Many cookbooks contain nutrition charts. Take time to study them so that you know whether or not your meals provide a nutritionally sound diet. Daily intake should include the following:

Vitamins. B vitamins enhance energy. E helps healing and heart. C retards bruising and may help prevent colds, and so forth.

Minerals. Our bodies are dependent upon delicately balanced minerals. We are literally made of earth.

Protein. This substance is the basic body builder.

Carbohydrates. These are necessary to make vitamins work properly.

Fats. Fats contribute to food assimilation and to healthy skin and hair.

Fiber. Fiber is the key to a healthy digestive tract.

Water. Our bodies are largely composed of water and demand generous daily liquid intake.

A selection of foods, including something from each of the main food groups (meats, dairy, grains, fruits, and vegetables), ordinarily supplies daily dietary needs. A good multiple vitamin can be an effective *supplement,* but not a *replacement.*

Buy wisely when shopping for food, taking advantage of food bargains. Look for markdowns on older vegetables or slightly darkened meats. Learn the markdown schedule of the store or stores you patronize and plan your shopping trips accordingly. Careful shopping can feed your household well without depleting your pocketbook.

Food Fads

Common sense in eating is better than faddism. There are food fads just as there are fashion fads. New books are constantly being written proposing some wondrously effective diet. The trouble is, hardly any two of them agree! Each author spends a chapter or two trying to convince us that the other self-proclaimed authorities are wrong and he is right; he then proceeds to set forth his own ''discoveries.'' Most fad diets shortchange you in one or more of the needed dietary components and thereby endanger health. Prevalent in Christian circles, unfortunately, are ''food evangelists'' who try to convert others to dietary dos and don'ts. It's wiser to hang on to your wallet and your common sense than be converted to food fads.

Food Preparation

Food preparation affects flavor. Most of us must choose the tougher cuts of meat for economy's sake. But we can increase their palatability by proper cooking methods. For example, low-heat, extended-time cooking makes meats tender. Also, some new flavoring tricks may help. The fact that you are accustomed to a certain combination of flavors for pot roast doesn't mean you must always do it that way. Marinating meats is an excellent way to flavor as well as tenderize them. Try different marinades to find several that work well for you. Vegetables, by contrast, retain both flavor and nutritional value better when cooked just to the crisp-tender stage.

Physical Exercise

Exercise, in combination with a balanced diet, makes for stamina, strength, and weight loss/maintenance. Some Christians (especially the very sluggish) like to present a "spiritual" excuse: "Well, the Bible says 'exercise profiteth *little.*'" Actually, Bible scholars tell us the better rendering of that verse puts an *a* between *profiteth* and *little*—to read, "Exercise profiteth a little." In other words, physical exercise does provide some profit. Moreover, the Apostle Paul lived in a day when the whole tone of life was physically active. Imagine, for instance, walking the distances Paul covered! In contrast, we are sedentary people, tending toward softness, excessive weight, and heart attacks. For us, planned exercise is necessary to keeping physically fit.

Exercise yields specific benefits for body, brain, and emotions.

Body. As youth slips away (or sometimes before it does!), muscle tone declines. Even if not an ounce of weight is added, bulk seems to shift; what was firm becomes flabby. Exercise helps maintain firm flesh and good muscle tone. It also extends physical energy. Who among us Maidservants could not use the thirty-percent extra energy that experts tell us comes from consistent exercise?

Brain. Blood moves through the body more quickly when we engage in strenuous physical activity, and the mind profits from that surge of fuel. It's as if cobwebs get swept out of the mind, leaving room for fresh ideas and attitudes.

Emotions. Certainly one of the most important benefits of exercise for a woman is its contribution toward emotional balance. While not being qualified to present a scientific explanation, Bobbie and Beneth both have experienced its reality. The Creator made us humans wondrously complex beings in whom the mental, physical, and spiritual are tightly intertwined. Daily pressures grind us down physically and emotionally. Instead of succumbing, we should force ourselves (we'll seldom *feel* like it) into some strenuous physical exercise. By putting demands on our exterior, we can lessen pressure's stress on our interior.

While encouraging exercise, we urge moderation. Some persons become so enamored of physical activity that they allow it to outgrow the relatively small part it should play in life. A regard for proportion and moderation should govern even so beneficial an activity as physical exercise.

The type of exercise you choose is a matter of individual preference. What fits your life? Would you enjoy jogging, walking, bicycling, swimming, gardening, or jumping rope? There are many other beneficial forms of exercise to choose from. Whatever form you choose, **establish a habit.** Make exercise as regular a part of your day as eating and sleeping. When you let yourself say of exercise, "It can wait till tomorrow . . . or next week . . . ," you'll soon drop the whole endeavor—to your detriment.

Sleep

God so designed our bodies that they must be renewed by sleep each day. That being the case, we need to consider both quantity and quality of sleep.

Quantity of Sleep

Men generally don't need as much sleep as women. If a Maidservant tries to maintain a man's schedule and pace, weariness sets in. Her mind loses its alertness; her spirits take a nose dive. Heed the sleep experts who tell us that a woman requires about an hour's more sleep per night than a man. Moreover, needs for sleep vary widely among individuals. Your friend may regularly get by with only five hours' sleep a night and stay fit as a fiddle. But the five hours that leave her energetic and alert leave you dragging and dopey. Rather than be discouraged by the difference, acknowledge that your sleep-needs design is **God made.** Heed it.

Quality of Sleep

Each of us wakes up feeling better on some mornings than on others. That's mainly due to the difference between quantity and quality of sleep. Amount of sleep does not always equate with *effectiveness* of sleep. Sleep quality is affected by air, temperature, quiet, and mattress condition.

Air is a simple but often overlooked need. Open your windows at night and get fresh air into your bedroom (unless, of course, you have terrible allergies).

Temperature influences quality of sleep. If your room is cold, you don't rest well. You stay wound up in a tight, shivering ball trying to get warm. Too much heat, on the other hand, leaves you feeling wrung-out and groggy.

Quiet also contributes to good rest. Assign the children bedrooms on the noisier side of the house. They have the wonderful ability to sleep through all sorts of adverse conditions. Also, the demands of their lives don't compare with those of adults. Choosing the quieter bedroom is not selfish but sensible.

Mattress condition has much to do with the quality of sleep. Soft, sagging mattresses make for hard nights and stiff days. They let you sleep like a parenthesis. By morning, you may be a *painful* parenthesis. If your mattress is oversoft and you can't afford a new one, put a sheet of plywood between mattress and springs.

Naps

A short daily nap can be a preserver of mood, marriage, and ministry—not a one- or two-hour nap, but a mini-sleep lasting from ten to thirty minutes. Bobbie met a living advertisement for the napping principle: a ninety-year-old ''retired'' missionary lady who still traveled for speaking engagements several times a week. Amazingly energetic in body and sharp in mind, she declared, ''I've taken care of my body—the only vessel God gave me. No matter how busy the schedule, I take a thirty-minute nap every afternoon. I've outlived scores of fellow missionaries who tried burning the candle at both ends.'' There spoke a *wise* Maidservant!

Experts tell us that a thirty-minute nap during the day compares with *three hours'* sleep at night. You can train yourself to fall asleep quickly during the daytime. The secret is to relax both body and mind, not focusing upon anything at all—including sleep.

Diversion

Perhaps this area is the most neglected by those in full-time Christian service. While creating the world, God took the seventh day for rest. He also stated that His creature, man, should henceforth do the same. But we modern ministry folks seem to forget or ignore that divine intention. It is interesting that, whereas rest is structured into the secular work week, it is not in the religious work week. When Sunday must be a day of labor for God and in behalf of His people, are we laborers exempted from the day-of-rest principle? No. God nowhere says we who minister can bypass His commandment for Sabbath rest. In this area as in every other, "to **obey** is better than sacrifice." When the day of rest is a day of ministry work, we must adjust by converting a workday to a rest day.

First Corinthians 3:16 reminds us that our duty to God includes regard for our bodies. "Know ye not that ye are the temple of God, and that the Spirit of God dwelleth in you?" The Lord gives each of us only one temple—with a mind that is supposed to monitor its care!

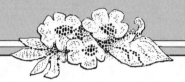

Chapter 4

Woman's Wasteland

Attitudes

Like other human beings, we ministry women experience attitude problems. What are attitudes, anyway? They are mental states and habits affecting our selves, our work, and other people. Sometimes we excuse bad attitudes by claiming helplessness— "That's just the way I am!" Not true. There is a split second in any situation when we choose an attitude. It's a bit like driving a car: when our street meets a cross street, we decide whether to turn right, turn left, or continue straight ahead. Stand back and observe your attitudinal travels. You'll soon recognize that the sharp turns at crossroads incidents are not automatic; they are *choices.*

Attitude choices made repeatedly become habits. For example, when Herkimer Husband uses a certain (irritating) vocal tone, Winifred Wife makes a hard left turn onto Stubborn Street regardless of what he's saying. Or when Rhonda Roommate indulges in an idiosyncracy (of which she is unaware), Sally Servant abruptly swings onto Acid Avenue. Those reactional attitudes come quickly because they've become habits. But are stubbornness and acidity characteristics of holiness? Obviously not. Neither are any of the other destructive attitudes that plague us.

There are general principles for dealing with whatever attitude challenges we face. Let's follow through with the roadway/crossroads concept.

First, mark each trouble spot—*your* tough places for attitude control. Put up a *stop sign.* Then obey it: idle your mental-emotional motor, and choose not to turn onto the destructive side street.

Second, change the road signs. Remove the well-worn one pointing left: "Crabbyville, $\frac{1}{2}$ moment, steep downhill grade." Replace it with a new one directing you right: "Quietdale, 2-mile climb."

Third, on your personal road map, highlight the *scriptural routing* that specifically applies. (For example, haven't you noticed how many times the Bible warns against anger?)

Fourth, turn your attitudinal vehicle in the new direction. It will be bumpy at first (the road's not very well used, is it?) and long (yes, you really have wandered that far from the desired route!). But the more you choose the proper turn, the smoother the road becomes.

Contrary to wishful thinking, victorious Christian living has less to do with miracles than with **work.** It is hard work to change poor attitude habits.

Our focus contributes to attitude problems. Our dusty, earthen selves tend to focus on whatever irritates or displeases; we mentally poke and prod until we make an attitudinal sore spot. Walk through the following scenario:

You are moving smoothly through your morning's work, humming the chorus of a hymn, basking in the rosy glow of contentment. All at once you call to mind a remark someone made. You replay the sarcastic tone of voice; you renew the sensation of hurt that you originally felt. Oh yes, your hands go on working. But inwardly you run and rerun that painful scene. Your mental video enhances color, proportion, and intensity. By midafternoon, though your body may be cool, your spirit is steaming. By evening, when you happen to come into contact with the offender, or with an imagined offender-sympathizer, you either blow up or freeze him or her knee-knocking cold. Your foul mood is a puzzlement to the other person, who has of course forgotten the incident if indeed he had anything to do with it at all. You have enlarged, or even created, a problem *by your choice of focus.*

Where we look determines what we see. Far too many of us (yes, we ministry women) concentrate on negatives: we look at the ugly rather than the lovely, at shortcomings instead of strengths, at deprivations rather than blessings. With that kind of focus, it's no wonder we chafe, complain, and sulk.

The **way** we look at things influences our reactions. If Sally Servant looks at life through suspicious eyes, she's going to distrust people, think them insincere, and credit them with wrong motives. If she's bitterly envious, she'll see others as worldly, proud, put-on, and so forth. When Sally feels particularly timid, she may look at a person who often speaks to groups and think, "Oh, what power! She just breezes through what she does with no nervousness at all." Or, should Sally feel discontented and bored with her life, she reads glamour into others' lives.

Where we look, the way we look—these "eye problems" all too easily develop, thus producing attitude problems. We each need the **eyeglasses of love** to correct our vision and enable us to see reality. There is, of course, something called "love" that is a syrupy, gushy pretense. Biblical love, in contrast, reaches out through our own faults and failings without focusing on them; it reaches out, moreover, to those around us without focusing on *their* shortcomings. That love sees deeply, looking past the surface, into hearts and needs. What a wonderful possession those eyeglasses of love are for any woman in full-time Christian service! God's Word writes the prescription: "Brethren, **love one another.**"

Why should we analyze, challenge, and change attitudes? Because of their many-faceted importance.

Attitudes say something of our self-mastery, our self-control. Secular authors are producing shelves of books touting positive thinking. Although their thrust is humanistic, they usefully remind us of the importance of attitudes. Our approach to attitude control as born-again Christians is not theirs—a pull-yourself-up-by-your-own-bootstraps concept. We have a personal relationship with the God who created the mind. We enjoy communication and companionship with Him. It is incredible, therefore, that Christians should so often whimper, "I just can't change my attitudes." Isn't that denying the Bible's wonderful assurance that "I can do *all* things through Christ" (Phil. 4:13)?

Attitudes have strong positive or negative effects: upon ourselves, making us blessings or banes to those around us; upon our homes, creating atmospheres of sweetness and warmth or sour coldness. Our attitudes also color our public ministries. We choose the colors ourselves, whether bright or dim. A personal relationship, a home, a church—each has a spirit, a personality. In each case, the outstanding contributor to that personality is the leader's attitude.

First Peter 5:2 presents the ideal attitude for any Maidservant: "Feed the flock of God which is among you, taking the oversight thereof, not by constraint, but willingly; not for filthy lucre, but of a ready mind."

Emotions

Emotions are a complicated and complicating part of female personality. We female creatures tend to operate more according to feel than to fact. In response to a logical explanation we are likely to maintain, "Yes, I know all that . . . but I *feel* . . . " The very fact that head knowledge collides with our "feel" knowledge adds to our internal conflict.

Contrary to the laity's assumption, a Maidservant is every bit as human, as earthen, as anyone else. Women in ministry at home and abroad agree that the most intense spiritual battles they wage are in the area of attitudes and emotions.

Our emotions as women are closely linked to the body's cyclical functioning. Take, for instance, the difficulties of premenstrual days: everything appears gloomy; a cross word (real or imagined) can trigger a weeping fit. Such monthly doldrums are fairly manageable when we keep track of our cycle. Sometimes, though, time slips by unnoticed, and suddenly a woman finds herself floundering in raging seas of downheartedness and oversensitivity, wondering how she got there.

There are no magical means to avoid our cycle-related emotional variations, though extremes can be somewhat lessened by certain medications. Most of us can help ourselves by remembering that there *is* a physical cause; the difficult days "come to *pass.*" An eye to the calendar also can help us avoid scheduling super-demanding tasks for premenstrual days. When enduring the monthly tough time, we need to blend prayer, will power, and rationality so that we do not become victims of our emotions and consequently victimize those around us.

Monthly fluctuations are not the only time-related emotional upheavals a woman must undergo. Another follows the birth of a baby. This emotional "down" is so common to new mothers that it has been given a name: postpartum blues. It may last several weeks while the body readjusts to its nonpregnant state. A third life-seasonal upheaval is menopause, which, like the onset of menstruation, is marked by emotional mountains and valleys. Again, the cause is physical: tremendous changes take place in the body as it exits the fertility mode.

And so it goes throughout life. Female emotions travel uncharted terrain where the topography presents constant challenges.

Somersaulting emotions are harmful not only in what they do to us but also in what they do to others. Proverbs 25:24 tells us, "It is better to dwell in the corner of the house top than with a brawling woman and in a wide house." *Brawling* not only connotes loudness and argumentativeness but also carries the sense of emotional upheaval. Brawls are conflicts begun without premeditation as a person takes offense at an attitude, word, or action of another. A brawler is someone who reacts as if his interior self were heaped with tinder: any little thing can torch it into flame.

Although as feminine creatures we cannot *escape* emotions, we can and should *encompass* them. How? By the Word of God and the Spirit of God. It takes daily study and absorption of God's Word to keep us sensitive to our emotional barometer and in control of our emotional weather. Scripture in mind and heart can do wonderful things to keep these skittering selves in check. As we daily commune with the Lord, His indwelling Holy Spirit convicts us when our emotions run amuck. He points us to Christ, the Altogether Lovely One, into whose likeness we are to be growing.

Attitudes and emotions are a woman's wasteland—a field of battle the seriousness of which those unaffected may discount or, at best, underestimate. But our heavenly Father knows their strategic importance for life and service.

> He that hath no rule over his own spirit is like a city that is broken down, and without walls (Prov. 25:28).

> He that is slow to anger is better than the mighty; and he that ruleth his spirit than he that taketh a city (Prov. 16:32).

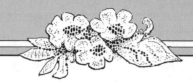

Chapter 5

Soap and Sachet

The book of Exodus contains God's instructions for building the wilderness tabernacle and preparing the priests for service. It is impossible to read the passages without being impressed with His personal attention to detail. He is concerned about materials, color, texture, pattern, beauty, cleanliness—in a word, *appearance*. The reason? The tabernacle was to be God's earthly dwelling place—a sanctuary that pictured outwardly the character of God and the attitudes appropriate to His worship. God's inward view of these realities and man's outward view were to be in agreement. Today God dwells within born-again believers in the Person of the Holy Spirit (I Cor. 6:19-20). Has God's demand for special care of His dwelling place been rescinded? Is He now satisfied with carelessness and neglect? Not for a moment.

Every Christian woman's appearance should be clean, modest, and fittingly attractive, and none more so than those in full-time Christian service.

Some Christians protest that care for self is unspiritual. Scripture indicates otherwise. That *nonpareil* of godly womanhood, the virtuous woman of Proverbs 31, takes pains to keep herself attractive while providing for her household. Of the seventeen or eighteen verses describing her, one deals with her appearance:

"Her clothing is silk and purple." Those words tell us directly that she wears the top-quality clothing of her era. They also indirectly tell us something else. If the statements of these verses are correlated with her waking hours, one hour a day is given to self care. In all her industry and efficiency in the service of others, God's virtuous woman does not neglect herself.

A Maidservant's good grooming is important in several ways. First, appearance has an effect on the servant herself. When she *looks* dowdy, she *feels* dowdy. Recall an incident in your own experience when, for example, you had to run an errand without having time to "whip yourself into shape." You rushed through your business, hoping not to see anyone you knew. And when you crossed paths with Miss Super Neat, you felt resentment toward her and embarrassment about yourself. It comes to this: our sense of self influences our attitudes and actions. The Scripture verse "Thou shalt love thy neighbour as thyself" presupposes a healthy (sensible, balanced) view of self. Numerous studies show correlation between appearance and performance.

Second, appearance is important to marriage. For those of us Maidservants who are married, our most eternally valuable ministry is not in the church, not in the community, but in the **home.** Marriages can shatter while husband and wife zealously minister to other homes and hearts.

This may be a sensitive area for some women, but a man likes to have his wife stay at least recognizable as the girl he married. Wrinkles and gray hair are inevitable; sloppiness and neglect are not. Though age may dim a husband's eyesight, it doesn't rob him of it. God created men with a strong visual trigger to their sexuality. The wife who ignores or discounts that fact invites marital suicide. A wife's daily appearance proclaims to her husband and to the world, "He's not worth the effort to keep myself looking good" or "He's *well* worth it!"

Third, personal appearance makes up an important part of our testimony to the world. Someone has wisely said, "You never get a second chance to make a first impression." Impressions make points either for or against the Lord we represent. How can the world glimpse our Altogether Lovely Lord in an Absolutely Awful Ambassador? Objectors will hastily trot out the text, "Man looketh on the outward appearance, but the Lord looketh on the heart" (I Sam. 16:7). This consideration, far from being a reason against, is an argument *for* meticulous grooming. The outward appearance is all that other persons are able to see, the only basis they have for judgment.

It is no wonder that God cares about the appearance of His tabernacle. We should care too, and there is not one of us who can't profit from a quick run-down of grooming basics.

The absolute minimal necessity is **cleanliness.** The Christian's blood-washed heart demands a clean exterior. Whatever the inflation rate, soap is cheap; and "elbow grease" is free.

We each must consistently guard against **body odor.** A daily bath or shower is a must. When the weather is hot or there is strenuous activity, a second shower may be required. Perspiration creates body odor; body odor is offensive. A testimony can be "aromatic" in the wrong way!

Proper **skin care** is important. Don't go to bed with makeup on; skin needs to "breathe" freely through the night. Oily skin needs cleansing several times a day; dry skin may do best with cleansing by cold cream. About the age of thirty, most skin begins requiring moisturizer.

Mouth care should be a constant consideration. Have you had someone with garlic breath try to witness to or counsel you? If so, you know how bad breath negates good counsel. Besides regular, careful tooth brushing, we who deal with people need to keep breath fresheners handy. Many types are available. Chewing gum *does not* qualify! A woman chomping gum is as unattractive as one puffing a cigarette. A student passed along an inelegant but succinct lyric:

> A gum-chewing gal
> And a cud-chewing cow—
> There's hardly a difference,
> I will allow,
> Save the intelligent look
> On the face of the cow!

The importance of personal appearance was demonstrated in an experience the Yearicks had. Dave and Bobbie, with a small group of their church members, were traveling home from a mission trip to Africa. All of them felt dishevelled, and most of them looked it from their long journey. At various airport stop-overs Bobbie noticed a fellow passenger: a neatly dressed, well-groomed young woman. Her bearing and grooming were such that people were drawn to her, as evidenced by their asking her questions and engaging her in light talk. Striking up a conversation, Bobbie learned that the young woman had been serving as a missionary in Africa and was on her way home. When asked her denomination, the girl said, "I'm with the Unification Church." The lesson hit home with power. Here was *falsehood's purveyor* exerting positive attraction, while those who represented the Lord of Glory did not—all because of *her grooming and carriage*. The Yearicks' group rushed immediately to the airport restrooms to try to remedy their negligence!

Our **clothing** deserves careful attention—not only in its choice, which will be discussed in a later chapter, but also in its care. The clothes we wear should always be clean, pressed, and neatly worn. A couple of simple rules are helpful:

1. Wash washables after each wearing.
2. Protect and inspect "Dry Clean Only" clothing.
   a. Wear an apron when in the kitchen and underarm dress shields as needed.
   b. Air the garment before returning it to the closet.
   c. Inspect carefully after each wearing; visible soiling demands a trip to the cleaners.

Don't leave clothing care for that last, hurried moment when you snatch an outfit from the closet. Build into your daily/weekly schedule a routine checking for snags, runs, picks, loose buttons, split seams, or drooping hems. Fix what's found—right away.

Avoid being fooled by "wrinkle free" tags. Synthetic fabrics do not make the ironing board obsolete. Easy-care fabrics vary in their wrinkle-shedding ability according to fiber content/combination, weave, weight, and quality. Getting synthetic or synthetic-blend garments out of the dryer as soon as it stops is an important preventer of wrinkles but is not foolproof. A brief steam pressing may be needed to give the fresh smoothness that says good things about the wearer's personal care and character.

Hair is the woman's crowning glory, is it not? That depends on the woman under it. Because our heavenly bank accounts are greater than our earthly, most of us Christian workers do well to learn to manage our own hair between cuts: it saves hours and dollars. Our regal adornment should be clean, attractively styled, and manageable.

Shampoo your hair as often as necessary to keep it shining and bouncy. Rinse thoroughly; residual shampoo dulls shine. An attractive hairstyle is one that flatters its wearer. Don't choose a hairstyle just because it's pictured in a magazine. Make a careful, creative study of your own needs. Here are the factors to consider:

1. *Age*. Ponytails and long, free-flowing tresses are flattering to youth but frivolous and aging for maturity.
2. *Body proportions*. A too-full look overpowers a petite figure; a head-hugging cut can make a tall woman look pinheaded.
3. *Profile*. Hair can camouflage, or emphasize, weaknesses.
4. *Face shape*. Hairstyle should contribute to "ovalizing" your face and equalizing its proportions by either counterbalance or disguise.

Manageable hair comes either by nature or by treatment. In the latter category are perms, straightenings, shaped cuts, and conditioning.

Remember the extremities—**fingers and toes.** Nail care need not take a great deal of time and effort, but it should be given weekly. Fingernails should be smooth and rounded, toenails smooth and cut straight across. Cuticles should be pushed back. Nails should shine either from a careful polish job or from buffing. If you use polish, whether it be clear, natural, or subtle color, redo your manicure whenever there is chipping or growth. Otherwise, your fingernails will scream careless grooming.

The twentieth century is not the day of the hairy female. Be meticulous in keeping **legs and underarms** hairless. Can women with very blond hair skip de-fuzzing legs? No. Sunlight shows up leg hair of whatever color. And unshaven legs under hose look absolutely abominable.

If you have a daughter, do some of your beauty routine with her as she enters her teens. Teach her proper principles of feminine appearance soon enough to counteract wrong input from media and peers. You also might consider teaching a short grooming and beauty course for the teen girls in your congregation. We find that Christian girls are eager for the right kind of advice *and example.*

Finally, we would remind you to wear a girdle and/or hose when appropriate. Consider the following:

1. The dressiness of the occasion.
2. Your weight and shape.
3. The fabric and fit of the garment.

Always check your outfit in a full-length mirror *from behind.* That front-fine dress may look awful from the back because of hip humps, dimples, and droops.

An effective overall grooming routine can be reduced to three basic ingredients:

Principle. Know the principles of good grooming.

Priorities. Build careful grooming into your schedule, recognizing its importance to your testimony and ministry.

Practice. Make your personal care a firmly held habit.

To help remember the contents of this discussion, we present the following acrostic:

> The **B**est appearance . . .
> at **A**ll times . . .
> demanding the **L**east time . . .
> in order to reflect my lovely **L**ord.

May that **b-a-l-l** roll along with each of us throughout the years of our Christian service.

Chapter 6

A Creative Closet

In the Old Testament, God instructed that His priests be dressed "for glory and for *beauty*" (Exod. 28:2). As we have noted, the virtuous, highly esteemed woman of Proverbs 31 wore "silk and purple." We are reminded in Isaiah that when God bestows salvation, He clothes our souls in the beautiful robes of righteousness—the finest, richest, most glorious garments imaginable. With such strong biblical implications about quality of appearance, it is impossible to justify a feed-sack clothing philosophy. It is important that we Maidservants strive for balance in the matter of wardrobe. Clothing is to be lived *in,* not *for.*

Although we would not dream of building a house without a blueprint, women's wardrobes often are accumulated haphazardly. The wardrobe that works is built according to a plan.

Color

Essential to any building is a foundation. A wardrobe's foundation and the building blocks that rest upon it have to do with **color.** Color works for or against its wearer in two major ways: distribution and integration.

Distribution. Colors in dress yield impressions of size and proportion. Lights and brights attract the eye and say "larger." Darks do the opposite.

Integration. Colors in a wardrobe should, first of all, integrate with the wearer's own coloring—hair, skin, and eyes. Second, they should integrate with one another—making *coordination* possible.

Fashion researchers have identified four color palettes, each of which integrates with certain personal colorations. Staying within your prescribed color palette ensures the most flattering effects. If you don't know your best colors, analyses are widely available. The color palette approach is not a frill; it saves time, money, and frustration.

A closet needs only *one* color coat, shoes, and purse for warm seasons of the year and *one* for cold. Your color palette will determine whether the foundation color is brown, black, or navy for cold weather, white or creme for hot. It's a good idea to include in each set (a) a basic dress and (b) a suit.

With the color foundation in place, building blocks of color may then be added. As you know, any one color has different shades and tones. Your personal palette will determine which of those work best for you. In the case of red, a spring-palette woman should choose a clear or an orange red; a summer should reach for watermelon, blue reds, or raspberry; an autumn looks best in orange-reds, bittersweet, or dark tomato; and a winter should stick with true- or blue-reds.

While these color considerations may seem complicated, they really are not. Take time to learn the basic scheme as it applies to your personal coloring. It will lend confidence and simplicity to your clothing choice.

Line

Another factor in building a wardrobe is *line*. Line in clothing can be used both to direct and to disguise. Unlike many of the unsaved, who emphasize breasts, hips, and legs, a Christian woman wants eyes to be drawn to her face, the main indicator of personality and character. Line can help do that.

Line also can disguise less-than-ideal physical features. Most of us have some physical feature we'd like to de-emphasize. A garment's line can be the answer. For instance, a short-waisted woman should avoid a snug natural waistline: it emphasizes her misproportions. A lowered waistline or a waistless sheath, on the other hand, streamlines her appearance. A short woman is enhanced by strong vertical line; a six-footer is not. A thin woman can wear horizontal stripes; a heavy woman should avoid them.

Line in garments is created by silhouette, seams, color contrast, waistline, and hem or edge. Each can be used to camouflage body length, breadth, and proportions.

Coordination

A well-planned wardrobe is a *coordinated* wardrobe. Coordination creates variety with relatively few clothing pieces, making the contents of a closet flexible and practical.

It's easy to check the coordination quotient of your closet. Pack for an imaginary fourteen-day trip in *one small suitcase*. The **greater** the number of outfits you can put together from the the pieces that fit in the suitcase, the better.

Individuality

Individualize your wardrobe. Contrary to the fashion industry's ballyhoo, there is no reason for you to dress like everyone else. Each piece of clothing you own should enhance your unique self. For the Christian woman, of course, the scriptural principle of moderation is to be followed; in being individualistic, we should never be ''kooky.''

Another aspect of individualization has to do with purpose. No two people have work schedules, domestic responsibilities, social involvement, financial circumstances, and travel obligations exactly alike. That means differentiation in wardrobes for practicality. Your clothing needs to fit *you*—not just with regard to your physical shape and personality but also in keeping with your unique lifestyle.

Be aware, also, that clothing should reflect different ages and stages in life. Eventually high-school and college casuals will give place to more tailored outfits; washable mother-of-toddler dresses are replaced by some dry-clean-onlys.

Modesty

The outstanding characteristic of a ministry woman's wardrobe must be **modesty**. Plunging necklines and miniskirts are not the only violations of the modesty standard. Too-tight clothing is immodest. Fabric that clings to body outlines is immodest. Dresses and skirts worn gracelessly (for example, when sitting with knees apart) are immodest. Culottes worn to climb mountains or ride horseback can be extremely immodest. In every instance of clothing choice, we need to analyze an outfit carefully for modesty *in the activity for which it will be worn.*

Unified Tone

Within any one outfit of clothing there needs to be a single tone or level of formality: sport, casual, tailored, dressy, and formal. The principle here is simple: *don't mix any two.* For instance, the appearance of a formal gown is ruined by wearing klunky casual shoes.

Choice of outfit tone is made by considering the occasion for which it is to be worn. Office work calls for tailored clothes, church for tailored or dressy, and so forth.

Time and Season

Some types of garments and accessories are considered "evening only." (The term *evening,* as applied to fashion, generally refers to after 5 P.M.) Among the "evening onlys" are sequins, rhinestones, satin, and gold or silver shoes. Seasonal guides are quite common-sense ones, but nevertheless they are frequently violated. Patent leather, chalk whites, voile, and straws are for summer only. Velvet, velveteen, and felt are for winter only. (The fashion calendar knows two basic seasons: "winter," October to April; "summer," May to September.)

Permanence

Clothing of course will not and cannot last indefinitely; but careful choices mean usefulness for years rather than weeks or months.

Permanence in connection with clothing is not a word fashion designers and manufacturers relish. They are in the clothing business to make money. Therefore, they try to convince us that last year's style is obsolete this year. *Do not* be herded into that corral! Only the extremely rich can empty and restock closets yearly. Ministry women must have wardrobes that serve well for as many years as possible. Your authors both have the joy of wearing some outfits or pieces that are twenty-plus years old. The secrets for building permanence into a closet are the following considerations:

Quality. Quality is more important and practical than quantity. A stuffed-full closet is seldom a *good* closet. In fact, most of the things in it probably are just taking up space and represent wasted dollars. Learn the hallmarks of quality: the "feel" of a fabric; generous seams with pinked or bound edges; well-fitting linings; generous, smoothly-hanging hems done with blind stitching; plaids and stripes that match at seam lines.

Basic or bold. You can wear a classic style more often than you can wear a striking outfit. If you wear the striking outfit every week, for instance, people will remember that you have just worn it. That principle should be applied to colors, patterns, and distinctive cuts. For example, dark and medium colors are less memorable than brights and are therefore more serviceable. How many days in any one week could you wear a red suit? A navy, black, or brown suit could be worn often simply by changing the accessories.

Plain or patterned. Particularly in the primary stages of wardrobe building, think in terms of "basic" garments—those with no contrasting trims or eye-catching details. Choosing plain over patterned extends a garment's usefulness by making it adaptable through accessorizing.

Fit. Be precise about the fit of any garment. Poorly fitting clothes neither look good nor feel good. They irritate the wearer and are soon abandoned. A misfit is a waste of money, time, and space.

Simplicity. Those pieces that become the real backbone of your closet are the ones that are simple or "basic." They have self-belts, self-buttons, and uncluttered lines. If that sounds dull, it's not. A basic piece of clothing works much like an artist's canvas. Upon it you can "paint" a great variety of pictures by adding interesting jewelry, scarves, and belts.

Financial Considerations

Put the most money into what you most wear. An outfit used only once or twice a year should be inexpensive; the suit or dress worn weekly deserves (indeed, *demands*) better.

All our money belongs to the Lord. We are to be good stewards of it. Buying top-quality clothing (which ultimately proves less expensive than cheap-quality) does not mean paying top dollar. A workable, effective approach we've found is this:

1. Pray about clothing needs.
2. Resist impulse buying.
3. Exercise patience.
4. Watch for sales in better departments and stores. (Their markdowns are more significant, and their quality is superior.)
5. Browse outlets, yard sales, and resale shops.
6. Put into your closet a great deal more thought than money.

A Maidservant's prudence, femininity, and modesty are reflected in a wardrobe that is appropriate, practical, adaptable, and of good quality. She may rightly be likened to that estimable lady of ancient praise whose clothing was silk and purple.

The
Maidservant's
Home

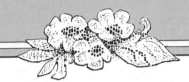

Chapter 7

Critical Clockwork

Is there any mortal woman in full-time Christian service who doesn't occasionally wish for lengthened hours to do the things she needs to do? Alas, that wish can never be fulfilled. We can, however, learn to use the time we have more wisely and thereby extend and enrich our service for the Lord.

Time is a precious gift from God. It is the framework for all He wants us to be and to do. This fact is brought home to us in Scripture by such reminders as "My times are in thy hand" (Ps. 31:15) and "What is your life? It is even a vapour" (James 4:14). Yet often we let time slip through careless fingers.

We can rise to the challenge of time management, ignore it, or flee from it. The choice is made repeatedly throughout each day as never-to-be-repeated opportunities come to us. Proverbs 27:1 warns, "Boast not thyself of to morrow; for thou knowest not what a day may bring forth."

Perhaps Scripture's most thorough treatment of time management is Ephesians 5:15-17: "See then that ye walk circumspectly, not as fools, but as wise, Redeeming the time, because the days are evil. Wherefore be ye not unwise, but understanding what the will of the Lord is."

To "walk circumspectly" means to look all around, to consider (not *do*) everything. Twice in this passage we're told to bring wisdom to bear—an urging we often ignore, causing numberless problems for ourselves. "Redeeming the time" means to rescue from loss: investing rather than wasting time's gold. "Understanding what the will of the Lord is" gives the crucial point: seeking His pleasure in whatever decisions we make about our time.

Actually, of course, we do not and cannot manage time itself. A minute will always contain sixty seconds. An hour can hold only sixty minutes. No day can be stretched longer than twenty-four hours. What we really mean by the term *time management* is *self*-management—ti**ME** management.

As faithful stewards we must make each day count for eternity. The psalmist said, "So teach us to number our days, that we may apply our hearts unto wisdom" (Ps. 90:12). Try this sobering exercise: subtract your present age from the normal life expectancy as given in Scripture, seventy years, and then multiply by 365. The result is days *remaining to live* (as the Lord wills)—a shockingly brief time, even apart from an early homegoing. Life certainly is the vapor God calls it!

Thoughtful time management yields benefits in three vital areas:

> Personal peace of mind
> > Others' comfort and care
> > > Joyful accomplishment and service

The principles of time management are simple to state, but applying them is quite another thing. It is up to the individual to make the decisions and exercise the discipline necessary to plug them into life's current.

Setting Goals

Time management is time marksmanship. Aimlessly waving the gun of intention will have the obvious "pointless" result. Someone has wisely said, "Aim at nothing, and you're sure to hit it."

Be specific in setting your goals. Make the goals time-oriented: hourly, daily, monthly, yearly, lifetime.

Perhaps the most important thing to realize is that the Christian servant's goals should be of the "to be" nature as well as "to do." We're familiar with to-dos such as "Do the laundry," "Lose five pounds by Christmas," "Make dress for banquet." We hear less of goals concerning personality, character, and spiritual growth. Those to-bes are more important than to-dos; yet they usually get overlooked.

If specific planning seems mechanical rather than spiritual, we need to remind ourselves that human plans and divine guidance are not by nature incompatible. Proverbs 16:9 tells us that our planning and God's ordaining can actually work hand in hand: "A man's heart deviseth his way: but the Lord directeth his steps." Luke 14:28-30 speaks approvingly of forethought in life's undertakings. Nehemiah's wall-building project could hardly have even gotten started without his outstanding organizational talents.

Priorities

Goals set willy-nilly without regard for proper priorities are an exercise in futility. Modern American women generally have turned their priorities upside-down; that makes it all the more important that we Christian women hold firmly to divine intention. God's Word gives women the following areas of responsibility:

Closet (personal spiritual life)   Church
Castle (home)   Community

Such a listing becomes unwieldy and frustrating when we try to rank its components and apply it. Instead, picture your areas of responsibility as a wheel.

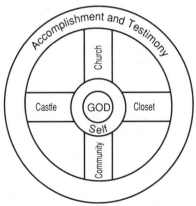

Note, first, that God is the hub of the wheel—*central* to all of life. When His centrality is maintained, He touches every aspect of our being and works out through us into every area of our lives. Should God be pushed off center, the wheel cannot turn smoothly. Each spoke's importance as a God-ordained responsibility can be verified by specific Scripture passages.

Notice that each spoke has two ends, two points of connection. We can think of this connectivity as interaction: God working outwardly through us to others enabling accomplishment and testimony, and the recipients of this ministry in turn dependent upon and controlled by God as we hold tightly to Him.

At various stages, each of the spokes will be in a greater weight-bearing position than the others. For a number of years the married Maidservant will necessarily concentrate upon her castle responsibilities. Her children will demand the bulk of her time and attention. As they grow older, she will be freed for more active participation in church and community ministries.

Note that the "closet" spoke is as solid and important to the wheel as any of the others. Should active spiritual life weaken or collapse, the whole would be affected.

Some may sigh, "My life turns so fast it's like being caught in a cyclone!" Each of us experiences "cyclonic" times. But where, in a cyclonic storm, is quiet and peace? *In the center!*

Having established the necessity of God's centrality in our lives, let's move on to consider the specific areas of responsibility. How much should we be expected or feel obligated to do?

Busy is one of the most often heard words of our time. Instead of sitting calmly on the front porch, we clear it in one bound, charging in and out of the house. Today's woman is typically up to her eyebrows in commitments, and the ministry woman is no exception. She can feel driven rather than called—a deadly, joyless state.

A first step toward correcting overcommitment and bettering stewardship of time is **getting things into black and white.** Putting commitments into writing helps put them into perspective. A sample commitment chart follows. Fill it in and adjust the list of categories according to your needs.

Listing these areas of involvement makes them seem almost manageable. Why then doesn't everything get done? Why do we feel frazzled and frustrated? Problems most often come from falling into one or more time traps.

Time Trap 1—Doing Too Much

Christian workers are notorious for this. Realizing how much needs to be done for the Lord, we try single-handedly to do it all. But Satan is just as victorious when we play Super Saint as when we take the role of Slothful Servant. "Super" too often ends in a soup of damaged health and unstrung nerves.

Each of us must draw the line against overcommitment and learn to say no. But how can we sort through the flood of demands, requests, and opportunities, rightly choosing from among them? We must ask, "What is the primary function God has for me right now? What is the reason for my involvement in each activity?" Applying that measure will eliminate some of our activities, though the deletions may cause pain. For instance, your husband or supervisor may ask you to curtail activities in a well-loved area in order to be more useful in the place he needs you. At such times, it is imperative to overlook the hurt of the moment and, in faith, trust God's direction through that one He has placed over you. Compliance in the right spirit will be rewarded.

On the chart, notice the column called "Possible Replacement." *No one* is absolutely indispensable. Each of us can be replaced in some manner or fashion. Yet there are degrees of dispensability. For example, the married woman is *most* important to her husband and children. She certainly does not want to call in a replacement there! But, as for playing the piano, there probably is someone else who can take her place accompanying choral and congregational singing.

Rather than feel guilty about letting another take over some of your involvements, realize that trying to function in too many areas not only decreases effectiveness but also deprives others of the opportunity to grow and to serve.

Time Trap 2—Doing the Wrong Things

Almost every opportunity that comes to a ministry woman could be considered good. But there is an old saying, "The good is often enemy of the best." A Maidservant can so load herself

AREAS OF RESPONSIBILITIES

Home

	Present	Future	Reason for involvement
1. Husband			
2. Children			
3. Parents			
4. House			
5. Hospitality			
6. Yard			
7.			

Church

1. Membership			
2. Secretarial			
3. Bookkeeping			
4. Flower arranging			
5. Janitorial			
6.			

Women's ministries

1. Missionary society			
2. Bible study			
3. Visitation			
4. Banquets			
5.			
6.			

Children's work

1. Nursery			
2. Sunday school			
3. Awana			
4. Teen group(s)			
5.			
6.			

Music

1. Pianist			
2. Organist			
3. Vocalist			
4. Choir			
5.			
6.			

Christian school

1. Administration			
2. Teaching			
3. Secretarial			
4. Bookkeeping			
5.			
6.			
7.			

Other

1.			
2.			
3.			
4.			
5.			

Present   Future   Reason for involvement

Possible Replacement

down with good involvements that when the best comes along, she is unable to accept it or give it anything but cursory attention. Re-evaluate by asking, "What is my **best,** my **most effective** means of serving the Lord in this ministry, with these people?" Don't expect the answer to be unchanging. Adjustments will be required according to age and stage of life, locale, and cultural differences.

Time Trap 3—Doing Things the Wrong Way

We human beings are creatures of habit, and much of life reduces itself to habit. But habitual methods are not necessarily the best: they may waste time, motion, and concentration. Do an efficiency study of your everyday activities. Let it last for several weeks in order to yield a true, inclusive reading. You may be surprised at the wasted time you discover: golden moments that can be rescued from loss by simple method changes. For example, the woman who leans on the countertop with one hand while she unloads or loads the dishwasher may realize that she is **doubling her work time.** By tackling the task with two hands, she could sooner free herself for other jobs.

Time Trap 4—Wasteful Preferences

Worry. In our concern for details, we women tend to worry. There are even women who worry about not being able to think of anything to worry about! Mental nail chewing can immobilize performance.

Procrastination. When we rationalize, "There will be time to do that later," "later" slips into the distance, and the postponed task either gets buried in forgetfulness or is done haphazardly.

Compulsive activity. How recently have you had an "irresistible" urge to do something other than that important thing you'd planned to do? Succumbing to those urges sidetracks priority tasks.

Distractions. There you are, managing nicely with your morning vacuuming . . . until you pick up a snapshot from the floor. Looking at it, you're reminded of the occasion. You pause, sink into a chair to enjoy the nostalgia, and . . . so much for vacuuming! The truth is, we are surrounded by potential distractions. We must conquer them rather than let them derail accomplishment.

For that arch-distractor, the telephone, lessen its effectiveness by (a) limiting conversation time (yes, even if it means saying, "I'm sorry, but there's just not time to talk anymore right now"); (b) keeping small handwork jobs nearby (materials for manicuring, mending, crocheting, etc.); and (c) installing a superlong telephone cord, which will let you move about to cook, clean, and so forth, while conversing.

Indecision. Chunks of time are lost while we try to decide what to do and how and when to do it. The loss can be avoided by planning.

Idle conversation. Whether over the telephone or the backyard fence, idle conversation "speaks for itself."

Disorganization. A haphazard approach to responsibilities lowers accomplishment and heightens tensions. "Let all things be done decently and in order" (I Cor. 14:40) can apply outside as well as inside the church. We're told in I Corinthians 14:33, "God is not the author of confusion." Surely the Lord desires orderliness in the life of the believer, His living tabernacle.

Television-itis. Is there any greater time thief in the world than TV? Its dramatic offerings are increasingly unsavory. Its news coverage is ever more blatantly biased. Yet numbers of Christian women succumb to television's addictive powers. TV's influence is progressive. The more you watch, the more you want to watch. The more you want to watch, the more you tolerate. The more you tolerate, the more you imitate. Ultimately, television steals much more than time!

Perfectionism. Though we should put our best efforts into our tasks, we must realize meanwhile that perfection in this world is impossible. While chasing a "final" dust particle or re-re-re-redoing a bulletin board or straightening a bedspread a quarter inch, we can miss opportunities of eternal significance.

Individual Limitations

We must *honestly* acknowledge our limits. We must recognize the fact that capacities differ among human beings. Overload for one Maidservant may seem as nothing to another. These differences in personality, physique (strength, stamina, etc.), and emotional capacity are God's creative fingerprints. The boundaries they represent must be respected. If we consistently violate them, we court physical, emotional, mental, or spiritual disaster. On the other hand, they may not be so narrow as we represent them to ourselves or to others. What a pity to meet the occasional ministry woman who enjoys "poor health" as an escape from involvement.

Working the Plan

Goal setting, analyzing, charting, and determining will not accomplish anything until we put **feet** to our intentions. To make implementation less daunting, consider the following suggestions.

Simplify and unify.

There are a number of ways in which this principle can be profitably applied:

Cooking. Are your work areas well planned, or have you built unnecessary steps into your kitchen routines? What about the cooking utensils untouched for years except to be fumbled through each time you reach for favorites? Simplify by rearranging cabinets and appliances and by getting rid of unused items.

Do you wonder at five o'clock what to whip together for dinner at six o'clock? Simplify. Plan your menus a week in advance. Better still, establish three or four weeks' menus and rotate them (varying which weekday a certain food appears in its particular week). Simplify and unify. Keep a permanent shopping list for each week's menus.

Prepare part of an upcoming meal while cleaning after the current one.

Could your recipe collection use some attention? Is it making three drawers bulge or five bookshelves sag? Can you possibly use all or even most of it? Get rid of the overflow.

Closets. Whatever the size of your closet, chances are its space is crowded by clothes seldom worn: six outfits too small (waiting for unlikely weight loss); fifteen hangers holding items that coordinate with . . . nothing; oldies but goodies that just might come back into style twenty-five years from now.

Placement of clothing in the closet also can complicate life. Coordinates hanging far apart, unseeables at the bottom of stacks, belts tangled around each other—these snarl time and you.

Simplify and unify in your closet. Some of that comes automatically as you work toward overall color coordination. But also get rid of clutter: unworn clothing and nonclothing items. Place coordinates together (or at least close). Arrange stacks so that all items are visible. Keep belts neatly and conveniently stored.

General clutter. Get rid of it wherever it collects in your house. "A place for everything and everything in its place" is not an impossible dream; it can keep you from living a nightmare of frustration.

Change screamers to routiners.

Suppose you hate cleaning the refrigerator. You successfully ignore the task until that awful moment when, with company coming for dinner in half an hour, you must make room for the cold foods on your menu. With nerves twanging and teeth grating, you attack the job with all possible haste, only to find that the accumulated drippings on the shelves are impervious to suds and scouring. You spill two containers, and the contents run down into the vegetable bins. The gray-green mold on the applesauce makes your stomach churn. *That job* has become a screamer.

Why not put disliked tasks on a regular schedule or break big, tough jobs into manageable small chunks? In refrigerator cleaning, for instance, you might wash and straighten one shelf each day during regular meal cleanup.

Adopt efficient methods.

After analyzing your habitual methods with regard to time and motion required, decide how to streamline each task. Adopt the new, more efficient method and stick with it until it becomes habitual (twenty-one days, experts tell us). You might begin with the following areas of possible improvement.

1. *Setting and clearing the table.* Cut down the number of trips to and from the table by taking stacks or trayfuls of items.
2. *Drying/folding/putting away clothing.* Take no-iron items out of the dryer as soon as it stops running and fold them. Put away clothing in one trip by using a clothes basket or laundry cart filled with sorted clothes.
3. *Food preparation.* Keep it simple. Work for variety by changing seasonings and garnishes. Prepare two dishes of the same food and freeze one for later use.
4. *Room cleaning.* Have all necessary cleaning supplies with you in a tote bag, bucket, or huge-pocketed apron. Work around the room methodically; don't backtrack.

5. *Grocery shopping.* Standardize menu lists. Itemize in the order of your favorite store's food arrangement. Learn not to backtrack.

6. *Bed making.* Try the hospital method of making up one side completely before moving around to the other.

7. *Shirt and blouse ironing.* After ironing collar, cuffs, and yoke, place the shirt flat on the ironing board, back down and front halves closed as if to button. Iron the fronts after being sure there are no wrinkles in the back; you will be pressing front and back simultaneously. For any necessary touchup, open the shirt/blouse and lightly iron the inside back.

Eliminate or consolidate errands.

Errands are time gobblers. Use the telephone and mail (for instance, in paying bills and buying gifts). Designate only one day a week for running errands. On each errand day, plot your course: go to the farthest point first, then work your way toward home, taking care of all your business in one trip rather than making a separate trip for each transaction.

Utilize energy peaks.

Each of us has high- and low-energy times throughout the day. We make things difficult for ourselves and unnecessarily extend work by ignoring those body rhythms. Tackle tough jobs when you are energetic. Leave the less demanding ones for your sluggish moments. Highs and lows also occur within a week. Why must thorough house cleaning be done on Saturday morning? If you're a zombie on Saturday morning and a zoomie on Thursday evening, make the obvious adjustment.

Concentrate.

We dawdle over the simplest tasks if we let our minds wander. A self-disciplined worker keeps her attention on what's being done. If certain things consistently distract, put them out of sight. For instance, if you cannot pass that book you're currently reading without stopping to snatch fifteen or twenty minutes' enjoyment, put the book in a drawer while you do your "shoulds." Save the "coulds" for later—as a reward for tasks well done.

Be aware, however, that peak concentration can be maintained for only about thirty minutes. Waning concentration drains efficiency and extends time. Adjust to concentration limits. Instead of working doggedly for three hours preparing a Sunday school lesson, break your study time into thirty-minute segments. Sandwich a physically demanding activity between them (for example ironing or scouring). You will accomplish more in both projects.

Finish the job.

There are some tasks so big that it takes several work periods to complete them. But keep returning to a big job until it's done. Unfinished projects, like clouds, cast unflattering shadows upon our character's landscape—and upon our peace of mind.

Reconceptualize time.

Conceptualize short-range and long-range time more vividly and intensely than as weeks and months. Thinking of time in relation to life and of life as a totality of minutes will help you not to squander the treasure of allotted time. You'll also be more likely than otherwise to make choices that move you toward your life goals.

Compartmentalize planning.

Compartmentalizing is akin to simplification and unification. Here is how it can work. Keep looking ahead on your monthly calendar. Buy greeting cards and gifts for an entire month at the beginning of that month. Then use low-energy times to write the enclosure notes, stamp and address the cards, wrap and address the packages, and write the date each should be mailed or given. Assign a waiting place for these items, and note on the calendar the sending date for each.

Also, prepare for the unforeseeable. It seems that half the world is getting married in any given season and the other half is having babies—and *all* send invitations or announcements to Maidservants. Stock up on suitable wedding and baby gifts three or four times a year when they go on sale. Wrap them and mark them by contents. Keep greeting or enclosure cards handy for individualizing the gifts as needed. This method is a great time saver—vastly superior to the last-minute-run-to-the-store-can't-find-anything approach.

The key ingredient to compartmentalized planning is a calendar notebook, whether purchased or personalized. In size, it should suit your needs, but portability is important. When you have your paper "memory" with you, your mind is freed.

In case you've never found a commercially made calendar notebook that suits your needs, consider creating your own. Design your calendar sheets to reflect your day's normal divisions and duties. Make a master copy and reproduce it in quantity at an inexpensive printing shop or by spirit duplication, xerography, mimeograph, or computer print-out.

On the following page is the design Beneth used before she found a suitable commercial schedule book.

Besides daily sheets, a schedule notebook needs a yearly calendar with monthly pages, enabling quick checks backwards and forwards. Otherwise, a Maidservant can get herself into conflicting obligations.

Replace piles with files.

One of clutter's greatest contributors is paper. Bills, catalogues, school papers, maps, Sunday school lessons, mail, speech outlines, and magazines proliferate at a fantastic rate. If papers are piled here and there around the house, you can lose time and temper riffling through the stacks looking for that one piece you're sure you remember seeing somewhere.

Like your calendar notebook, a filing system should reflect your own routine. Start now. Work your way through one of those paper mountains, making a folder for each category of should-keep papers. If you have no filing cabinet or drawers to hold the folders, store them in a box that will hold them upright, with labeled tabs easily in view. Categories might include these:

- School information
- Boy/Girl Scout or AWANA schedules
- Stored items (lists made according to location)
- Gifts (lists of people, dates, ideas, catalogues)
- Cents-off coupons
- Insurance information
- Dental/medical materials
- Taxes
- First-aid techniques
- Household hints
- Financial records

Day _____

Date _____

Pray for

_____

"This is the day which the LORD hath made . . ."

General To-dos	Errands
Writing	Speaking
Supper Menu	Calls

Once you've established your filing system, keep it alive and well. Never revert to piling. Instead, sort incoming paper items immediately, either flinging them into the wastebasket or filing them in their appropriate folders.

Besides those day-to-day necessity folders, we would also urge you to set up a separate filing system for collecting **ministry resources**. It might include these topics:

- Addresses for equipment/materials sources
- Bulletin-board designs/ideas
- Church bulletins of various types
- Clip art (reproducible for printing)
- Banquet ideas/materials
    General banquets
    Mother-Daughter banquets
- Wedding information (etiquette, etc.)
- Women's retreat/seminar materials
- Women speakers

Such collections will prove invaluable not only to you personally but also to those who serve with you and whom you serve.

Use two-in-ones.

Many of our activities can be done at the same time. These are only some of them:

Drying hair (hood or rollers)/manicure

Typing/facial

Ironing/listening to Scripture tapes

Waiting/note writing, needlework, or reading

Cooking and baking for self/for shut-ins

Create people times.

Don't organize yourself into inhumanity. *People* are the earthly focus of Christian ministry. Consider our family members. We naturally take time for them, don't we? Surprisingly, no. Pressured ministry schedules may give us barely enough time with our families for casual acquaintance. That's not just sad; it's tragic. Times with spouse, children, parents, and extented family must be provided and protected. *People* should take precedence over *projects*.

Outside the family, too, people should be kept central in your concerns. With some thought, you can maximize your availability to persons in need of help. Those requiring special encouragement, for instance, should be favored in your before-or-after-service visiting over those who merely want to chat. If someone needs counseling, you (and your husband) might take them out for lunch. You must be available to your people in order to serve them, and serving people is what ministry is all about.

Systems and schedules are wonderful things—to a point. But be sure to allow mental-emotional leeway for the unexpected. Don't let a dent in neatly jotted plans cause nervous prostration. Adjust to the interference; then restore the interrupted schedule as soon and as completely as possible. A schedule is a sketch, not a finished picture. It is a means to an end, not an end in itself.

Let's also guard against being depressed by what doesn't get done when we'd like it done. Most of us tend toward idealism in our planning. Intentions outrun implementation. When obligations seem to clash head-on, it's important to remember that "to-dos" can wait; "to-bes" and "to-helps" cannot.

The purpose of time management is the heightening of efficiency and the lowering of frustration—obvious enhancers of ministry. But if we let schedules become our masters rather than our servants, we've defeated our purpose in service and missed the entire point. Let's never forget that our times are in His hands. The God whom we serve in ministry has the right to rearrange our schedules as He sees fit!

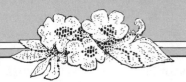

Chapter 8

Domestic Decoration

Home furnishings are important because they constitute our most constant surroundings. The believer's home décor has additional importance as part of her Christian testimony.

There is no set formula or recommended style for furnishing a ministry home. It is wise, however, to aim for a median: a level neither greatly above nor greatly below the comfort and beauty of the average congregational member's home.

Developing Tastes and Knowledge

Other than moderation, the only rule for home furnishings is the personal taste of the ministry person, couple, or family. Whatever the style of another's home, choose yours according to what you like and feel comfortable with. In that way, the structure in which you live will be more than a house or a parsonage. It will be a home reflecting your unique personality.

Our lives and selves are not static. Our preferences change with the rest of us. Therefore, young people are wise not to purchase a full complement of furniture right away. Actually, the "make-do" of furnishing one's first home is a colorful part of life's tapestry. Both authors look back fondly upon various pieces of adaptive furniture in the early (and succeeding!) years of marriage.

Home furnishing choices are rooted in personality make-up. Some delight in the country look. Others shudder at the thought of being surrounded by calico.

A married Maidservant might ask, "What if my husband doesn't like the same type of furnishings I do?" Always consider his preferences as well as your own. A wife who furnishes a house strictly according to her own wishes is unwisely creating a place where her husband doesn't feel fully comfortable. There are homes whose furnishings are so feminine one wonders how a man can endure them. At those points where you and your husband are unshakably opposed in your ideas, work toward compromise. Concessions may be carried out either in overall décor or by decorating some rooms from the "his" standpoint, others from the "hers." We recommend that the master bedroom be an "ours" room.

To learn specifics about home decorating, consult books, articles, and other sources in your spare moments. Become knowledgeable about styles and periods of furniture, shapes and fabrics, and coordination of types, woods, and periods. Happily, you don't have to spend a dime for taste development (unless you forget the library due date!).

Basic principles of interior design can be garnered through observation. Look in women's magazines, newspapers, and other publications; collect pictures of furniture arrangements, window treatments, decorative touches, and color combinations that appeal to you. Browse furniture store displays. Visit model homes, observing what professional decorators have done in them. When you're actually ready to purchase something, browse pawn shops, yard sales, and classified newspaper ads—sources of the *look* you want without the *expense* of buying retail.

In doing your informal study of home furnishings, don't get bitten by the "I-want-one-just-like-that" bug, becoming dissatisfied by comparing your home unfavorably with the slick examples you see. "Godliness *with contentment*" (I Tim. 6:6) should be operative.

Developing "Craftiness"

The more of *you* in your home, the more comfortable and individualistic it will be—to both you and your guests. Your own handiwork throughout your home lends a distinctive personality.

If you have not done handicrafts but feel you'd like to start, do so on a small scale. Learn one craft well and complete its projects rather than jump into several different crafts at once. Beware the high prices of some craft specialty shops. Compare prices. Haunt antique and used-furniture outlets; follow garage sales; keep your eyes open for craft materials in discount stores. *Personalize* needn't mean *pauperize.*

Collect ideas. Talk to practitioners of various crafts. Compare appeal, quality, expense, and difficulty. Booklets, magazines, and books are also good sources for ideas.

Women usually are eager to teach others a craft they themselves enjoy. Craft shops and departments or civic activity groups offer courses in various crafts, either at nominal cost or free with purchase of materials.

Acquaint yourself with the wide variety of handicrafts available for helping you decorate your home inexpensively. Just to whet your appetite, consider the following brief list:

calligraphy	furniture refinishing
ceramics	needlepoint
crocheting	quilting
cross-stitch	rug making
decoupage	sewing
embroidery	tole painting
flower making	upholstering

No ministry woman can count on an abundance of free hours in which to do handicrafts. Much can be done, however, in time slivers that otherwise would be wasted.

Developing Adaptability

Pastoral or missionary housing is determined by the local situation, the specific ministry, and the people. Few ministry women will have the experience of owning a brand-new home built to their dream blueprint.

In some instances, the Maidservant goes into a prefurnished home: a residence owned by the ministry and decorated accordingly. The key to living happily in such a home is *genuine gratitude for what has been provided, balanced by refusal to be enslaved by it.* The fact that a sofa has had brown plaid upholstery for thirty-five years doesn't mean it everlastingly must be so. A furnished home (even if obviously resulting from the emptying of several attics) can be made cozy and individualistic by added touches of your own smaller possessions and by rearranging, refinishing, and recovering of furniture. When outside personalities involve themselves, be sweetly firm in making the décor reflect you and your family. Don't become defensive or angry.

On the other hand, you may be put in an unfurnished house or apartment. For those who have been in the ministry a number of years, that may pose no great problem. But for young people just entering their pathway of service, it is a different story.

When neither the dwelling nor dweller comes equipped with furniture, take your needs *first* to the Lord in prayer. Then do your part by using some of the suggestions above about crafts and bargain hunting. By all means, do not expect to acquire a houseful of "ideal" furnishings right away. Avoid the unrealistic expectations of a regrettably large number of young moderns, even of many dedicated to lives of sacrificial service.

If the rooms of your home are furnished with love, humor, and praise, the floors covered with a thick carpet of gratitude, the whole insulated with prayer, yours will be a *mansion*—regardless of the stick-and-fabric items it may contain or lack.

Chapter 9

Homeside Homiletics

Decorating a home is only the beginning of home care. Whether married or single, serving in America or on a foreign field, she whose life is spent in Christian ministry must figure housekeeping into her time-and-effort demands.

The Principles

Happy and *housekeeping* are not mutually exclusive terms. When God's Word instructs women to be "keepers at home," or housekeepers, it is not consigning us to misery (Titus 2:5). We should acknowledge our housekeeping role and accept it gracefully. Without personal acceptance, the dailies of housework can seem a tyrannical imposition.

Housekeeping should be wisely prioritized—positioned neither at the forefront nor at the tail end of our concerns. The houses we care for are things—material possessions. While it is right to be interested in our homes, our lives must not center upon them. Any material item is God's entrustment, important only in that He has allowed us stewardship over it. That which we hold too tightly actually holds us.

69

While avoiding imprisonment by housekeeping, we must not be escapees from it. No Christian woman, especially one in full-time service, should be so "other worldly" or so ministry driven or so slovenly that her unkempt home blots her testimony.

The purpose of housekeeping, from the Christian perspective, is three-fold:

First, we should desire our home to be a warm haven for its occupants. A carefully tended house provides a shining framework for a loving, nurturing atmosphere.

Second, we should desire our home to extend hospitable welcome to friends, acquaintances, and strangers. Cleanliness and order make significant contributions to godly hostessing.

Third, and outstandingly, our housekeeping should be a tangible testimony of our dedication to Christ. A well-kept home complements Bible studies, Sunday school lessons, and sermons. A poorly kept one just as surely contradicts them.

The Practicalities

The principles of housekeeping appear in its practicalities.

Clean is half the battle.

Establish whatever cleaning schedule works best for you: one that ensures thorough cleaning of the entire house on a regular basis. Designate cleaning jobs as daily, every-other-day, weekly, every-other-week, monthly, semiannual, and annual.

Within the regular cleaning routine, two places in your home should be cleaned every day: the entryway and the bathroom. The entry is seen by all who come to your door, whether they actually enter the house or not. A doorknob bearing caked-on grime, a glass storm door made opaque by grubby handprints, or an entrance hall littered with the flotsam and jetsam of living do not say good things about the home's mistress—or about its Master!

When people come into the house for any but the shortest length of time, count on someone's asking to use the bathroom. When you go into the bathroom of someone else's home, do you not form conclusions about her housekeeping? Don't imagine that others visiting your bathroom are any different. Behind that closed door they make a careful, private evaluation.

There are three "specials" for cleanliness we want to mention: dishcloths and towels, animals and their hair, and general unpleasant odors. Dishcloths and towels should be laundered daily; because of their perpetual dampness while on the job, they quickly sour. Beneth has visited in a ministry home where the dishcloth could be smelled from *clear across the kitchen.*

Animals and their hair are usually taken for granted by the people who live with them daily. Owners become impervious to offensive sights and smells and behavior of their pets. Not so with any outsider entering the house. Animal smells are instantly noticeable and hairs readily visible on furniture and floors. Even if guests are not allergic to dogs and cats, they probably don't relish their smell, their manner of welcome, and their clinging hairs.

Be constantly on guard against general, unpleasant odors in your home. Again, the house's occupants may not even sense the odors that are so familiar to them. However it's not your own nose you are to consider but the visitor's. Simple, consistent cleanliness helps to eliminate the odors of living, but we would urge you to go a step further. Use deodorizing sprays, candles, or potpourri so that the air of your home says "Welcome!" to any entering nose.

Eliminate stacks and steps.

Just as you clear the house of stacked papers, clear it also of stacked paraphernalia. Assign a place for everything; then train family members to return items to their proper place immediately after use.

When you can reduce the number of trips needed to accomplish any housekeeping task, you reduce time and effort. Watch waitresses, bus boys, and professional cleaners for inspiration.

Persistence beats procrastination.

Small cleaning jobs done systematically are more effective, as well as easier on the housekeeper, than a panic-stricken cleaning binge just before guests arrive. The same principle holds in big jobs, such as washing windows and cleaning rugs. It is more effective to do them piecemeal than to delay, hoping for a time segment long enough to complete the whole.

The persistence principle likewise works on a moment-by-moment basis:

1. Think of yourself as a human vacuum cleaner, picking up lint, cat hairs, bits of thread, and so forth as you move about the house doing other things.
2. Take out-of-place items from a room each time you leave it (and teach your children to do the same).
3. Straighten a room occasionally as you move around it doing something else.
4. Clean one cupboard shelf each morning with the breakfast cleanup.
5. Straighten a drawer or shelf between scheduled tasks, or while doing something else, such as baking.

Consider doing a quick mini-clean at three crucial times during the day:

- before leaving the house.
- before the family comes home.
- at bedtime.

While at first glance those may seem "a bit much," look at them again with an eye to improved spirits when you (a) rush back into the house with friends unexpectedly met while shopping, (b) greet your tired husband at the end of your own tired day, and (c) drift off to sleep knowing you won't wake to face a messy house.

Alternate your tasks.

This principle, mentioned in our time management chapter, bears repeating because it can contribute to optimum attention and efficiency.

Housework is a constant factor in our lives. A positive attitude joined with practical efficiency can keep it from becoming drudgery. We must keep before us the eternally important fruits of these seemingly trivial, temporal tasks: a public ministry accredited by the private ministry; children's lives positively imprinted by a religion just as vital during ironing as during the teaching of a Sunday school class; friends, acquaintances, and strangers blessed by what they see and sense in the home.

Surely one of the greatest encouragements to faithfulness and diligence in housework comes from Hebrews 6:10:

> For God is not unrighteous to forget your work and labor of love, which ye have showed toward his name, in that ye have ministered to the saints, and do minister.

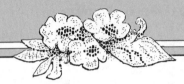

Chapter 10

Ministry Mates

One of the most disheartening realities of our times is the breakup of ministry marriages. Infidelity and runaways have become commonplace. It is no wonder that the breakup of marriages is a prime strategy of Satan in his war against God, for marriage is crucial to the program of God in this world.

Satan works hard against marriage, first, because it is the God-created basic unit of human society. Human community dissolves as the home disintegrates. Satan works especially hard against *Christian* marriage because it is the picture of Christ and His bride, the Church, and also because Christian marriage is meant to perpetuate and enlarge Christ's kingdom by godly offspring. Satan, however, works hardest of all against *ministry marriages*. These marriages are his special targets because they have all the importance of the first two categories plus the significance of being *core or foundational qualifications for ministry*.

The dangers of the day and the strategic importance of the marriage relationship in ministry make it imperative that each of us wives take a new, careful, sensitive, honest, and prayerful look at her own marriage.

Let's begin at the beginning. No matter how many anniversaries we've celebrated, there is always value in considering the basics.

The Creation of Marriage

Women's liberationists direct withering scorn against what they term the manmade or socially imposed institution of marriage, an arrangement designed to "enslave" women. They are, of course, totally mistaken: it was **God Himself** who brought marriage into existence.

In the second chapter of Genesis we read the beautiful story of the divine origination of marriage. The Creator God, seeing Adam's isolation, made for him a strategic counterpart. That premier wedding ceremony brought threefold delight: to Adam, to Eve, and to God. Woman made for and brought to man was creation's completing, crowning moment. Why, then, do some Christian women adopt the world's viewpoint on marriage rather than God's? Surely it is because the serpent Satan is still at work on the Eve within each of us!

God's pronouncement in the Garden of Eden was that a man and his wife would be one flesh. If put into an equation, it would look like this:

$$1 \text{ man} + 1 \text{ woman} = 1 \text{ flesh for life}$$

Marriage brings together two entities that are to make a whole— a **unit** of heart, mind, spirit, and body.

Besides physical, emotional, and mental unity, God designated that the woman's role be supportive: she was to be a **helper fit** for (suiting or adapting herself to) the man (Gen. 2:18).

Scripture sets forth three purposes for marriage: propagation, protection, and pleasure. Genesis 1:28 gives God's directive concerning *propagation:* "Be fruitful, and multiply" (see also Genesis 17:1-8). Malachi 2:15 makes clear that God had in mind more than just the spread of humanity over the earth. God made man and wife "one" for the propagation of godly offspring. Whereas the ungodly avoid conception and abort babies, faithful Christian couples raise up "a godly seed" for the Lord.

The second purpose for marriage is *protection* (or prevention). God designed us as sexual creatures, with inherent desire for physical and emotional fulfillment via intercourse. **Only** in marriage is sexual union beautiful and blessed. First Corinthians 7:1-5 commands spouses to respond generously to one another's needs "to avoid fornication": "Defraud ye not one the other . . . that Satan tempt you not for your incontinency."

The third purpose for the marriage bond is *pleasure*. Sexual pleasure within marriage is defended in Hebrews 13:4 ("Marriage is honourable in all, and the bed undefiled") and encouraged in Proverbs 5:18-19.

In the light of these facts, how should the Christian wife respond to the physical aspect of married life? Unquestionably, in **joyful acceptance** of God's creation of and blessing upon sex in the marriage relationship. That acceptance, however, is difficult for some women. If you happen to be one of those wives who brought into marriage wrong thinking about the husband-wife physical union, and who remain obstinate in this thinking, you need to confess it as a sin. A born-again couple living in poor sexual adjustment is a spiritual, mental, and emotional tragedy, for God pronounced His plan "very good" (Gen. 1:31).

An additional, especially strategic, significance of Christian marriage is God's intention that it picture the beautiful relationship between Christ and His Church (Eph. 5). The capacities of marriage for propagation, moral protection, and pleasure have their spiritual counterparts in the benefits and joys of our relationship with the Lord.

The Creatures of Marriage

Marriage unites a man and a woman: two beings with God-created sexual differences. Modern sociologists perform intellectual gymnastics in downplaying gender differences while scientific research ever more clearly reveals them.

Physical Sex Distinctives

From basic cell formation to major body systems, sexual differences are integral and pervasive, extending to skeletal structure, fat distribution, muscle mass, skin thickness, and other important features. Neither sex is shortchanged by the differentiations. They proclaim God's intention that men and women be mutually completing: complementary.

A man, generally speaking, is more frequently and more strongly eager for physical love than is a woman. For example, tiredness may drive a man *toward* lovemaking, a woman *away* from it. But let this be understood by every wife: the greater male sex drive is God-created; it is not "crude." A physical need akin to hunger for food, it is to be satisfied by the wife.

Men and women have different sexual triggers. Men respond to *visual* stimulation; women to *tactile* (touch).

These observations are given by way of explanation and reassurance. Many times women express puzzlement and frustration over the distinctions discovered in bedroom behavior. There is a twofold message for every ministry wife in these facts: (1) don't expect your husband to act or react sexually as you do; (2) realize the importance of satisfying his sexual needs.

Sexual temptations in modern society are numerous and strong. Don't render your husband vulnerable to those temptations through unfulfilled needs. The ministry man faces sexual temptation in two primary areas. First, women are attracted by male authority figures; some are not reluctant to try enticement. Second, every ministry deals with hurting women; in their pain, they can feel drawn to a man who offers concern and comfort. The proper wifely response is neither unreasoning jealousy toward her husband nor suspicion and denigration of other women in his world. We must instead do everything possible to **armor our men against sexual temptation.** Someone has said, inelegantly but accurately, "A man who gets steak at home is not likely to go out looking for hamburger."

Mental Differences

Here the distinction has to do with mental processes, not capacities. Male mental machinery is strongly logical, comprehensive, and long-range. The female mind, on the other hand, operates more in the realm of feelings and intangibles, including intuition. It is details oriented. Recent studies show that these differences have their roots in actual physical operations: in the distribution of functions between the brain hemispheres. Men are predominantly left-brain-oriented, women right-brain. The statements so often made, therefore, about men not being able to understand women's thinking, and vice versa, have a basis in physical fact. There is no "better" or "worse" involved in the diverse mental responses. One is not more *intelligent* than the other. There is simply a difference. Again, however, we should focus upon the purpose for God's creating us with these mental distinctives: compensation and completion as husband and wife blend their diverse mental perspectives.

Emotional Differences

Generally speaking, men are stable in their emotions. Their logical mental orientation and noncyclical physiology spare them the emotional variations common to women. They do not personalize words and actions as women do.

The masculine objective bent is a positive factor in his God-assigned leadership role. Consider a hypothetical situation, to illustrate. A family of five is ready to leave for vacation. Just as they near the door, the telephone rings. The owner of the town's only boarding kennel is calling to tell them not to bring their two dogs and four cats for vacation boarding; a fire during the night destroyed the kennel. At the news, five-year-old Lillian cries in the certainty that their vacation is ruined; eleven-year-old Lizzie cries imagining how their pets might have been killed; eight-year-old Larry has run ahead to the car and is honking the horn with one hand while holding the leashed dogs with the other, all the while keeping one foot atop the loose lid of the cats' carry box. Mother Marcia comes unglued emotionally, wailing "What can we do?" Father Fred marches through the mayhem and picks up the telephone directory. In such a moment, because she's immersed in personal and family concerns, Mother may long for Father's gentle comfort for herself and the children, becoming irritated by his focus on finding a viable solution.

When mental/emotional cogs fail to mesh between the sexes, as in the example given, the woman should carefully guard against two destructive judgments: first, that the man is *uncaring;* second, that he is *unmanly.* In the male, caring and manliness are most naturally and automatically expressed through practicality.

Men steel themselves against overt emotional demonstration; women have the need to express what they feel. This latter distinction offers particular challenge to marital communication. Someone has noted that women are **body** modest; men are **soul** modest. Just as a husband's accepting, loving, appreciative spirit eases a woman's innate reluctance to reveal her physical self, so the wife's proper spirit encourages a man to reveal his inmost self.

Gender-oriented differences are not the sole distinctions that become obvious in marriage. Because no two **people** are alike, marriage inevitably creates areas of necessary adjustment and possible conflict.

Innate Characteristics

Every child is born with complicated genetic coding; he or she is a product not only of father and mother but also of earlier generations. Like a fine vase whose one-of-a-kind design and mold are unique, so too is every human being. In marriage each partner's individuality must somehow meld with the other's into a lovelier whole. What a challenge to patience, perception, and prayer!

Background

Studies indicate that personality and character are formed by the age of three. Throughout succeeding years, formative factors make ever deeper impressions.

Suppose a man brings into marriage the background patterning to drop clothing, reading materials, and other articles wherever and whenever he's through with them. By contrast, his wife may have grown up in a house where neatness was a cardinal rule.

Imagine a wife whose home training about the Lord's Day was easygoing; relaxation was its main ingredient. The husband, however, came from a home where observance of the Lord's Day was very stringent; letter writing was the only allowable activity.

Whatever the differences, the partners' attitudes toward adjusting are crucial. Flexibility in both husband and wife is a must. Should either retain the "I'm right; you're wrong, and I won't budge an inch" attitude, the other will suffer emotional bruisings. There cannot come the true unifying God desires. Harmony depends upon both partners obeying the scriptural command, "Yea, all of you be subject *one to another,* and be clothed with humility" (I Pet. 5:5).

No matter how compatible a man and woman may seem before marriage, later actualities reveal differences. At each point of contrast, meshing demands freedom for and acceptance of the other's individualities plus mutual concession for the sake of love's bonding.

External Pressures

In-law Interference

The challenge of in-law interference must be met by obedience to the scriptural principle of leaving and cleaving—leaving parental jurisdiction and forming a new entity as man and wife. Each marriage partner must leave his or her family not only physically but also emotionally as far as dependency and primary loyalty are concerned.

None of the above, however, means that a ministry woman ever is justified to harbor bitterness toward offending parents, whether they be hers or her husband's. Nor is she to forsake them in the sense of abandoning or rejecting them.

Friends

Like families, friends can pressure a marriage. Friends may feel commissioned to offer unsolicited advice. Their motives are not always suspect: it may be genuine sympathy and good will that prompts them to interfere. It is up to each marriage partner to restructure personal friendships in the light of the marriage relationship. If either partner holds tightly to friends from single days without incorporating the mate's friends, a kind of mental/emotional tug of war may result. A couple should, from the outset, endeavor to have not *"my* friends" and *"your* friends" but *"our* friends."

All friends should be excluded from intimate, detailed sharing of the marriage's inner workings. Sometimes a partner (particularly the wife) is tempted to betray marital privacy. To do so imparts a threefold burden: upon listener, speaker, and marriage.

A final word about friendship: it is destructive to harbor the attitude "You're my husband/wife, but my real supporters, helpers, confidants are my friends." None of us should have a dearer, more highly treasured friend than our life's mate. Nor should our social involvement reach the point of straining that essential friendship.

The Ministry Itself

A third source of pressure on ministry marriage may be the ministry itself. This pressure is increased by unfulfilled expectations. If, for instance, we have pictured the ministry as an idealized side-by-side partnership, the reality of constantly conflicting schedules can be crushing.

It doesn't take long to realize how energetically demanding and emotionally draining full-time Christian service is. There is so much to do, so many long hours, that little may be left but exhaustion. Dealing with people means giving out emotionally to them. Our emotional reservoir can run dry before we get it home.

Pressure comes, too, as the marriage partners experience unforeseen dimensions of the ministry in people, profession, and place. The "ideal" congregation does not exist. Instead, every group of believers sooner or later reveals its self-appointed critics, its deacon-devils, and its assistant-antagonists. The unperceived, unpublicized aspects of ministry can seem overwhelming. Whatever the locale, Christian workers usually refer to some characteristic making their place of ministry "hard." The battles and batterings can have repercussions in the ministry marriage.

Every woman in the Lord's work must guard against resenting the pressures inherent in ministry. Instead, we should recognize and accept them, all the while working carefully and prayerfully to so strengthen and beautify the fabric of our marriage that pressure smoothes rather than causes wrinkles.

Wives' Working Outside the Home

The twentieth century has added yet another challenge to marriage: wives' working outside the home. The decision about the wife's outside employment is a private matter to be decided as husband and wife agree before the Lord. However, the marriage partners should be aware of three possible complications:

1. Distraction from the wife's main purpose.
2. Competition with domestic time and attention.
3. Increased opportunities for temptation.

Let us say just a word about the third point. The work place is a classic site for temptation. There may be the temptation of money itself as the paycheck begins to look good, and then essential. If job promotions come, the expanding responsibilities bring fatter pay envelopes, increased self-confidence, and greater independence. There is also occasion for temptation toward marital infidelity. The possibility seems unthinkable, of course, but the secular work world has become a cesspool of immorality. The average man or woman hardly knows where to find *decency* in the dictionary. A Christian woman in the work place can be an intriguing challenge to the seductive abilities of worldly men. We may gasp in astonishment, "Me? Never!" However, Scripture has something to say about one who feels herself impervious to temptation: "Let him that thinketh he standeth take heed lest he fall" (I Cor. 10:12).

It is unfortunate that the issue of working wives has caused recriminations and divisions in the Christian community. In some quarters the stay-at-home wife has become an *extrascriptural* fetish; its worshipers not only bow down to their idol but also criticize any who refuse to do so. While outside work is not ideal for a Maidservant, it cannot be condemned out of hand. Sometimes a wife and mother must work outside the home. There are areas of the country where the cost of living is so high the wife must help support the family or finance the children's Christian schooling. Are those areas to be abandoned, left untouched by biblical ministries? Can God's keeping power not be trusted to offset the difficulties?

In order to be fair and reasonable, we must note the positives that can come from outside employment. Ministry wives who work tell of wonderful opportunities for testimony among unsaved whom they would otherwise never touch. The experience of outside work, as well, may enable the Maidservant to empathize with congregation women who work, thus expanding her ministry to them. Finally, the Lord can actually strengthen family unity as members draw together, each shouldering part of the burden created by Mother's outside job.

Nevertheless, if at all possible, avoid taking outside work before the children start school. The early childhood years are strategic, fleeting, never to be regained.

Imperative employment should be agreed upon, chosen, and hedged about with prayer by both husband and wife. Unless the couple has come to the empty-nest stage of life, any outside employment should be considered **temporary only** and discontinued as soon as possible so that husband and wife can return to wholehearted, unified concentration upon and dedication to the joint ministry God has given them.

Internal Pressures

Personal Differences

Personal differences, if allowed to do so, can become battle-grounds. Marriage partners become vulnerable to wounding words and lose the ability to laugh off inevitable minor conflicts. The daily pressures of marriage demonstrate that love involves much more than appears in its dictionary definition. The Christian couple do not head for divorce court when troubles arise; they turn to God's Word, seeking His definition rather than Webster's. The thirteenth chapter of I Corinthians must be operative in their relationship if they are to weather the storms on matrimony's sea.

Titus 2:5 speaks to the purpose of the wife's management of personal differences. Wives are "to be discreet, chaste, keepers at home, good, obedient to their own husbands, that the word of God be not blasphemed." These qualities have some interesting and demanding nuances as they are translated in the Amplified Version.

discreet = self-controlled
chaste = pure
keepers at home = homemakers
good = good-natured (kindhearted)
obedient = adapting and subordinating themselves

If those clarifying words don't give each of us Christian wives something to chew on, we've lost our spiritual teeth!

Finances

Finances rank high on the list of marital trouble spots. Despite an engaged couple's having discussed future economizing, the reality of skimping may prove unpleasant. Few Christians are rich in this world's goods, and those who dedicate themselves to any area of full-time service are likely to face particularly short finances. *Reactions* to financial pressures become crucial: both spiritually and maritally, they will have a telling effect. We can allow penny-pinching to be a worrisome burden or a motivation to greater dependency upon and delight in God's promises. A wife can choose to let financial strictures press her away from or closer to her husband.

Do your parents or your husband's family lament your financial hardships? They may even be so thoughtless as to hint that there would have been plenty of money had you married someone else or were you not in the ministry. Be sweet to them, but *don't listen!* Happiness and effective service are not synonymous with a sizable bank account.

Ministry Characteristics

Ministry characteristics likewise can pressure the marriage bond. It is not particularly easy, for instance, to move frequently, to live in a house chosen and furnished by church committees, to adjust to different areas of the country, to survive an always-on-call schedule, to rear children with an audience. And yet, rather than let these "adverse" circumstances become destructive, we can allow God to teach us something special in each instance. The constructive attitude is "All right, Lord, you've ordained this as part of my life and service. Control my thoughts and reactions so that I may grow spiritually and bring glory to You in the midst of it." In the face of ever changing circumstances, how sweet is the personal relationship focused upon our never changing Lord Jesus Christ!

The Changes in Marriage

Marriage is not static. Its inevitable changes move the relationship either toward betterment or disintegration. The wife, to a great degree, determines the direction, because God created woman to center upon the home. It is her primary realm of responsibility, concentration, and interest. The man, by contrast, focuses more upon matters outside the home—again, in accord with God's creative plan.

Marriage also mirrors change according to larger blocks of time, or states of life, four of which are more or less clearly definable: newlywed bliss, toddler blitz, school-years blurs, and empty-nest blahs. Let's briefly think about each of these.

Newlywed Bliss

Newlywed bliss takes in the honeymoon, post-honeymoon, and playing-house days. During this time, the young couple's world is generally fresh and rosy. But as days go by and life leaves the rarified heights of romance to settle into normalcy, the rosy glow may be shadowed by leaves, stems, and thorns. Most of the shadows are cast by *unfulfilled expectations*. We all enter marriage with preconceived ideas about how situations—and people—will be. But mental pictures have little if anything to do with reality. Most of our expectations are illusions. When they do not materialize, we experience *disillusionment*.

Toddler Blitz

The toddler blitz usually follows hard on the heels of the newlywed period. The arrival of little people means abrupt, drastic changes for big people. Suddenly there are mountainous demands day and night. As a result, the wife may experience physical and emotional exhaustion.

Within this period lies a very real but little-recognized danger: transferring *too* much attention to the child or children. As babies arrive upon the domestic scene, a husband may have the uneasy feeling of being crowded out of his wife's affection and attention. This results from contrasting adjustments to parenting. It is said that with the coming of the first child, the man remains 75% husband while becoming 25% father; the woman, however, becomes 75% mother and remains only 25% wife. The possible clash is obvious. One young woman confided, "I have a real problem since the baby came. I consider my breasts the source of food for my baby rather than the source of joy for my husband." Common problem!

The husband's uneasiness over his wife's change of emotional focus may cause him to make unreasonable demands of her as he tries to regain the centrality he formerly enjoyed. The wise wife will recognize her husband's actions as the plea they really are. It is essential that she so arrange her busy days that she has time and energy to spend on being an ever better helpmeet.

Here are a few suggestions for keeping attentions to husband and baby properly balanced:

1. Don't overdo telling of Junior's exploits. Extol Senior's as well.
2. Don't be loath to turn the baby over to a sitter so that you and your husband can go out for dinner or on another type of "date."
3. Take a nap while Baby does so that you can be fresh, not frazzled, when Hubby comes home.

School-Years Blurs

Following toddler blitz comes school-years blurs. Diapers are put aside. Now Mama needs a chauffeur's license. Infant wails give way to a ringing telephone and endless conversations in giggling voices. Progress through school and its extracurriculars, plus church involvement, music training, dental and medical care for the children, amount to nonstop schedule-juggling for their mother. When the children reach high school or college age, the wife may find it necessary to work outside the home in order to provide tuition. And throughout the teen years there is the indescribable strain of parenting teens, whose intensity, volatility, exuberance, independence, and insecurities make the parents realize their own fast-advancing years.

Empty-Nest Blahs

After the rush-rush-rush of the family-filled years, there comes the hush-hush-hush we call the empty-nest blahs. All at once the children are gone from home, pursuing their individual, mature lives. The empty quietness may leave the parents mentally and emotionally disoriented. Their world for twenty years or more has turned upon the axis of child care. Husband and wife must make another abrupt adjustment—this time back into the original twosome. Ideally, marriage partners will have so concentrated attention and care upon their relationship through the years that the children's departure, though saddening, simultaneously frees them for the joy of unhindered togetherness.

It is a shocking truth that many marriages break during the empty-nest period. Marriages of twenty-five or thirty years' duration are shattered by infidelity and divorce. What may seem sudden to outsiders, however, actually reflects a gradually weakening marriage bond throughout the family-busy years. The childless house merely exposes the marriage's cracks, thinnings, and strained spots. We will repeat a point made earlier: the wife who possesses godly wisdom will spend her child-rearing years reserving special attention for her man. In that way, time's passage will strengthen rather than weaken the marital bonding. God said, "The *two* shall be one flesh," not three, four, or five. That elemental entity must be constantly and tenderly nurtured.

The Criminals of Marriage

Sometimes marriage partners guard against external dangers while harboring hidden, shadowy enemies within. These, like the others, must be diligently exposed and opposed.

Attitude

The primary marriage criminal working from the inside is attitude—particularly the wife's. Her world, the home, is colored by her attitude as it seeps through words, actions, and thoughts. Specifically, Maidservants are afflicted by—and afflict their homes with—three attitudes containing the explosive equivalent of TNT: indifference, discouragement, and resentment.

A wife sometimes adopts *indifference* as a protective mechanism. She finds things in her mate, their relationship, their place, or their calling that she dislikes or by which she is hurt, and she takes shelter in cool detachment. Emotional coolness is difficult for a man to accept. He may react by bringing out the only weapons he knows to use against it: anger, recriminations, jealousy, or indifference of his own. If the cool . . . cooler . . . coolest trend goes unchecked, the love relationship that God intended for supreme beauty becomes a tattered, battered, and ugly thing.

Or consider the second inside criminal: *discouragement.* Obviously the wrong attitude for a Maidservant, this internal criminal is born when a woman's focus is in the wrong direction: upon herself or her circumstances.

Women tend to be insecure and highly critical of themselves. A wife's brooding over what she considers her inadequacies can drag her into the pits of discouragement. Add to that a few random critical comments by an unwary husband, and she plunges deeper. When a wife *feels* discouraged, she begins to *act* discouraged. Her husband may, at first, try to cheer and encourage her. But if she holds stubbornly to the weights on her heart, he may feel that the job is hopeless. His giving up will plunge her deeper still . . . and so it goes. Eventually a man becomes self-protective by

- ignoring the perpetual gloom,
- meeting it with forced and phony joviality,
- feeling guilty thinking he has caused it, or
- fleeing its depressive presence.

Similar discouragement can grip a wife if she looks too long and critically at her circumstances: the threadbare furniture, the cracked china, the dusty road too close to the house, the church members with oversized curiosities and undersized manners. There are many things in any locale or setting that can become sources of discouragement. But we must remember that no challenges, privations, or circumstances are bigger than the God who promises to make us *more than conquerors.*

A third destructive attitude cropping up in some ministry women is *resentment and bitterness.* Like discouragement, bitterness comes from wrong focus and negative feelings pandered to instead of purged. One feels badly treated—cheated, as it were, by life. More accurately, the bitter woman feels God Himself has let her down. A ministry woman can grow bitter over any number of "causes"—running the gamut from irritating isolation to pressuring publicity; from too-great involvement in the ministry to feeling isolated from it. The single Maidservant may become bitter over her singleness. That particular heart gall often produces enmity against others' reputations and marriage. On and on it goes . . . seeds of bitterness are as numerous as the women who allow them to be sown in heart and life. That is, in fact, the key: the *woman herself* is to blame for the bitterness filling her breast. While she accusingly points at things or people or circumstances, the real fault rests in her own *chosen* outlook and reactions.

All of us make mental evaluations. We classify some things as "good" or "blessings"; other things as "bad" or "burdens." But for the believer, *all things are good* in that they have (a) come from the hand of the Father, either through direction or allowance and (b) are meant for our growth and His glory. With that truth tempering our spirit, we can accept life's less desirable elements with rejoicing rather than resentment.

The Bible addresses the problem of bitterness with inescapable directness as we are told to be "looking diligently lest any man fail of the grace of God; lest any root of bitterness springing up trouble you, and thereby many be defiled" (Heb. 12:15).

Immaturity

Another criminal working from within the marriage relationship is immaturity. Perhaps because in many cases the choice of marriageable young people is small for a born-again teen, many marry before they have the mental and emotional maturity to build a strong, enduring relationship. The outstanding characteristics of immaturity are selfishness and oversensitivity. Any marriage will suffer intense strain if the partners are emotional juveniles.

Acid Tongue

One of the most energetic internal criminals of marriage is an acid tongue. This enemy seems more often found in the female than in the male mate. Recent studies have shown that the female brain tends toward greater facility with verbal expression. Structural gender differences can become a Goliath in our lives. Specifically, this enemy works through four C's:

- criticizing
- complaining
- counseling
- clamming up

Let's briefly examine each of those deadly instruments of marital warfare.

It is easy to extend our self-critical tendency toward others. The nearest, handiest object is the man with whom we live. The criticism probably begins early—when the bride realizes the groom is not Mr. Perfect and begins trying to redesign him by force. A man's selfhood is a fragile thing. Critical jabbing at his faults mangles the fabric of his being. To the extent the home's *head* is weakened or wounded, so too is the entire home.

Perhaps your tongue does not take the direct attack of criticism but instead prefers the sneak attack of complaint. If you complain about low salary, unsatisfactory housing, hectic schedule, and so forth, your husband's heart interprets those gripes as his *unsatisfactory provision* for you.

It is, of course, right that the wife, while daily growing in her knowledge of the Word and her walk with the Lord, should take an active interest in things that interest her husband. But growth and interest can motivate unsolicited advice or instruction to the husband. The ministry home can become one in which the man is advised, directed, corrected, and generally steamrollered—all with the stated motivation of "helping" by Mrs. Sweetie Perfection. And pity the man who gets himself maritally enmeshed with a female theolog! Homes where the wife holds sway as combination conscience/Holy Spirit/mother adviser are unhealthy. As a result, the husband may swing either to sentimentality or harshness—both evidences of his being driven by the emotional half of the unit. A manly man resents feeling he's being instructed by his wife, and rightly so. According to God's Word, that is an upside-down situation. The man weak enough to accede to his wife's advice giving grows weaker; the strong man may react by hardening himself not only against her advice but also against her. Either way, the counseling tongue of a ministry wife is destructive.

Although there are marriages in which the wife's counsel is eagerly sought and gracefully accepted, our contacts overwhelmingly indicate they are rare. There are several possible reasons: the husband's insecurity, poor communication skills in one or both mates, or the wife's negative spirit.

Women often ask, "Shouldn't I ever state my opinion? What about when he asks me for advice?" Certainly, a wife is to use her mind, with her mental ability complementing her husband's. She should think clearly and pray deeply about the various aspects of the life and ministry they share. Nevertheless, volunteered input should be carefully rationed, and requested input restrainedly presented. A wise wife guards the spirit with which she states opinions and observations, avoiding anything that smacks of superiority, badgering, challenge, "putting down," or pressuring. Should her husband ultimately fail in the discussed endeavor, she must avoid having an "I told you so" or "you should have listened to me" attitude.

Rather than "overtalk," some wives "undertalk." For whatever reason, a woman may have developed an uncommunicative trait during her growing-up years. This trait, during marriage, can exert itself at times when open communication is most needed—for example, when misunderstanding arises between husband and wife. Whether to maintain control or to insulate herself against hurt, the wife may "clam up." She locks her husband out of her mind and heart so that he must try to guess at her feelings, thoughts, and reactions. More often wrong than right in his guesses, the poor husband proceeds upon an incorrect assumption, thus heading for even greater trouble. The uncommunicative wife herself suffers. By not expressing the problem, she prevents its exposure and dissipation. Instead, she harbors it for further brooding and bother.

The Wife's Charge in Marriage

Building a Home

Proverbs 14:1 provides the challenge: "Every wise woman buildeth her house; but the foolish plucketh it down with her hands." The wise woman of God will so concentrate upon, pray over, and live within her home that the atmosphere will be positive, warm, pure, loving, open, and protective. A positive spiritual atmosphere is not something you "work up." It is, rather, something you *live out.*

The foundation upon which a ministry wife must build her home is the Lord Jesus Christ Himself. The central pillar, humanly speaking, must be her husband. That is his rightful, God-ordained position. Yet many a woman tries to remove her husband from centrality. As a result, the roof begins to sag, the walls to buckle. Rather than building her house, she is pulling it down, bringing it to ruin. She will prove the warning of Proverbs 11:29: "He that troubleth his own house shall inherit the wind."

Kindness and courtesy—simple as they are—make constructive contributions to a home. In its discussion of husband-wife relationships, I Peter 3:8 urges sensitivity and gentleness: "Finally, be ye all of one mind, having compassion one of another, love as brethren, be pitiful, be courteous." Family members should enjoy our very best manners, our most thoughtful attitudes and actions. Lack of courtesy indicates carelessness—the Devil's crowbar against the home. Some of the most important words in the English language are very small ones—"please," "thank you," and "I'm sorry." Shouldn't we ministry women excel in the sincere, daily use of those mighty midgets?

Constructing Emotional Unity

Women desire to be loved. But few seem to realize that love must be *extended* as well as *enjoyed.* No one enters marriage an expert on love. Genuine love is a growing, learning process. Contrary to a fond false theory, marriage in and of itself does not, *cannot,* create happiness. Marriage partners must work together to make a happy marriage. Because the wife is the partner whose emotional sensibilities are the more tender, she is the one whose contribution to the emotional bonding seems most apparent.

Wives can weaken emotional "glue" by wishing their husbands would express their love in ways more nearly like their own—the gentle touch, the secret glance, the loving word. When, instead, the man gives his wife a new washing machine or a vacuum cleaner, she may wrongly judge him lacking in love. The masculine expression of love, however, is often practical and solid: the lawn work, the savings account. He is saying "I love you" *in his own way.* Treasure that fact, and rejoice in its expression.

Enhancing Physical Completeness

The components of our human make-up are so closely intertwined as to be inseparable. Mind, heart, soul, and body are meshed so tightly that one cannot be neglected without the whole suffering. Conversely, when one is benefited, all profit. A wife contributes to her husband's *total* well-being when she meets his sexual needs. Failure in this area pulls bricks from the walls of her marriage by denying needed support to her husband's emotional self. A wife's joyful, uninhibited, avid meeting of her husband's physical needs in the bedroom is the best human insurance she can provide against his infidelity.

Supporting a Positive Self-Image

Men seem self-possessed, emotionally secure, take-care-of-themselves creatures. They have, instead, tremendous needs in the area of self-concept. A wife acts as her husband's mirror. He sees himself in her representations of him. If she represents him negatively through speech, attitude, or action, his self-image is shaken. The prudent wife—a gift from the Lord (Prov. 19:14)—is ever *building* her husband's sense of self. She does not give in to the temptation to snipe at him—for example, by commenting on his expanding waistline, receding hairline, or colorblind clothing choice. Instead, she will tell him and show him positive things about himself—his looks, his spirit, his actions, his provision for the family. In other words, she works at encouragement. Encouragement arms a man. A wise wife buckles him into that armor each day as he goes out to face the world and polishes it each evening when he comes home weary and battered from the fray.

Extending Spiritual Well-Being

Primarily, the wife helps her husband spiritually by praying for him. Supportive, intercessory prayer is the most important responsibility we have as ministry wives; yet probably it is the most neglected. Our prayers for our husbands should address both practical and spiritual matters. An excellent pattern of prayer for spiritual well-being is Colossians 1:9-12.

Some years ago Dave composed the following prayer guide. Bobbie has since found it an effective pattern for her daily prayers for him.

A Prayer for Pastor

Pure in life
Joyful in heart
Mighty in spirit
Strong in conviction
Honest in motive
Prevailing in prayer
Powerful in preaching
Effective in witnessing
Abundant in wisdom
Selfless in service
Patient in trouble
Victorious in battle

—David Yearick

A wife's praying through that petition several times a day for her husband could make the difference between his becoming a mighty preacher or a mediocre one; a triumphant battler against temptation or a struggling, capitulating weakling.

A husband's spiritual well-being also is enhanced as his wife follows his spiritual leadership. Sometimes a Maidservant may feel awkward recognizing her husband as her pastor as well as her life mate. Human nature's perversity would have us react to that awkwardness by challenging, resenting, or denying his leadership. But if the wife does not follow her husband's lead, others will have a hard time doing so.

The essential element in a wife's right spiritual contribution to her husband is *reverence*. Ephesians 5:33 reads, "And the wife see that she reverence her husband." That word *reverence* is a tough one to demonstrate in the "everydayness" of marital living. We make excuses such as the husband's flawed personality or unsatisfactory performance. But according to the Bible, we are to reverence him because of his *position:* his God-designated headship. It is important, then, that we know what reverence entails. The Amplified New Testament renders the passage this way: "And let the wife see that she respects and reverences her husband—that she notices him, regards him, honors him, prefers him, venerates and esteems him; and that she defers to him, praises him, and loves and admires him exceedingly."

Proper reverence for her husband obviously cannot be given by a wife who judges his spiritual condition. It would be foolish to pretend that all ministry husbands are what they should be spiritually. Sadly, there are some who are wretched hypocrites: they preach one thing while living the opposite. Nevertheless, a wife's scornful judgment of such a one does not help. She should redirect her energy into *intercessory prayer*. The changes needed in his life are *spiritual*. They must be wrought by God Himself.

A final duty in support of a husband's spiritual state is encouraging his time alone with the Lord: guarding the place and time of his devotional life against invasion.

In conclusion, let's allow ourselves to be challenged by another verse from Proverbs: "A virtuous woman is a crown to her husband; but she that maketh ashamed is as rottenness in his bones" (12:4). Each of us might well ask herself, "Right now, at this moment, would God judge me to be a *crown* or a *corrosive* to my husband and consequently to the ministry we share?"

Chapter 11

Parsonage Parenting

It is essential that progeny validate preaching. God's Word makes it clear that ministry leaders should have children who are a credit to the ministry. Speaking of the "bishop," or preacher, I Timothy 3:4-5 says he is to be "one that ruleth well his own house, having his children in subjection with all gravity; (for if a man know not how to rule his own house, how shall he take care of the church of God?)"

A Maidservant is called upon to instruct others about rearing children. More effective than her advice is her *demonstration* of proper godly child rearing. As with so many other things, however, the proclamation of proper parenting is easier than the practice.

Ministry Kids—Their Reputation

Ministry children are burdened with negative stereotyping, which they must be taught to disprove rather than to reinforce. Let's consider the negatives attributed to ministry children. Forewarned is forearmed.

Maidservants should be prepared to deal with the common perception that *ministry kids are spoiled brats*. All too often it's true. Obnoxious children not only bring difficulty and dislike to themselves but also adversely affect the ministry. Members of the congregation resent child-rearing admonitions from leaders who fail with their own young.

Ministry parents must discern between earned and unfounded criticism. At times, of course, the charge of brattiness is unfounded. The critics may be motivated by a "squirming" reflex: trying to deflect criticism of or dissatisfaction with their own children. But automatic disbelief that our child *could* be bratty will do him tremendous harm: like a bad apple, he will get progressively more rotten himself and infect others.

Perhaps the main contributor to spoiling is publicity. A Christian worker's child automatically experiences a certain amount of spotlight that spills over from his parents. Church and staff members may flatter and pamper him. He may be called on to answer most of the questions in Sunday school; be favored and protected from normal social badgering common to youngsters; be given starring roles in musical or dramatic presentations; have his looks, talents, personality, and actions glowingly and ceaselessly touted; be urged to perform his latest piano piece, and so on. Such favoritism will reap the inevitable harvest: a brat who feels he is "different," "special," above criticism.

Overall, the best things Christian leaders can do to encourage normalcy in their children are to

1. Insist that they be treated like everyone else. Uphold rules, policies, and authority. Ministry children must be subjected to standards required of others; their violations must bring identical punishment. They should not be allowed to benefit from their high connections—from opportunities for high-level interference on their behalf or from access to special channels of appeal. The question is sometimes asked, "What if my child really is treated unfairly? Don't I take his side against the authority?" The answer is *no*. Instead, use the experience to teach him that many things in life are unfair. Special leniency in demands, flexibility of standards, partiality in rewards, or opportunity for appeal destroys respect and invalidates testimony.
2. Keep them out of the spotlight. (Yes, involve them in the ministry, but in behind-the-scenes *service* roles.)

Another negative stereotype of ministry children is that of "goody two shoes." This usually is a false charge. Children are too bent toward naturalness to be concerned about perfection in appearance and action. The charge may be motivated by resentment of a real or imagined spiritual superiority over the critic's own children.

Still another negative in the stereotyping of ministry children is their future prospects—they will reject their upbringing and live worthless lives. Skeptics have their list of Christian leaders' children who have become *reprobate, renouncers of the Faith.* This allegation comforts those who are looking for excuses for failure with their own children. "Look how kids from Christian leaders' homes turn out! There's no use trying to rear a decent kid in my home; it's hopeless. I'll just relax and forget all this Bible-and-discipline stuff." It is interesting that, of those who have made worthwhile contributions to American life in various professions, three times as many have come from preachers' homes as from any other family background.

Ministry Kids—Their Requirements

Brooding over the reputation of ministry children is fruitless. Engaging in practical, prayerful efforts for their successful rearing is what is required. A good starting point is Proverbs 22:6, perhaps the most often quoted Bible verse about child rearing: "Train up a child in the way he should go, and when he is old, he will not depart from it."

Digging into the verse uncovers a parenting treasure. The word *train* has threefold meaning in the original language:

1. To control and guide, as with a horse
2. To create a taste for
3. Dedication

We parents often misinterpret the *train* verb—usually by putting into action only the *first* of those meanings. We will have more success if we implement the full definition.

Some Bible scholars point out that the phrase "the way he should go" not only refers to the way of decency, purpose, and service but also to the child's God-determined bent: his talents, interests, personality. The verse then supports a consideration for the child's personal capacities and inclinations and a tailoring of his training to his individual nature. A wise parent notices the strengths and propensities of this child and educates him in the direction of his natural grain.

Specifically, what do ministry children require to grow to faithful, useful maturity? *They require precisely what a child in any Christian home requires*, with a few extra considerations.

Love

Simple as this necessity may seem, its actuality is complex. Perhaps the preeminent rule for parents in Christian work is that *love for the ministry and the people must never be (or seem to the child to be) greater than love for the child*. Full observance of that rule can come only with effort and prayer. The difficulty lies in the amount of time necessarily spent in ministry. Children equate time with love.

Love for our children must be clearly communicated. Touch is particularly potent in this. Scientific studies show that cuddling is vital even to a tiny baby. Without it, he actually can sicken and die. Though cuddling and tender touching would seem to be natural for a mother, such is not always the case. A mother's behavior toward her children reflects her own upbringing. If it was of the "touch-me-not" type, she may have difficulty communicating to her own children physical security and warmth.

The built-in need for physical closeness and warmth continues throughout the difficult teen years and must be met if the child is to reach his full potential. The mother's quick hug for her gangly teen-age son can do more to give him a sense of security and well-being than any lengthy treatise. The parents' loving touch also serves as a restraint and protector. At the time the young person's body is undergoing the sexual maturation that so changes and shapes him or her, the loving hugs, kisses, and pats from the parent of the opposite sex act as an anchor against the surging tide of sexual need until it can be rightly fulfilled within marriage.

Touching should not be the sole means of communicating love. We need to be *telling* our children we love them—often—throughout the years as they grow up. Few things are nicer to a child than "Bye, Honey, have a good day—I love you!" or "Good night, Johnny—I love you" or "Love you, Sweetheart" stuck to the refrigerator door or written in soap on the bathroom mirror. Through the tempestuous teens, those three little words *I love you* do so much to smooth the transition to maturity.

Proper Christian parental love is also *considerate*: it is concerned for the child's good. Genuine love asks, "What can I do for you? What do you need?'' For instance, how wise (or spiritual!) is the ministry mother who drags a sniffling, feverish child to every session of a week-long evangelistic meeting?

It is particularly important that a mother be finely tuned to her children so that she can sense the needs they're unable to express. How sweet to draw a grumpy, restless child down on the sofa beside you, put an arm around him, pull him close, and say, ''Things haven't gone too well for you at school today, have they, Honey?'' Sure enough, the tears begin to flow as he tells of some disappointment or embarrassment.

We also should respect individualities. Proper parental love recognizes differences and loves each child for what he or she is as an individual. It *does not have favorites* or compare one child unfavorably with another. To favor any of our children is to misuse all of them. Wise love recognizes that the treatment of the child must be specially tailored to his individual capacities, personality, and interests. The parent with a ''one-size-fits-all'' approach will suffer frustration and failure. As in the case of snowflakes, no two children are the same. None can be forced into another's mold.

Allowance also must be made for the child's good growth. Genuine love does not hold a child too close to its breast, thereby suffocating it. ''Smother'' love is not godly parental love. Wise love gives its children room to breathe, to develop, to learn— even, when necessary, painfully. Though smother love looks upon itself as sincere, actually it is ill-disguised selfishness. Too-close binding is for the parent's emotional benefit rather than the child's. Pity the child so used and abused!

Love for a child should be consistent and unconditional. Because we in ministry desire our children to be all they can be for God, we sometimes use love like a bone for a dog—giving it for actions and attitudes that please us, withholding it when they don't. A child—any child—desperately needs to know *he can always count on his parents' love*. Failures, mistakes, rebellion, or stupidities must not change that basic, essential framework of love within which the child's life unfolds.

Punishment must not communicate withdrawn affection. The spirit with which a parent administers punishment is crucial. Do not punish while you are angry. Without a cooling down period, the punishment may be overly severe; the child may interpret the anger as hatred. Love speaks in those moments when, after a spanking, the child is gathered into warm parental arms to sob out his hurt and repentance.

The Bible speaks of using a *rod* for punishment (actually a reedlike implement). *The parent's hands should represent love.* The use of an inanimate object for spanking, such as a wooden spoon or small paddle, preserves the association of hands with love. It is distressing to see a mother slap her child, pull his hair, or pinch him.

Discipline

Discipline is a function of genuine love. Parenting is not a popularity contest. We cannot be "buddies" with our children during their growing-up years. It is temptingly easy to avoid rousing a child's wrath or dislike, to sidestep confrontations which bring a scowl to his smooth young brow. But in that direction lie delinquency and disaster. We have only to look around at the world's version of parenting to see the ugly results: rebellious, bitter young people wandering about the countryside and through life, sustaining barren lives with the dismal props of liquor, drugs, and immorality. We may hear the objection, "But mine is a *Christian* home, a *preacher's* home!" And so? There is no safety in the mere fact of Christian parentage, even of ministerial parentage. A preacher's child is just like everyone else's: a sin-natured human being whose moral bent is toward evil. Moreover, because parents are dedicated to Christian service, Satan is more determined to destroy their children than those of others.

Proverbs 22:15 says, "Foolishness is bound in the heart of a child; but the rod of [or *and*] correction shall drive it far from him." The Old Testament word *foolishness* means something more serious than a cute, mischievous characteristic. Various passages make clear that the *foolish* child is one who

- despises discipline.
- hates instruction.
- is quarrelsome.
- is licentious.
- is morally bad and wicked.

What is meant by *discipline?* Many, unfortunately, limit discipline to punishment. Its meaning is far broader than that. Discipline is training that develops self-control, character, orderliness, and efficiency.

Proper, effective discipline has several characteristics. First, it is **undergirded.** Its primary support must be *faithfulness to Scripture*—what the whole Word says about immediate and long-range training of children. There are more than a few wrecked, wretched children of ministry parents whose child rearing ignored all but the "rod" Bible passages. That is totally unlike our heavenly Father—He who is to be our pattern for parenting. Parents' consultation of God's Word cannot be a once-over-lightly-now-I-have-the-idea matter; the text must daily discipline us before we can rightly discipline our children.

Discipline should also be undergirded with *love.* Harsh homes produce hard, or crushed, young people. A child who senses love in his parents' control and punishment will respect his training, though he won't always enjoy it.

Third, discipline must be undergirded with *reasonableness.* That is, account must be taken of

- the child's age and natural capacities.
- his comprehension of the infraction.
- the spirit and seriousness of the infraction.
- his reaction to being caught and reprimanded.

A commonly seen example of unreasonableness is the punishing of a very young child for not sitting adult-still through a long church service.

Second, discipline should be **undivided.** If a child senses disagreement between his parents over the need, type, or severity of his discipline, he will use the disunity to his own advantage, playing one parent against the other. When one parent is not in accord with the other's discipline, the disagreement should be handled when the child is not present.

Mothers may tend toward softer discipline—especially with sons. Basically, your husband knows more about the internal workings and external indications of boys. He once was a boy himself. At the same time, however, a ministry father may have difficulty separating his preaching role from his parenting role. His expectations, especially regarding his sons, may be impossibly high. In driving toward those unreachables, he may violate the "lest they be discouraged" warning of Scripture (Col. 3:21). In such cases, the mother's wise and gentle intervention can make the difference between success and failure with the children. Her intercession, though, must be done prayerfully and *privately* with her husband.

Third, discipline must be **unwavering**. Strictness one day and marshmallowing the next day is deadly. A child needs to know where behavioral boundaries lie, that they are constant, and that violation of them will *always* bring unpleasant consequences. Otherwise, he comes to all the wrong conclusions about both human and divine guidelines, rules, and laws.

Effective discipline is not easy. It demands determination, hard work, and earnest prayer. It requires a clear view of the goal: *obedient, effective servant-soldiers for the Lord Jesus Christ.*

Communication

Children are children, adults are adults. It is difficult for parents to remember the rawness, vulnerability, instability, and kaleidoscopic changes of youth and to empathize with the oversized importance of insignificant happenings. On his part, it is impossible for the child to understand what makes an adult tick. He hasn't been one. Sometimes he wonders whether he'll ever arrive at maturity or if arriving will be worthwhile.

God ordained that maturity train immaturity. But if the "generation gap" has overtones of resentment, silence, and coldness, things are not as they should be. The most effective bridge between generations is easy communication. The primary responsibility for building that bridge belongs to the *parent*, not to the child. In fact, the interpersonal domestic communication system is mostly constructed by you, Mother, because the child talks first and most to you.

Infant days are delightful times of earnest, awkward, humorous efforts in communication, as parents respond to the vocal venturings of their little ones. But as children grow and responsibilities multiply, communication may deteriorate. If the mother discourages communication, if her distracted response is "Uh-huh" or "Wait till later to talk . . . ," the child will get the real message: "What you have to say is not important." Verbalizing thoughts, feelings, and experiences is essential to a youngster's development.

A mother must not only establish a good communication system but also maintain and upgrade it constantly. This means one thing in particular: *really listening,* taking genuine interest in what the child says, whether he's describing a caterpillar or the woes of dating. It means *being with* the child in circumstances, times, and settings that encourage open communication. It means maintaining a general home atmosphere that is relaxed, accepting, and warm. It means giving the child your *attention* when he talks to you, not half-listening, eyes elsewhere. It means allowing him freedom to express what he is thinking and feeling (no matter how shocking) without interrupting him to condemn or criticize. It means responding with

- gratitude for his talking to you about the matter.
- recognition of his immaturity and humanity.
- prayer for God's control and guidance in your responses.
- reasonableness.

It means *focusing* on the child—not only with eyes and ears but also with parental radar to detect nonverbals: eye expression and direction, physical agitation or repose, vocal tone, overall body language.

When we consistently encourage and attend to a child's talking, we are drawn to him as a listener and, ultimately, as an adviser.

Time

Child rearing costs dearly in parental time. It takes only weeks to grow a cabbage; *it takes years to grow an oak tree.* Too many ministry parents spend cabbage time hoping for oak results. It never works.

Priorities come into play in the time we spend with our children. In the biblical scheme of things, children come before outsiders in order of importance. They come before the formal "ministry." In fact, *they are our most immediate and important ministry after our marriage relationship.* Successful Christian parenting is the process of making disciples of our children. Discipling takes time and effort.

We must *plan* for time with our children. Full calendars must not drain the reservoir of our primary human relationships. The busier our schedules, the more imperative it is that we write our children into them.

Promises, too, have a place in time considerations. All of us make promises to our children: "Anita, tomorrow Mommy will take you to the zoo." "If you'll be patient while things are so busy, Tommy, next week we'll . . ." There is nothing wrong with promises—if we keep them. Promises sometimes are necessary for adjusting the desires of children to the demands of adult lives. Also, they can help teach children patience and responsibility. But if we repeatedly break promises, we scar our image for that ever observant youngster. He may come to the following conclusions:

- The parent is not trustworthy.
- The child is not worth the keeping of a promise.
- God's promises are suspect.

Intellectual Stimulation

Recent studies show that much can be done by parents in developing young minds. The world strives merely for intellectual brilliance. Christian parents should aim for full realization of the divinely bestowed intellectual potential of each child, with the additional controlling dimension of godliness.

Children come equipped with tremendous curiosity and imagination. A very young child minutely explores his physical world, storing data by means of sight, smell, touch, hearing, and taste. Meanwhile, he exults in the breadth and brilliance of his imaginary world. Parents must recognize curiosity and imagination as doors: wonderful open doors to both intellectual and spiritual learning.

Reading should play an important role in a child's growth years. In fact, some studies indicate that reading to a child even while it is still in the womb can have positive effects! Unfortunately, many parents, absorbed in their professions, whether secular or sacred, fall into the snare of allowing their children's major source of intellectual "exercise" to come from television. That is no exercise at all. TV is a numbing, addictive medium of stagnation, by means of which a youngster (or an adult, for that matter) not only vegetates mentally but also decays morally.

Well-chosen books do much more than entertain. They develop imagination, stimulate thinking, expand horizons, strengthen vocabulary, and present character challenge. Especially are these important in early youth. Children's personal creative roots take hold in the early years, and their reading needs to be the richest possible. Search out the best writing styles in each genre and subject field. Your purchases will not only benefit the children but also encourage writers toward higher standards. The contents of a good home library range from light entertainment to the classics and should be particularly strong in Christian biography. See that your home has a good supply of books—not only in view but also within easy reach. The world of books is wonder-filled; build a sturdy bridge to it for each child God lends you.

Turn your child toward reading by your example. He should see *you* reading each day—for your enjoyment—as well as enjoy your reading to him. Read aloud to him from his youngest days, gearing choices to age interests as he grows. Read expressively— enter into the material and, by vocal and facial expression, draw your young listener into it. Even after the child begins reading for himself, continue reading aloud to sustain growing appreciation for the written and spoken word. Don't be afraid to move several steps ahead of him in terms of concept, expression, and language.

Take special care to see that your reading of the Bible is as fresh and expressive as reading any adventure story. Intoned, preachified, or monotone reading of the Word will make it burdensome and unappealing to the young ear.

Supplementary reading tools should be kept in the home as well. Encyclopedias, dictionaries, world atlases, and other reference works can expand the child's knowledge of specific subjects as his interest in them is stimulated by school responsibilities or from his reading of other books. Bible dictionaries, geographies, and commentaries also have an important place.

The home environment is also enriched by good music. The presence of good music in the home yields future benefits as well as immediate pleasure, for exposure develops appreciation and taste. Ultimately, cultural bent is not so much "I know what I like" as "I like what I know." Surround your offspring early with fine music.

A love of good music can be morally protective. Satan is enjoying enormous success in the area of modern music. Its devotees have their consciences as well as their hearing dulled. Churches advertise spirituality while promoting fleshliness. Our efforts against this threat must be more than passive complaining. We must consistently direct our children's tastes toward good music while banning the objectionable. The objectionable includes rock music, but more than rock. The Devil also uses country and western music. The tunes and rhythms may not be so obviously offensive as those of rock, but the lyrics are trash: deadly input for impressionable minds!

What music should we offer our children? A realistic range would include classical, light classical, *selective* easy-listening, and *good* Christian music. Children who learn to love good music will have less difficulty resisting the bad. For those who have missed this opportunity and have been blind or lax concerning the music of their children, establishing listening standards at this point may seem daunting. It *will* be difficult. But it is not hopeless. If under the Lord's direction you must force change from corrosive to constructive music, your children will resist. But hold on. Pray for strength to endure and for their hearts and their tastes to turn higher.

Emotional Development

A child's emotional self is delicate, impressionable, and consequential in all that he does. It is sensitive to both negative and positive input.

One emotionally harmful tendency in ministry homes is forcing a child toward a predetermined adult role. A sad product of modern Christianity is the number of parent-called preachers and missionaries. Certainly, we desire to see a son go into the ministry, a daughter into full-time Christian service. But parental desire must not determine a child's path in life. Our duty is to see that each child is faithfully trained to love and live for the Lord—with the specific calling left to God Himself. A child herded down the chute of parental determinism may react in one of several ways:

- outright rebellion
- external capitulation but inward frustration
- bitter renunciation of his parents' faith

A child needs a healthy image of who and what he is. Foundational to that self-image is the security afforded by love. A youngster shortchanged on love concludes that he's not worth loving. Upon that unstable ground rises a life haphazard in design, inadequate in construction, and unseemly in influence.

A healthy self-identity rests upon three support columns:

- a sense of belonging
- a sense of competence
- a sense of worth

A child at any age needs to know that he belongs, that he is a highly valued, integral part of his family unit. If, for instance, one child is so unlike the rest of the family in appearance, temperament, or whatever as to draw teasing charges of being a misfit or adopted, parents must focus extra time and energy on pointing out family likenesses. In other words, it is important that a family be a unit—a "we" rather than a "you-versus-us" thing.

A sense of competence comes through accomplishment. We need to teach our children useful skills. Girls can be taught household duties, handicrafts, and other skills. Boys can make their own beds, keep their rooms in order, carry out the trash, care for the yard and car, and develop hobbies. Hobbies and special pursuits should be encouraged but left up to the child. (If a boy enjoys cooking or baking, let him learn!) Teaching is more than telling. It may mean repeated demonstration and close supervision. Supervising, of course, takes time. It is easier, as a rule, to do a task ourselves than to oversee the child's work. But he needs to learn proper techniques, to be thorough, to strive not just for acceptability but for excellence. These, once learned, not only contribute to his future good as a knowledgeable, proficient adult but also build his present sense of competence.

While parents should encourage accomplishments, they also need to let a child be a child. Sometimes in their wish to teach responsibility, parents demand so much of a youngster that he misses the glorious freedom of childhood. Responsibility settles soon enough upon everyone in adulthood. Imposing its weight upon childhood is cruel.

In order to have a sense of worth, a child needs to know he is treasured by his family and by God. This valuation should be based not upon good looks, intelligence, or cute personality but upon the building blocks of Christian character: thoughtfulness, sensitivity to others, kindness, patience, diligence, and so on. Even a well-loved child needs to have his good qualities extolled.

This is not to say he is to be praised constantly and indiscriminately. Nor should he be praised for something he's not responsible for—good looks, athletic ability, intellectual superiority. A balanced approach must be taken to building a child's positive self-concept: valid criticisms for his weak points, warranted compliments for his strengths.

It is important to give children individualized, specific assurances. In the Jones family, for example, we've seen positive results from quiet, simple revelations of the specialness of each child. With Roxane, we offset her young teen query, "Why can't I run fast—am I crippled?" with the story of the glorious sunset sky on the day of her birth—so unusually glorious that her grandfather captured it in a snapshot and announced, "I feel God has something very special for this baby!" A part of that "something" is a physical handicap. For Bob IV, struggling under the burden of an inherited identity, we countered by telling of our long, earnest prayers for a son to replace the firstborn, whose stay with us was only hours long; of our assurance that God's answer means His special creation of mind, body, and heart. And finally, with Stephen as he entered the bewildering maze of adolescence, we told how the difficult pregnancy and threatened miscarriage assured us of Satan's designs against but God's overpowering design for him as His servant.

Communicating a sense of worth is a particular challenge in the case of a handicapped child. Whatever the specific handicap, its facts, though certainly not ignored, must be offset by spoken and demonstrated assurances that he is special to each member of the family in the very best sense of the word. Over and over again we have had the joy of seeing Christian homes radiate Christ in a sweeter, richer way than might have been possible apart from the blessing of a handicapped child.

Physical Well-Being

Because it seems so obvious, this facet of child rearing can easily get shortchanged. Physical well-being has both internal and external ramifications.

Eating proper food heads the list as a necessity for internal well-being. Mothers must see that children eat well. Nutrition demands neither overabundant nor terribly expensive foods. It does mean a well-balanced diet. It also implies protecting children from a junk food diet. Hamburgers, hot dogs, pizza, and carbonated drinks should be exceptions rather than regulars. Daily fare draws properly from each of the main food groups discussed in Chapter 3.

The human digestive mechanism is helped or hindered by the emotional atmosphere of mealtimes. It's wise to make a household rule that mealtimes will be pleasant. Arguments, scoldings, talk of problems, illness, and death can ruin everyone's gravy!

Children need to feel comfortable and secure in their home. One contributor to that feeling is the mother's presence. Pity the latchkey child! Coming home from school to an empty house does nothing for his internal well-being. But neither does coming home to an atmosphere of hostility, unrest, or depression. Furniture, color schemes, and material things mean little to a child. The home's emotional décor means much, and its effects are lifelong.

A child's heart knows peace when he feels at home in his home. That means keeping him surrounded with the familiar—even if the familiar must often move from one locale to another because of the nature of your ministry. Your home needs to be distinctively yours, wherever its actual physical location. The big old chair in which a son loves to sit should accompany your moves, no matter how much its bulk may complicate arrangements in the moving van. Beloved pictures that have hung on your daughter's bedroom walls since toddler days should remain until she herself wants to change them. The battered but sturdy and beloved bed should be kept rather than exchanged for a new contemporary model. In fact, one of the most important aspects of womanly "nest building" is surrounding the family with feathers of familiarity.

A child's physical well-being is influenced by the sanitary quality of his surroundings. A dirty home contributes to physical ills. In this regard, we would urge you to raise pets and children separately. We have visited ministry homes that reek of dog odor, where babies share dogs' toys, where cat hairs appear in visitors' scrambled eggs.

Mothers regularly react to hurts ranging from scraped shins to broken arms. But they should also practice preventive care, anticipating dangers to physical health and safety—keeping poisons and sharp objects out of reach, maintaining sanitation in kitchen and bathroom, teaching good hygiene. These safeguards are necessary not only in the home but also in the neighborhood. Physical and moral problems can come from unsupervised relationships. An important multipurpose safeguard is to deny children close friendships with those who would lead them into unclean thinking, rebellion, smoking, drinking, sexual immorality, and drugs. The hedge against destructive friendships is crucial because peer pressure is a major factor during adolescence. Undesirable friends may be in our own church members' families or in other ministry homes. Although prohibiting these friendships poses special difficulties, the standard must remain in place: "I will do what's necessary for my child's protection and well-being even at the risk of losing others' warm feelings."

The manner in which you handle forbidden friendships makes a great difference. The declaration that "So-and-So is a rotten kid, and you'll not associate with him" will cause repercussions in the child's peer group, in the other family, and even throughout your entire Christian circle. It would be more sensible—and more spiritual—for you to take this approach:

1. Pray for godly discernment. Personal dislike for a child's friend is not sufficient reason to separate them.
2. Pray for the right spirit. A supercilious attitude can detonate emotions and demolish communication within and without the family.
3. Pray and prepare to meet with the parent(s) for discussion.

The meeting between sets of parents should be calm and nonaccusatory, marked by genuine Christian love. The other parents should not be made to feel that their child deserves all the blame: problem friendships result from fault on both sides. Stress that the combination, the "chemistry" of the personalities, is the trouble, the reason the association must end. Let it be known that your decision is not an easy one, that both you and your child regret what must be done.

Restrictions on friendships do not mean isolation. The Bible makes it clear we are not to withdraw from the world. Recent tendencies toward isolation have had sad results. Christians who refuse to associate with the unsaved develop near-hysteric fear, lose their heart burden for souls, and become bloated with self-righteousness. We need to walk through the world with hearts that love, eyes that see needs, and hands that reach out to help. How can we who claim to be imitators of Christ do otherwise?

Sexual Preparation

Parents should provide children with proper sex education. Too many Christians think they have carried out their responsibility as parents in this regard by removing their youngsters from ungodly sex-education programs of public schools. Not so. It is vital that we teach God's viewpoint on sexuality: that it is "very good" within the bounds of marriage but uniquely destructive in all other relationships.

In our Minister's Wife class, we have been dismayed to find how ill-prepared many Christian young people are for marriage. Usually their parents have fallen short in either or both of the following ways.

Silence. Many parents are embarrassed to talk openly with their children about sex. The wall of silence may shield adult sensibilities, but it leaves youth pitifully vulnerable. Ignorance, vague ideas, and misinformation open the way to premarital experimentation or postmarital shock.

Earlier in this chapter we discussed communication. Its nature and quality become crucial in sex education. In most cases, parents can simply answer questions as the child asks them, sensing how much he can understand. Children typically ask questions only so far as their interest and understanding extend. When answering, use proper technical terms. Reluctance or embarrassment in dealing with the subject conveys the feeling that it is somehow "not nice."

The character of modern life is such that rudimentary sex education is important very early as a safeguard against molestation. Even a small child must be taught that his body has private parts, that anyone (including a relative) who tries to see or touch those parts is (a) to be repulsed and (b) to be reported to the parent. Without raising unnecessary fears, we must caution children about situations, places, and people that represent danger.

Imbalance. Emphasis upon God's demand for sexual purity, badly needed as it is to counteract the satanic distortion, must be balanced by an emphasis on the wonder, beauty, and rightness of the sexual relationship within marriage. Too many Christian young people are made to feel that all sex is disgusting. Taking that concept into marriage robs them of joy and riddles their relationship with problems. The message should not be "Avoid sex, period!'' but ''Avoid sexual intercourse before marriage, with purpose in your heart to obey God's command and provide for untarnished joy in marriage's blessed union.''

Ministry Kids—Their Response to Ministry

Negative Responses

Some children of ministry homes grow up resentful and bitter. Several factors contribute to that attitude. The first is **wrong focus.** Parents present others' opinions or the importance of family reputation to their ministry as the reason for good behavior. Instead, children need to be told, ''The standards we hold are in place because we are Christians; we want to please God by the way we live.''

A second possible cause is **unwise rules.** Parents can be mistaken in the nature and in the number of family rules.

The nature of rules. Parents sometimes twist Scripture to make it support personal preferences. Not all the rules in our homes have to be directly scriptural. Consider the following types:

1. Directly scriptural: spiritual or moral-ethical, clearly stated in God's Word
2. Social and cultural (using good manners and correct English— not chewing gum in public, not using *lay* for *lie, good* for *well,* etc.)
3. Expedient (being on time for meals, keeping the bedroom neat)
4. Respectful of taste (not cracking knuckles)

The number of rules. Parents may make too many of them so that the child is overwhelmed and discouraged.

A third cause of a child's resentment is **unwise priorities.** Children resent the ministry if they feel they are competing with it for parental attention and affection. If such resentment exists, parents should consider whether their children are not victims of sincere but misguided ministry priorities.

A fourth cause is **unwise example.** Parental patterning really is the key to successful child rearing. Fatal flaws include the following:

Inconsistency in mother or father or both. There is nothing more deadly than for a child to hear a parent mouthing marvelous things from podium or pulpit while living miserable things at home.

Derogatory talk about congregation members or other ministries. By example, he learns that "the ministry and God's people are something you criticize."

Parental poormouthing. Complaints such as "We can't afford what we'd like because we're in the Lord's work" make a child feel that God mistreats those who serve Him.

Unreasonable demands. The child knows, as parents may pretend not to know, that no mortal can be perfect—that "preacher's kid" or "missionary's kid" or "Christian worker's kid" cannot translate as "faultless kid."

Positive Responses

Ideally, parsonage children mature with two *R*s characterizing their attitude toward the ministry: *realism* and *respect.* Certainly there are difficulties and pressures in ministry, but what occupation is without them? It's all too easy to talk of the negatives of full-time Christian service rather than considering its special blessings and privileges. If we surround our children with an atmosphere of complaining, it is little wonder they chafe at privations and shun the thought of full-time Christian service. A youngster should see in his mother and father positive examples of Christian adulthood: effective, consistent, and emotionally mature people who obey God and rejoice to serve Him. That kind of parental living is beautifully magnetic.

Ultimately, respect for the ministry grows out of reverence for God. How amazing that the great God of heaven, the eternal I AM, would allow us fleeting, frail, and flawed beings to serve Him!

Ministry Kids—Their Potential

There is, first, the opportunity for a strong present testimony. Our children's obedient lives can bless and challenge their peers and adults. Second, for them the future stretches out with its vast and rich possibilities. The darker the world grows, the more brightly shines the remaining light.

In closing this chapter, we wish to return to the emphasis made throughout: that a Christian worker's child is simply a child and therefore his successful molding depends primarily upon what his parents are rather than on what they claim to be or tell him he should be. Ministry parents must take special care to be parent-examples to their children, not "Mr. and Mrs. Preacher." There is no stronger, clearer challenge for Christian parenting than that found in Proverbs 23:26: "My son, give me thine heart, and let thine eyes observe my ways."

How consistent, how transparent, how integrated parental spirituality must be! That is, after all, the point of Deuteronomy 6:6-9:

> And these words, which I command thee this day, shall be in thine heart: And thou shalt teach them diligently unto thy children, and shalt talk of them when thou sittest in thy house, and when thou walkest by the way, and when thou liest down, and when thou risest up. And thou shalt bind them for a sign upon thine hand, and they shall be as frontlets between thine eyes.

Chapter 12

Broken Boundaries

Children embody our highest hopes, our fondest dreams. Parents who are in ministry for the Lord particularly yearn for their children to follow the path of righteousness in Jesus Christ. But hopes, dreams, and spiritual yearnings can be—and are—shattered in parsonages just as in any other home.

Although the concept is not voiced, there lies deep within us ministry parents a bit of *contractual* thinking: the God whom we serve is obligated to make our children holy. Not so. Each *heritage of the Lord* is put into our hands. The heritage can be mishandled by us because of our sin-flawed humanity. The heritage itself comes packed in humanity's earthen vessel and is pathetically vulnerable.

Before proceeding with this discussion, let's be sure to lay aside any tendency toward superiority or self-righteousness. Do not allow yourself the attitude, "My child will or could never stray; other parents have just messed up somehow . . ." That is pride wearing a clerical collar—the object of God's hatred. There is no more painful destruction of pride than that caused by a straying child. Our prayer in presenting this difficult chapter is that God may use it to kindle compassion in your heart toward the parents of rebellious children, whether they be in the ministry or those who come to you for counsel.

The Reality of Rebellion

Humanity's earthen vessel sits on an uneven base: it leans toward sin.

Self-interest and self-will are evident in a child from babyhood and become more prominent as he or she moves toward independence. It is, of course, natural that progeny grow away from their parents' nurture; there must be some struggle and discomfort. Too, the personality and temperament of a particular child can make his growth toward independence more trying than that of his brother or sister. Parents need wisdom to discern between the normal and necessary process and a destructive one.

The age in which we live also presents children with general temptations toward rebellion. Ungodly elements are blatantly evident everywhere, and they focus with particular power upon the young. The god of this world surrounds our children with sights and sounds that tug at them to *do their own thing*, to kick over any restraints. The most pervasive and persuasive evil of all is rock music. Under its drugging influence (often *sniffed* in the form of Christian contemporary music), the youngster's spiritual sensitivity is dulled. Distinctions between right and wrong give way to personal preference and "right" to pleasure.

Besides the general temptation toward rebellion, there is also a special targeting of the Christian home. Satan's hatred of righteousness takes perhaps its most cruel form in the darts he hurls at our children. As parents, we wish that Jesus' assurance of tribulation in the world (John 16:33) could somehow exclude our children. But, as hard as Satan works against you and me, he works even harder against our offspring, diligently intent upon crippling and decimating the next generation.

The Range of Rebellion

Some rebellion in a child remains mostly internal: the *secret sins* open only to God's eyes (Ps. 90:8). Among its evidences are boredom with spiritual things and skepticism and cynicism regarding Christian people and precepts. (Nothing will more effectively plant and nurture the seed of cynicism than inconsistency in authority figures.) Humanistic thinking beckons our children from the time of its first appearance in cartoons and children's books. There may be a secret leaning toward and catering to the lust of the eyes and of the flesh. Pornography is easily available by telephone, by computer, and through print.

If inward rebellion is not recognized, admitted, and dealt with, there ultimately will be outward indications: alcohol, drugs, ethical or sexual immorality.

The Reaction to Rebellion

Christian parents hit by the blast of a rebellious child react in different ways. The first two to be discussed are useless and harmful.

Denial and willful blindness. Whether it be in the early stages of straying or in the time of obvious wickedness, some parents reach for the self-protective blanket. Apparently the idea is "If I didn't see it, it couldn't have happened." Perhaps fear lies at the base of this response: fear of what acknowledgment would mean—the personal struggle, the public disgrace.

Anger. The wounded parent may lash out—screaming, crying, accusing the child who has hurt him; attacking the person or circumstances that brought the child's sin to light. Underlying the anger response, many times, is pride. The rebellious child has dented the parent's public image, violated a stated precept, disrupted a comfortable lifestyle. After all, a Christian parent has a right to obedient children, does he not? A parsonage parent has a right to immunity from tragedy, does he not? Violation of those supposed rights can make a parent livid with anger.

Hurt bewilderment. This response is inescapable. The very fabric of the parents' hearts is torn when a child rebels. Their minds feel loosed from their moorings, blown in dizzying circles by hurricane winds of uncertainty.

The deepest wound comes to the soul: suddenly the Scripture passages memorized in Sunday school seem hollow. In an instant, Romans 8:28 is transformed from a passage glibly quoted to others—its words swim, incomprehensible, in agony's tears.

As the heaviness of having brought up a foolish son or daughter settles upon the parents, the very term God used increases the burden. Bible scholars point out that a *foolish son* is not the mischievous but lovable, naughty youngster we pictured. Remember, he is one who

- despises discipline.
- hates instruction.
- is quarrelsome.
- is licentious.
- is morally bad and wicked.

It is no wonder the parent of such a one experiences pain and confusion.

The Reworking from Rebellion

Although a breaking parental heart makes its bearer feel that surely death must follow, it doesn't. Life goes on—in a stagger.

Sadness and grieving are just as real for the Christian as for the unbeliever. There is, however, a major distinction: the born-again person's sorrow has within it the dimension of hope. Though the promises of God's Word may seem to have paled in the glare of emotional trauma, they are nevertheless the only point of light in otherwise impenetrable darkness. Feebly the broken-hearted parents must begin to grope their way toward spiritual recuperation and, ultimately, conquest.

The essential starting point is honest evaluation. God Himself raised the question concerning His rebellious people: "What could have been done more to my vineyard, that I have not done in it? wherefore, when I looked that it should bring forth grapes, brought it forth wild grapes?" (Isa. 5:4). The cry of God's own heart over His straying children echoes in the human heart when similarly aching. For the mortal mother and father, there most likely will be failings to acknowledge.

There may have been *undones*—a missing of the mark in parenting. Perhaps there was failure to divide time, love, and attention equally among the children, making the shortchanged one feel left out. The search for something to fill emotional emptiness can lead to tragedy.

There may have been *overdones*. This particularly tends to be true in the ministry home: the parents' desire for godly children blinds them to the fact that godliness is a spiritual work. They try to create or demand it. Insensitive authoritarian parenting yields the worst possible results: an unthinking, phony clone or a bitter rebel.

There may have been *inconsistencies*. Demanding a certain standard in one's child while missing that standard oneself is a proven way to *provoke your children to wrath*—a behavior against which we parents are warned in Ephesians 6. No matter how many Sunday school lessons, Sunday sermons, and mealtime homilies a child hears, the effective lessons come from seeing—seeing the truth active in his parents' lives each day.

There may have been a *failure to give reasons*. If, for instance, a child is being reprimanded for kissing someone of the opposite sex, a reasonable answer should be given to his question, "What's wrong with kissing?"

There may have been *no differentiation in the rules*. It is imperative that we parents distinguish between types of rules. To say or to imply that all our house rules are scriptural is to invite disaster. A rule against gum-chewing may simply be explained as a thing of personal and family etiquette. Eventually, a youngster is going to ask chapter and verse for the rules under which he lives. Some of those rules can rightly be attributed to books other than the Book, instead of being tied with a twisted cord to Scripture.

Inevitably, honest evaluation of our parenting is going to expose some flaws. Despite our earnest desires and diligent efforts, our humanity mars every undertaking. In fact, that realization and acknowledgment can be a key to recovery for both grieving parent and rebellious child. Our failures must be admitted, first, to God. We need to repent of the sins of omission and commission that have been part of our parenting. We also need to apologize to the child—not in a blubbering, breast-beating bid for sympathy but rather in simple admission of fault.

Be aware, however, that though hindsight is keen, it can magnify out of all proper proportion. While acknowledging their guilt in the situation, the parents of a rebellious child must not heap upon themselves all the blame for the problem. Satan loves to add the awful burden of guilt to that of grief. Afflicted parents may take heart from the example of their heavenly Father. In a wonderful, comfort-filled verse in the first chapter of Isaiah, God voices a parent's grief: "I have nourished and brought up children, and they have rebelled against me." God is Light. In Him is no darkness at all. In His parenting there is no flaw. But despite His perfect fatherhood, His children rebel. That fact helps us put our human family plight into proper perspective. As long as there is a literal devil, as long as human beings have free will, so long will there be the option for wrong choices, for sin.

After the parents examine themselves and accept their share of the blame, they should move on to a close examination of the rebellious child himself. His straying will have made them realize that, at least to some degree, they did not know him.

Exactly who is this child currently breaking his parents' hearts? What are his individualities of character, personality, and temperament? Now that easy assumptions have been shattered, correct understanding of his makeup can help shed light on where and why he veered off course. For example, a daughter in a ministry home, while appearing to be accepting the congregation's demands upon the family, may have been chafing for years at what she felt to be competition for her parents' love. Tired of being an *also ran*, she sought the wrong limelight. The fact that her brothers and sisters felt no such pressures and had no such inclinations is not a factor in the case.

The time for looking at the past with its flaws and at the present with its problem must come to an end. There ultimately must come the time to move forward, to ask, "What is the best thing to do now?"

There is no perfect plan. Each family will have to seek God's wisdom and will for their situation. Three ministry families in which a child rebelled and was expelled from a Christian school settled upon diverse solutions: one chose a local public high school; the second began home schooling; the third decided upon schooling in another state. In each case, the Lord put His stamp of approval upon the decision—all three children ended their waywardness and grew to be solid, dedicated Christians. Choosing the right protection-advancement course after rebellion can be extremely difficult because of unsolicited advice, hardhearted accusations, and rampant gossip. The focus must be kept on the child and what will provide the best opportunity for repentance and restoration. A helpful Scripture passage for such a time is Proverbs 3:3: "Let not mercy and truth forsake thee: bind them about thy neck; write them upon the table of thine heart." That balance of truth with mercy is a strategic factor.

While prayer and care are invested in the rebellious child himself, similar effort must come to bear upon the home's core: mother and father. The pressure of heartbreak over a straying child can and should force re-examination of the home's essence. From that, in turn, can come a strengthening and beautifying to benefit the testimony of the home both within and without. Four specifics need to take place.

Read. Each person in the family, in particular the mother and father, needs to go to the Word with determination and eagerness. God's voice must be heard above the sounds of weeping, whisperings, and suggestions. The Lord delights to speak in a special, tender way to broken hearts. He alone can give effective comfort and encouragement.

Heed. Obedience to Bible precepts should take on greater importance in the face of the ugly fruit of disobedience. As God impresses His claims upon wounded, tender hearts, renewed dedication results; the reality of His love grows warmer. Dealing with the *wild grapes* of rebellion (Isa. 5:4) can discipline the vine into bearing better fruit.

Kneel. Heartache caused by a rebellious child should drive parents to their knees both in humility for their failure and in dependency upon God's all-sufficiency. Obeying the injunction "Casting all your care upon him; for he careth for you" becomes absolute necessity. Expressing agony and bewilderment to the Lord not only releases the soul from their suffocating force but also begins to lift the soul's gaze from the dust of human failure to the universe of divine hope.

Heal. Rebellion of children in a Christian home demands healing in three areas: heart, home, and trust.

The deeper the heart wound, the slower will be the healing. Repeatedly the hurt-weary mind cries, "Will this pain never cease?" But time and the gentle balming of God's Word gradually ease the pain from agony to ache. The ache can be relieved only by the child's repentance and restoration. For some that comes soon. For others, it may not come in the parent's lifetime.

The home battered by rebellion's wind must be righted. Some parents actually further the destruction by so focusing on the prodigal that the other children are neglected. Too, there is the danger of trying to compensate for the strayer's failure by over-dominating the compliant stayers. Either parental reaction creates an atmosphere ripe for others' rebelliousness. It is essential to pull together, to strengthen, what is left: to re-establish the bond between husband

and wife, between parents and children. In this as in every crisis, the chance is given for betterment or embitterment.

Finally, there must be a healing of trust. When rebellion ends and the wanderer returns to the spiritual path, parents find it very hard to trust that child again. Memories of betrayed confidence loom in their minds. The dark cloud of suspicion shadows the restored one. That cloud must be dispelled, but its dissolving demands time and honesty. The returned prodigal needs parents who are open in admitting their difficulties in restoring trust. Too, he needs to know that the burden of proof lies upon him. He will need patience in rebuilding parental confidence in his restored heart.

Letting and Loving

Finally, we would point parents to the twofold need to let God be God and to love the rebellious child unconditionally.

We parents want *hands-on* child rearing—our own hands, that is. Perhaps the toughest lesson any Christian parent must learn is that when children grow to the age of accountability, our direct parenting takes a giant step backward. At that point our job becomes indirect. The child is personally, directly responsible to God. Our responsibility is to petition the Lord in the child's behalf. This puts trust to the test. Do we really believe that God loves the child more than we? Do we truly trust Him to work for the child's good and His glory? Assurances glibly uttered over a toddler are wrung from the heart when that child is a teen.

It is easy to get in God's way—to *protect* the child from the buffeting of life, to take his side against authority, to disbelieve warnings given by objective observers. Only harm comes from our attempts to hijack God's prerogative.

Unconditional love for a nasty-tempered, disrespectful, loose-living son or daughter is not easy. While not condoning any of the sin, parents must consistently extend their love to the sinning offspring. Apart from that anchor, the child may never be restored to the harbor. The anchor can be made to hold only by embedding it in God's own unconditional love for us. Let us confirm that principle, and conclude, by quoting a letter received by saddened parents from a concerned observer.

Dear _____:

I wanted to pen this to you from the viewpoint of a son, a restored son. Let me explain.

Quite by accident I learned of the circumstance you experienced with _____. Because of some similarities in my own testimony, I have wept and continue to feel empathy for your situation.

As a teen-ager I disappointed my parents in a similar manner and brought great heartache to the ones I loved the most. My parents were desolated by my action. I had disappointed them, disregarded their instruction, compromised their testimony, and broken their hearts.

In the midst of the family turmoil and the questions my parents asked themselves, something became very clear: my parents were far more concerned about me and the decisions I would make than the public embarrassment and pain I had caused them. My father and my mother made it plain through their tears that I was the most important consideration.

Their love broke my will. I gave myself unreservedly to Christ. With my repentance I also experienced a restored trust. Not more than I deserved, but enough to begin to rebuild my life.

What I wanted to share is this: I remember how reassuring and encouraging was my parents' love to me when my little world seemed to be in ruins. I sensed in all of their upheaval that I was more important than any of the other things I had set in motion. My wrong was never condoned, but I sensed their concern and their hope that I would do the right thing.

What I really want to transmit from my perspective is this: from a restored son, from the bottom of our hearts we will never forget or cease to be thankful for your love, support, and understanding. Thank you for believing in us when belief seemed so frail and shattered. Thank you for understanding when we couldn't find the words to explain why. Thank you for believing that in Jesus we will bear fruit to His glory because of your vision.

(Signed) A Son Who Knows

Powerfully reassuring and comforting as those human words may be, there is far greater power, far more effective comfort, in God's own precious Word:

Thus saith the Lord: Refrain thy voice from weeping, and thine eyes from tears: for thy work shall be rewarded, saith the Lord; and they shall come again from the land of the enemy. And there is hope in thine end, saith the Lord, that thy children shall come again to their own border.

Jeremiah 31:16-17

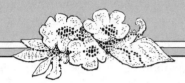

Chapter 13

Guesting Guidelines

The ministry home in itself is a means of blessing for others. This responsibility commonly takes the form of hostessing: as "first lady" of a ministry, the Maidservant must provide meals and/or housing for guests. Hostessing is one of the most typical and constant demands upon her strength and time.

The importance of hospitality permeates Scripture. A widow is to be judged eligible for support "if she have lodged strangers, if she have washed the saints' feet" (I Tim. 5:10). We are to "use hospitality one to another without grudging" (I Pet. 4:9). A bishop (church leader) must be "given to hospitality" (I Tim. 3:2). We must "not [be] forgetful to entertain strangers" (Heb. 13:2). How could God have been more plain in expressing His wishes about opening our homes to guests? If we accept this function as a matter of obedience, we need next to consider some how-tos of hospitality.

Principles of Hospitality

Start where you are. Whatever your age, wherever you live, whatever size and type of ministry you have, whatever your financial category, whatever cooking or serving skills and equipment you possess or lack, begin there.

The only woman in Scripture God Himself called great is the Shunammite who extended hospitality to the prophet Elisha in II Kings 4. Her equipment for hostessing was not ideal in the material sense of the word. She was, however, superbly equipped in the motivational sense: her heart was burdened for the itinerant preacher, and she provided room and board for him whenever he was in the area. She didn't wring her hands, bemoaning chipped or mismatched china. She didn't beg off because of her insignificance in comparison with Elisha's fame. Because her heart was open, her home was open.

It is true that many of us feel timid about doing something for which we feel poorly prepared. It is also true that few ministry women have extensive training in hostessing. But timidity and social inexperience are by no means restricted to ministry women. Most skills must be learned by doing. Indeed, our inexperience itself can make others sympathetic toward and uncritical of our efforts.

Adjust your attitude. We need to feed into our mental-emotional computer the terms *privilege, opportunity, enjoyment,* and *blessing* to describe hostessing and to let these displace *pressure, ordeal,* and *endurance.* Attitude lays the foundation for hospitality's superstructure.

Start with your own family. If your entertaining experience has been slight, begin having special meals for your husband and children or for your roommate or roommates—with fancy menu, best china, linen, flatware, centerpiece, and the rest. Then extend your guest list. Include Grandma and Grandpa, Cousin Suzy and Uncle Ed. As confidence builds, progress from the more to the less familiar relatives and acquaintances. Reach out further and further to extra mouths, expanded conversation, extended efforts, and polished manners. Your jitters will fade; your joy will intensify.

Use what you have. Don't wait to complete your china, silver, and linen. Intended guests may be under their tombstones before their feet get under your table. Instead, crank up your imagination. Use the table settings you have. (Table settings depicted in women's magazines often show imaginative combinations rather than pervasive coordination.) Wrap up the whole in a gleaming package of warmheartedness, and you will bless someone with the beautiful gift of hospitality.

Some of the most memorable experiences in both Bobbie's and Beneth's lives have been times when they and their husbands were guests in believers' homes abroad. Without exception, the living standards were far below the American norm. In some instances, the poverty was palpable. However, time spent in those homes was unexcelled for beauty and warmth. They were made to know the very essence of Christian hospitality.

Both authors also have experienced "authentic" Oriental meals in the homes of American friends. Those evenings have lingered long in memory for good food, warm fellowship, and uniquely enjoyable atmosphere. Only later did the truth come out: the hostesses chose and carried out the Oriental theme because their homes had no dining room furniture. As guests, we sat on cushions on the floor and ate from a coffee table. Great fun!

Purposes for Hospitality

Hospitality demonstrates friendship. "Come to our home for popcorn . . . dessert . . . lunch . . . dinner . . . " translates as "You're special; come; let's get better acquainted." That is a happy message for anyone to receive. Throughout their stay, make your guests feel as welcome as you possibly can.

Hospitality also shares the blessings of your home with others. Each of us can look about her home and thank the Lord for what it contains of the things that really matter. No apologies are needed for material items that may be missing. A hostess's good will outshines whatever is on the table.

Hospitality enriches your life and the lives of your family members. As various servants of God (and the unsaved) come into your home, they create memories and lessons that add an important dimension to family life. This experience can also be educational for the children. While absorbing the intangibles, they can be taught even while very young to accomplish set tasks on behalf of the guests and to contribute to the general spirit of friendship.

Priorities of Hospitality

People come first. They should be the hostess's main focus—not technique or technicality. Each ministry, with its built-in individualities, will help determine whom, when, and how we entertain. Generally, those in ministry should expect to extend hospitality to evangelists, guest speakers, and missionaries, as well as to those within their immediate ministry circle.

Motivation. That we should show hospitality has been settled already, but it may be useful to consider our motivations. First, of course, is human necessity. Ordinary decency does not permit letting folks go hungry or sleep by the roadside. The "hire" of which the laborer (evangelist, special speaker, etc.) is worthy surely includes food and lodging.

Second, there is the motivation of obedience to God's will, discussed above. Though we might downplay the importance of hospitality, the Lord evidently, from His urging toward it, understood the matter otherwise, and we should trust His wisdom over ours and submit to His authority.

Third, beyond the promptings of duty and obedience, each of us should be motivated by personal desire. Surely desire will bloom when we consider Jesus' words, "Inasmuch as ye have done it unto one of the least of these my brethren, ye have done it unto me" (Matt. 25:40).

Manner. Hostessing can take many forms. Individual circumstances will influence the choices. Besides meals and overnight accommodations, ladies might be invited for morning coffee or afternoon tea. When the congregation is so large that it's impossible to circulate everyone through your home for a full meal, one or more drop-ins a year might be the solution. For example, the Yearicks for many years hosted a Christmas Eve open house for which an invitation was extended to all of their thousand-plus members. They now host a gathering for new members following a Sunday evening service. Guests include some deacons and their wives plus other staff members. The list may number anywhere from forty to eighty. (Ladies in the church help with the food preparation.) For the Joneses, departmental buffets and weekly four-couple or eight-singles luncheons are a means of hosting, in installments, eventually all the University faculty and staff.

Find a strategy of hospitality that will enable people to get acquainted with *you* personally as well as positionally.

The Process of Entertaining

Now we come to the nitty-gritty of hostessing, moving from concept to details.

Invitations. If the guest is a speaker for the church, your husband may handle the invitation via correspondence, making sure that both you and the prospective guest know exactly what meal or meals will be served in your home. At other times you may prefer to use face-to-face invitations or telephoning. For a special occasion, invitations should be in note form and mailed two weeks to ten days before the scheduled event. Whatever the type of occasion, be sure the guests understand the time: are they to arrive at the given time, or does the meal begin at that time?

An entertaining record. Keep a record of the times you entertain. The method is up to you: notebook, loose sheets, file cards, computer. Whichever you choose, leave sufficient space for all useful information. This may include the following:

- names of guests
- place
- date
- type of meal
- menu
- other people in the group
- food allergies or dislikes
- left-handedness or physical difficulties
- special dietary requirements, etc.

Name(s) _____ Date _____

Place _____ Type meal _____

Menu _____

_____

Others there _____

_____

Special notes _____

_____

_____

It is important to note your times as guests as well as your hostessing. An entertaining record might look like this:

Name(s) *Brown, Fred & Mary*	
Hosted Us	**Hosted Them**
12/2/90	*3/16/91*
Greensleeves Restaurant	*Turkey dinner at home*

Whatever the method, take care to keep an accurate record of hospitality given and received. Memory failure can cause embarrassment and hurt feelings.

Service style and menu choice. Decisions concerning the type and service of the food may be dictated by a number of considerations. First, regard the nature of the occasion. A birthday might occasion a dessert party; induction of new church officers, a backyard picnic; welcoming a new staff family, a formal dinner.

Second, consider the number of people to be fed. Unless you have a very large dining room or an area that could be adapted as one, more than twelve is unwieldy for a seated meal.

Third, respect the limits of available finances—both yours and those of others who are asked to contribute food.

Fourth, take account of available time. The time required by the work and the time available in the social calendar must be appraised realistically. A church-wide party at the end of a relatively free week is practical. One at the close of a week's evangelistic services is not.

Service details. There are two basic types of service: seated and buffet. For a seated meal, a properly set table looks like this:

Food may be served either by passing platters and bowls or by the "blue plate" method, with food already on each plate. When serving blue plate, the plate should be placed in front of the guest with the meat at the seven-o'clock position.

For variety in seated serving, you may sometimes want your husband, as host, to serve the guests' plates at the table. In such instances, his place would look like this:

In a host-served meal, the host serves and passes a plate first to the guest of honor, next to the ladies at the table, then to the men, and then to the hostess. Last, he serves himself.

There is a conventional pattern for seating: (1) host and hostess at opposite ends of the table (hostess nearer the kitchen), (2) guest of honor to hostess's right, and (3) remaining guests in man-woman sequence. Etiquette books suggest that married couples be separated. The rationale is that the alternation of guests encourages greater conversational exchange. That according-to-rules arrangement, however, seems to be going out of favor in all but formal situations.

For buffet style, the following service table arrangement is often useful:

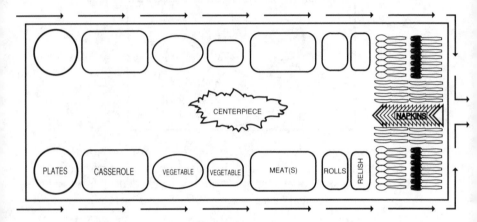

Since a buffet invites people to come back for second helpings, it is important to keep hot foods hot and chilled foods cold. Stone-cold casserole is no more appealing than melted gelatin salad. Also, it may be desirable to place the scarcest (or most expensive) item at or near the end of the food line. Usually that is the meat dish.

Planning ahead. Work through the entire meal on paper, scheduling the time for cooking each entry. That countdown list takes a load off nerves and memory in those final pressured minutes.

One of the many things to be decided ahead of time is the choice of table linens. Tablecloths range from casual to formal. Basically, informal cloths are of rougher texture and brighter colors than formal cloths. The latter are made of linen, damask, organdy, or lace. A proper-sized tablecloth has a ''drop'' on sides and ends that just clears the chair seats. For teas or formal receptions, tablecloths should be floor length. Napkins should match or complement the tablecloth.

Below are three covers (place settings) to accommodate differing menus:

1. Dinner plate
2. Knife
3. Spoon
4. Fork
5. Napkin (folded to
   open toward plate)
6. Individual salt/pepper
7. Water glass
8. Soup spoon
9. Soup bowl
10. Beverage glass
11. Bread and butter

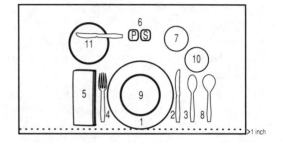

CHANGES
12. Salad plate
13. Salad fork
14. Cup and saucer

CHANGES
Using both salad plate and
   bread and butter
15. Dessert fork

Practical Pointers

Don't think too big too soon, either in number of guests or in extensiveness of menu. Instead, gradually enlarge your endeavors. Small successes are better than spectacular disasters.

Organize every aspect of your entertaining. Though planning takes time, it pays dividends. In the final analysis, too, it actually saves time.

Don't get caught on the cookbooks carousel. Your purpose is to choose a menu, not to spend hours poring over possibilities as presented in various cookbooks. We suggest having several standard menus that you alternate or adjust slightly from one entertaining occasion to the next. You develop confidence and ease by repeatedly following a plotted course.

Here are some "tried and true" menus used by Beneth and Bobbie.

Peanut Chicken with Mustard Sauce
Green Beans Almondine
Apricot Carrots
Spinach Salad
Yeast Rolls and Butter
Iced Tea
Rhubarb/Raspberry Pie à la Mode

***

Roast Beef
Broiled Mushrooms
Twice-Baked Potatoes
Green Beans Almondine
Orange-Apple-Pecan Salad with Maraschino Dressing
Italian Bread
Fruit Punch
Ice-cream Pie

***

Mandarin Orange Chicken Salad
Bread Sticks
Butter
Iced Tea with Ginger Ale
Individual Fruit Tarts

***

Roast Beef with Potatoes and Carrots
Lettuce and Boiled Egg Salad
Rolls and Butter
Fresh Fruit
Cookies or Pound Cake
Tea and Coffee

***

Chicken with Broccoli Casserole
Wild Rice
Corn
Congealed Salad

Rolls and Butter
Pie with Ice Cream
Tea and Coffee

***

(For a Crowd)
Baked Ham
Macaroni and Cheese
Potato Salad
Baked Beans
Applesauce or Waldorf Salad
Rolls and Butter
Dream Delight
Tea and Coffee

Having chosen your menu, organize your preparation with these helps:

- Menu card.
- Shopping card.
- Preparation schedule card.

The first two are self-explanatory. The third, the preparation schedule card, might contain the following information. (*Note:* the example given is for a seated lunch.)

Night before

- Make tea; refrigerate.
- Mix bread dough; refrigerate.
- Put meat in marinade.
- Set table.

Morning

- Knead and shape rolls.
- Prepare salad.
- Prepare side dishes.

Cooking times

- Meat: 1 hour (375°).
- Vegetables: 12 minutes.
- Bread: 30 minutes (400°).

It is also helpful to plan ahead

- which food items can be on the table ahead of time.
- which container will hold what food.
- centerpiece.
- seating.

Organization not only saves time and energy but also bolsters a hostess's confidence. Following a road map is more certain and comforting than wandering aimlessly through a strange countryside.

The principles we've presented in this chapter work—even for really huge crowds. For example, Beneth hosts an annual event called the Senior Lawn Buffet. Guests are graduating seniors, graduate students, spouses of married students, and a number of faculty and staff members. All together the guests number nearly one thousand. While the main portion of the picnic-type menu (prepared by the University dining hall) is being served and eaten on the back lawn, guests who have finished this part come into the house for dessert. Without organization and simplification, this event would be a hostess killer. Her sanity savers include the following:

1. A page-long check list of to-dos
    (call/see/notify/decide, etc.)
2. A page-long check list of house cleaning to be done
    (Seniors have been found peeking under beds!)
3. Four standard menus rotated from year to year
    (each with its own theme, color scheme, etc.)

Whatever the number of guests, entertaining's enjoyment can include the hostess via planning and organization. Part of the planning needs to include a few moments just prior to the guests' arrival wherein the hostess can compose her mind and undo any evidences of "slaving in the kitchen for hours" in hairdo, face, and dress.

Tips for Hosting Overnight Guests

A ministry woman may at times feel her real name is "Mrs./Miss Motel." She must make guests feel welcome and relaxed while simultaneously ensuring the household's continuing smooth operation.

As hostess, you are the one who determines scheduling; the guest accommodates himself to what you have planned. Give your visitor an idea of the schedule shortly after he or she arrives. For instance you might say, "The children catch the school bus at 7:30, but my husband and I will plan to eat breakfast with you at 8:15." Without an indication of what time breakfast will be served, the guest may be ready at 7:30 but have to wait until

8:15! If yours is a one-bathroom house, suggest a workable game plan. ("Do you prefer an evening or morning shower? Fine. The children will be bathed and in bed no later than _____.") Show the guest which bath linens he is to use. They can be hung separately on a rod in the bathroom or placed in his bedroom.

Besides meal and bathroom scheduling, find out how the guest prefers to spend free time. In this regard, realize that speaking and preaching (probable reasons for the visit) are hard work. Don't plan to keep your guest busy twenty-four hours a day. Allow plenty of time for study and rest. Recognize his need for privacy, and teach your children to respect the privacy of guests.

Keeping a guest may complicate your routine in another crucial way. It will be necessary, of course, to arrange not to be home alone with a male visitor. Perhaps a study place at the office or in the church can be provided. Make any necessary adjustment in order to avoid misunderstanding, embarrassment, and gossip.

Since few of us have homes with full-facility guest wings, some physical adjustments must likely be made for keeping a house guest. But be sure the changes are made before the guest arrives. He will be disconcerted if he stands in the entryway, suitcase in hand and body weary from travel, while little Judy drags her blankie, pillow, clothes, and toys out of what obviously is her commandeered bedroom. Keep any adjustments as inconspicuous as possible, and be sure the spirit behind the adjustments is gracious.

Think carefully about the foods you will serve your house guest. Find out soon after his arrival (or, if possible, even before) whether he has any food allergies or other special dietary requirements. Ask about food preferences—for example, tea rather than coffee for breakfast. Keep in mind that pre-speaking meals are kinder without spicy or flatulent foods.

Some things should be considered necessities for house guests. The first of those is a thoroughly clean house. Second is a comfortable bed. If the old mattress resembles a hammock, you need not buy a new one; put a plywood board under it. Clean linens on the bed are another must. Even though the previous occupant used the bed only one night, sheets and pillowcases need to be changed. Other necessities for the guest's room include a mirror, empty drawer and closet space (and empty hangers), something to hold the suitcase, house key, and access to laundry and ironing facilities. There also should be a provision for study and writing if at all possible. If a desk is not available, a lap board with armchair is a good substitute. The study spot should have good lighting.

Beyond the necessities are some niceties that make a guest room say "Welcome. You are special!" They include facial tissues, fruits or nuts, several books, an emergency candle or flashlight, fresh flowers, a personal bar of new soap, hand lotion, toothpaste and brush, paper cups, and an extra blanket.

Instant Hostessing

Rare is the Maidservant who doesn't occasionally face last-minute entertaining. Although such times defy planning in the truest sense of the word, they can be eased by having a few emergency entertaining rations on hand and some ideas for quickie foods in mind. Here are a few of the latter we've found valuable:

- Fruit plate with cheese and crackers
- Pita bread sandwiches with fruit salad
- Chili topped by corn chips, with vegetable relish tray
- Taco salad and gelatin dessert
- Baked egg dish (with bacon bits, sour cream, and chives); tossed salad
- Cheese soufflé with spinach salad
- Cottage cheese/flavored gelatin powder/fruit/whipped topping combination
- Ice-cream pie (crust of crushed cookies)
- "Dump" cake with ice cream and coffee

Simple and fast though the above suggestions are, they can be made attractive with easy, colorful garnishes. The suggested items obviously answer to varied needs. Add several ideas of your own to each category and make sure that you keep essential basic ingredients on hand.

Handling Disasters

Despite best efforts and careful planning there will be times when things go awry in your entertaining. No one has a one hundred per cent success rate in the kitchen and dining room. The best way to react to a hostessing mishap is to treat it lightly. Even the real biggies—like the dog eating the steaks—do not knock the world from its axis. Laughter is better on everyone's nervous and digestive systems than anger, abject apology, depression, or tears.

The Key Ingredient

When you've done all there is to do, done it in the right spirit, and worked with the highest efficiency, lay aside your apron as the doorbell rings, relax, and really enjoy your guests. A relaxed hostess is strategic to a successful and enjoyable visit, whether it be for a meal or overnight. Happy hostessing!

How to Be a Welcome Guest

Proverbs 25:17 contains an interesting concept: ''Withdraw thy foot from thy neighbour's house; lest he be weary of thee, and so hate thee.'' Clearly, the implication is that a guest should be considerate of those who host him.

Some types of Christian service demand a good deal of travel. Foreign missionaries log thousands of miles both in their initial deputation and in their subsequent years of furlough. Nearly every Christian worker, however, will have opportunity to be a guest in other people's homes.

General Attitudes

Consideration for the host or hostess must always be uppermost. You should never ''just drop in'' for a meal or to spend the night.

Do not invite yourself or hint for an invitation. No matter how close your friendship (or family relationship!), do not take hospitality for granted. Never feel it is your due. Do not consider one overnight visit an open invitation for repeats.

Hospitality always means extra effort and thought for the hostess. Thoughtfulness and gratitude should be hallmarks of your attitude and behavior.

Being a Guest for a Meal

Respond promptly to the invitation. If schedules must be checked before you can commit, make getting back in touch with the hostess a priority.

Attend to the wording of the invitation, whether verbal or written. There is a difference between ''We'll see you at 6:30'' and "We will plan to eat at 6:30." The first means you should arrive at that time. The second indicates you need to arrive no more than ten minutes ahead of the given time and no less than five minutes ahead.

A small hostess gift is in order. If you give a food item, make it clear that you don't expect it to be added to the menu.

Be genuinely complimentary about the meal, but do not gush.

Offer to help the hostess whenever she's at a pressure point (e.g., clearing the main course in preparation for the dessert). It is also proper to offer help in cleaning up afterwards. However, when the offered assistance is refused, do not argue or insist.

Do not overstay. Two hours is considered the proper time limit for a seated-meal visit. Once you decide to leave, don't delay your departure. Leave.

Overnight Visits

Principles for being a welcome overnight guest can be considered in three time frames: before, during, and after the visit.

Before the visit. Be sure you understand whether or not the family is expected. A hostess expecting to provide room and board for a missionary couple may not be expecting to do so for their seven children! If taking a small child, provide sleeping equipment yourself—including bed protection for bed wetters. Find out about any planned activities so that you will know what types of clothing to pack.

Be specific about your arrival time. If you are delayed or need to come early, call ahead and notify the hostess.

Don't unload all your luggage right away. It makes the arrival seem like that at a hotel rather than a home.

Take a hostess gift. (A book or cassette tape that has been a blessing to you is always a good idea.)

During the visit. Ask questions about essential information—for example, where your children are to play. Control your children at all times. Take along their own toys, books, and other diversions, rather than expecting the hostess to provide them.

Understand the meal schedule clearly. Check the type of dress expected for breakfast especially. Always offer to help with a meal, but be sensitive to the hostess's desires. Eat some of everything at meals. Do not let your children say, "I don't like this."

Be sure the hostess knows if and when you'll be somewhere else for a meal.

Be neat about your own belongings as well as those supplied by the hostess. Towels should be rehung neatly, closet doors kept closed, and so forth. When ending the visit, find out what the hostess wants you to do about bed and bath linens.

After the visit. Call back. Let the hostess know about your trip from the time you left her home. Send a thank-you note right away and offer (sincerely) to hostess a reciprocal visit.

Hospitality, for both giver and receiver, demands the observance of some guidelines and the operation of some principles which, together with the right spiritual desire and mental attitude, will bring blessing and enrichment to both.

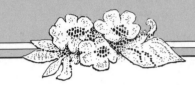

Chapter 14

Manners' Message

Whether hostessing, visiting, or simply following her daily routine, the Maidservant should recognize that etiquette is important to her personal testimony and the effectiveness of her ministry. Good manners are universally appreciated.

The problem most of us have is that we know, vaguely at least, what we *ought* to do, but we're too lazy, preoccupied, or careless to change poor habits. Social conduct really boils down to just that: habit. We do things the way we've learned to do them, and many of us grew up in homes where proper manners were not emphasized.

Should you discover from the following account that you now do some things incorrectly, don't feel resentful or rebellious. Instead, take up the challenge to change. A *polished* life vessel will more brightly reflect Jesus Christ. Realize, dear Maidservant, that as you obey God's will for your life, He may give you opportunity for witness to people at the highest levels of human society. If so, your manners will be scrutinized. Even more important, they will count either for or against the Lord at every social level. How sad if lack of interest today should result in missed opportunity and marred witness tomorrow.

But what, exactly, is etiquette? The common concept of etiquette as table manners is too narrow. It is rightly defined as *correct conduct under all circumstances of life.* Good manners and considerate behavior should go with us into every room of our daily living, not just into the dining room.

Mannerly behavior springs from *consideration for other people.* The woman or man who refuses to learn proper social conduct does so out of self-centeredness.

At least three distinct results come from learning etiquette:

1. You will personally benefit through increased social ease.
2. Your mannerly behavior will bless those around you.
3. *Most important,* you will enhance your life testimony for Jesus Christ. Salvation *refines* as well as *redeems.*

Many books deal with the subject of etiquette—several of them in great detail. As one (apparently unsaved) author points out, good manners rise from concepts presented in I Corinthians 13! The person trained in proper etiquette "does not behave [himself] unseemly." That is, he does not behave in an *unmannerly* fashion.

I Peter 2:9 reminds us that we are "a chosen generation, a royal priesthood" called to "shew forth the praises of him who hath called [us] out of darkness into his marvellous light." The words *shew forth* make clear that a Christian testimony is more than words. It is a *walk*—something we live out each moment of our existence. Our social conduct then is strategic to our representation of Christ. It should be the very finest because we are members of that blessed "royal priesthood."

Etiquette then is not a set of restrictions laid down by a staid octogenarian to make folks miserable. Good manners have, of course, been somewhat codified into rules. But these are not arbitrary pronouncements. There are reasons behind the rules:

- They keep us from offending others.
- They protect others' sensibilities.
- They oil the machinery of social interaction.

Common sense plays a large part in rules of etiquette. If, for instance, you are in a situation in which you don't know exactly what to do, choose the common-sense thing.

Women often complain about men who are ungentlemanly. But when tempted to make that complaint, we should analyze our own behavior. The *woman* sets the standard for mannerliness. In most cases, ladylike attitudes and actions will inspire gentlemanly conduct.

There are several situations in which women can expect a man's assistance:

1. *Seating at the table.* Wait quietly for the gentleman's help. Step away from his approach to avoid colliding. (In most cases the man will seat the lady who is to his right.) Slip gracefully into the chair he pulls out and keep most of your weight suspended by your thigh muscles as he slides the chair into place.
2. *Entering doors.* Pause long enough to give a man the chance to open doors for you.
3. *Entering and leaving automobiles.* Wait for the man to open the car door. Slip gracefully into or out of the seat. That means *knees and ankles together, moving legs in unison.* Allow the man to close the door.

If in any of the above you've become carelessly independent, polish your behavior. Give men the chance to be gentlemanly.

For *any* assistance given, *thank the man for his courtesy.* A woman who doesn't appreciate help doesn't deserve it.

Table Manners

Food moves *toward the right* around the table. When the hostess starts a serving dish or platter, she does not serve herself until after it has completed the entire circuit of the table. In cases where various bowls and platters of food are scattered about the table at the meal's beginning, the hostess may say something such as "Sam, please help yourself to the beans, and then pass them on." Or she may use a more generalized suggestion, such as "I'll just ask everyone to start the food that's nearest him."

Take the serving dish from the passer with your *right* hand; transfer it to your left; serve your plate; pass it to the receiver with your *left* hand. This crisscross action guards against jabbing table mates with your elbows or dumping food in their laps.

Take only moderate-sized helpings. Always use the serving spoon or fork—never your own—to take food from the serving bowl or platter.

If a table cover (place setting) contains more than the usual fork, knife, and spoon, use flatware **in order of its placement**

from outside in toward the plate: the pieces are arranged according to the sequence of courses to be served. Flatware above the plate is intended to be used for dessert.

Foods on the dinner plate usually are eaten only with a fork. Spoon foods are served separately. If a food leaves you uncertain about which silverware piece to use, check to see what the hostess is doing. (When you're the hostess, realize that others are looking to you as the example.)

The one hard-and-fast rule of silver usage is the one most often and badly violated: the proper way to use knife and fork. Variation from the standard proclaims boorishness. Study the following diagrams for proper American usage:

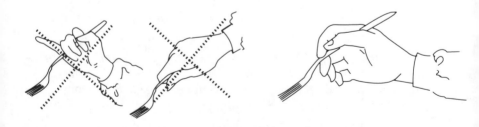

To cut meat, fork and knife lie **on their backs** diagonally across palms; index fingers provide pressure.

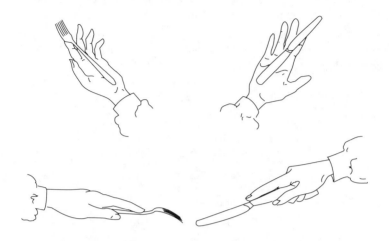

Fork tines go into the portion of food that will become your bite; knife cuts just to the far side of the fork position.

After a **single** piece of food has been cut, the knife is "cornered" on the plate rim while the fork is transferred to the right hand and taken to the mouth. Then another piece is cut, and so on, one bite at a time. The knife's resting position is not with blade on the plate, handle on the table.

Any piece of silverware, once used, should not be put back on the table surface, tablecloth, or place mat. Also do not use silverware in gesturing; no one enjoys a conversation punctuated by flying food.

Mouthfuls should be moderate in size—one fork or spoonful per bite. A stuffed mouth is singularly unattractive; tiny nibbles are silly. Chew with lips closed; table mates do not want to see or hear your food being pulverized. Never talk with food in your mouth.

A napkin is actually a *lap*kin: it should not be tucked into collar, vest, or belt. A dinner-sized napkin lies half-open on the lap; a dessert-sized one, fully open. A cloth napkin is *never* to be used as a handkerchief! After eating, place the napkin to the right of the plate, either crumpled or casually folded.

When a meal (or a course of a meal) has been finished, do not move the plate or bowl out of its assigned place.

Silverware position signals that you've finished eating. It should be placed across the center of your plate, parallel to the front edge of the table.

Social Conduct

Poise is an important part of social grace. Poise is simply the ability to appear comfortably at ease in any situation. Three ingredients combine to create a poised appearance:

1. *Quietness.* Physical and vocal quietness disguise nervousness or uncertainty.
2. *Control.* Your **mind**, not your jittery nerves, must be in charge of your actions and reactions.
3. *Concentration.* Concentrate not on yourself but on others. Forgetting yourself reduces nervous tension.

Be wise about time spent at any social function. People who know when to leave are worth their weight in gold. Discerning guests follow the wisdom of Scripture: "Withdraw thy foot from thy neighbour's house; lest he be weary of thee, and so hate thee" (Prov. 25:17).

A reception or drop-in requires no longer than a one-hour stay. Often it can be considerably shorter. Those hosting a drop-in expect visitors to "drop out" soon so that others can take their place.

For a seated meal you should stay only about two hours. No hostess enjoys marathon stays by guests. After they leave she must face the cleanup.

When you are a guest for a meal, offer to help the hostess. If she declines, don't insist. Stay alert, however, to do anything you can to make her job easier. This includes leaving within the accepted time limits. After saying a gracious good-by, **leave.** Don't linger. Always *send thank-you notes* to anyone who has hosted you socially.

Church Etiquette

As a Maidservant you naturally will spend a good deal of time in the church. Points of etiquette should be observed. *You set the example!* Church behavior should be dictated by the **purpose** for going there: worship of God. A spirit of true worshipfulness excludes giddiness, gawking, gabbing, giggling, and any kind of exhibitionism. Church behavior should reflect minds and hearts focused on the God of heaven. Church manners should contribute to the effectiveness of the preached Word. That means sitting still in the services. (Realize that *movement* steals attention from *speech.*) Perhaps the most common distraction in fundamentalist churches comes from **jaws**—jaws chewing gum. A gentleman or lady should never chew gum in public—and certainly never in a church service.

Conversation

In order to converse with people, we must be introduced to them. A few principles make introductions manageable as well as proper. In any introduction you make, it's important to know who is to be introduced to whom. Learn this simple formula for *whose* name to speak first. The formula has four parts:

1. The *lady's* name is mentioned first. ("Patricia, I'd like you to meet Mark Lewis.") If introducing two women of about the same age, mention a *married* woman's name first.
2. The *older* person's name comes first. ("Mr. Seventy-five, may I introduce Mr. Fifty.")
3. The more *prominent* person's name is spoken first. ("Senator Smith, may I introduce my mother, Mrs. Brown.")
4. The *individual's* name is mentioned first when introducing someone to a group. ("Sandra, I'd like you to meet my friends. Folks, this is Sandra Simpson.") Then, in giving names of those in the group, proceed in order around the room or gathering, indicating by gesture which name belongs to which person.

Finally, in making introductions, give *conversational clues* to those you introduce and then leave them to talk to each other. ("Katie, you and Nell share an interest in handicrafts.")

Communication is important for the woman in full-time Christian service. Ask and answer this question: how do you rate as a conversationalist? The standard of measurement is simple: good conversationalists *listen* more than they *talk*.

Christian conversation should be characterized by **tact**. A tactless person offends people. An offense is a hurt. Tactful speech does the following:

- It avoids asking prying questions (information that is not *volunteered* should be considered "off bounds" to questioning).
- It avoids discussing subjects that might cause someone pain. For example, a discussion of mortuary techniques in front of someone whose loved one has recently died is cruelly tactless.
- It does not compliment one person, excluding others in the group.
- It does not discuss an event enjoyed by only part of the group.
- It does not make comments that may injure a person's feelings about himself. For instance, calling the Large Sizes Department "Togs for Hogs" in the presence of someone who's decidedly overweight is coarsely insensitive.

All this is not to say that we should ever try to avoid the offense of the *Cross*. We must speak of sin to an unsaved person, despite the fact he may be offended by the concept.

Conclusion

We have chosen only a few points of etiquette to discuss in this chapter, those which we've seen Maidservants most in need of reviewing. Though commonly ignored and discounted, etiquette rules are grounded in consideration of others. This concern for others is especially expressive of Christian love, which demonstrates itself in the practice of the biblical injunction "in honour preferring one another."

Whose conduct should be more exemplary of humble deference to others than that of a Maidservant? Scripture makes it clear that the Christian **leader** should be a *servant* of others. A servant seeks the other person's honor, comfort, and enjoyment above his own. Servanthood, then, is the essence of etiquette—a condition of heart that adds vital, potent dimension to Christian testimony.

The
Maidservant's Handiwork

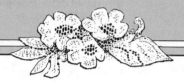

Chapter 15

Talk Techniques

Be prepared for people to make the following mental equation: "She's in full-time Christian service: she's a speaker." The two do not equate, but try to convince folks of that! Before moving into the subject of public speaking, though, let's think together about *private speech*.

Principles for Private Speaking

Scripture has much to say about personal oral communication. On the negative side, James 1:26 sternly warns, "If any man among you seem to be religious, and bridleth not his tongue, but deceiveth his own heart, this man's religion is vain." This test of spiritual integrity applies to those in ministry as well as to lay people. Like them, however, we often fail to control our speech.

Proverbs 4:24 enjoins against dishonesty of speech. "Put away from thee a froward [crooked] mouth, and perverse lips put far from thee." Notice that the verse does not distinguish between "big untruths" and "little untruths." It simply says to put away lying—period!

Proverbs 10:19 advises against superabundant speech: "In the multitude of words there wanteth not sin; but he that refraineth his lips is wise." Many of us get into trouble with our mouths simply because we say more than we should.

On the positive side, Scripture prescribes kindness as a controller of our lips. "The words of a wise man's mouth are gracious; but the lips of a fool will swallow up himself" (Eccles. 10:12). "There is that speaketh like the piercings of a sword: but the tongue of the wise is health" (Prov. 12:18). "Let your speech be always with grace, seasoned with salt, that ye may know how ye ought to answer every man" (Col. 4:6). Perhaps of all the characteristics of the virtuous woman of Proverbs 31, kindness is the most compelling and convicting: "She openeth her mouth with wisdom: and in her tongue is the law of kindness" (31:26).

The bridled tongue edifies. To edify is to build up, encourage, strengthen. Ephesians 4:29 commands constructive speech: "Let no corrupt communication proceed out of your mouth, but that which is good to the use of edifying, that it may minister grace unto the hearers."

Principles for Public Speaking

Yes, we know—public speaking scares you spitless (literally!). Be encouraged: you're not alone. In fact, studies show that fear of public speaking tops the list of terrors for American businessmen. The comforting fact, however, is that *stage fright does not kill*. It actually indicates that your physical system is preparing you for a more successful presentation than would otherwise be possible.

Stage fright's extra energy needs to be harnessed and directed toward your goal: *communication*. It's a bit like hitching a horse to a wagon rather than letting the wagon roll off by itself.

Mastering stage fright requires an attitude adjustment. The dread and reluctance with which most of us approach the speech platform needs to be adjusted. We should think "opportunity," not "obligation"; "gratitude," not "fortitude." Supporting this attitude adjustment should be diligent prayer for God's guidance and help throughout your preparation and presentation.

Material

The material you choose for public presentation can make or break your talk. Choose a subject that has meaning to you personally. Never just snatch a topic or an outline because it's neatly stated or because you heard someone else give it.

You may be asked to talk on a given theme. At other times you'll have the freedom to choose your own topic. Explore the possibilities: season, occasion, character study, personal experience, a specific verse or passage from the Bible, an idea from your devotional notebook.

Develop your topic with varied material types. Use a good mixture of facts, personal anecdotes, statistics, and illustrations.

Outline your material. Clear organization is essential to you in preparing and presenting content and to your audience in comprehending it.

Preparation

Do thorough, concentrated preparation for your talk. Practice aloud; rework weak spots; eliminate; adjust. But *do not memorize* anything except the introduction and conclusion.

Presentation

Choose platform dress that is appropriate, modest, attractive, simple, and conservative.

Walk and stand tall with weight mostly on the balls of your feet. Good carriage communicates poise and helps you command attention. Use bodily action positively, not negatively. Integrate gestures and eliminate nervous mannerisms.

Talk *to* your audience members, not at them. Look them in the eye. Determine that you will make yourself heard. Women gather to hear another woman speak, not to hear a mouse squeak.

Throughout your talk, keep your mind where it should be: on your message and on communicating that message. Thinking about yourself or about your hearers' reactions will make your communication ineffective.

Communicate on a person-to-person, woman-to-woman basis. Neither talk down to nor be apologetic toward your audience.

Obviously this chapter does not pretend to deal in depth with the subject of public speaking but gives only the barest principles. For thorough coverage of the subject from a uniquely Christian and feminine standpoint, consider acquiring the little handbook by Beneth entitled *Talk to Me, Lady*. Do, in any case, consider seriously the ministry of public speaking and the suggestions just offered. Christian women around the world feel tremendous need for help from other women in these challenging days. Speaking opportunities are everywhere. Our part as women in ministry is to accept, prayerfully and gratefully, the speaking opportunities God gives us. The Devil's women are ceaselessly spouting and shouting their falsehoods. How dare you and I who have the Living Truth be silent?

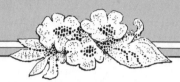

Chapter 16

Hearing and Helping

A large slice of a Maidservant's time and energy may be claimed by the delicate, demanding task of personal counseling. Women needing help naturally turn to someone in leadership. *Biblical* counseling is both a privilege and a responsibility.

It follows that those seeking counsel in difficulties are to be commended, not condescended to. They are wise in seeking counsel, according to Proverbs 1:5: "A wise man will hear, and will increase learning; and a man of understanding shall attain unto wise counsels." They are also wise in seeking as a *source* of counsel a person mature in spiritual knowledge. Isaiah 30:1-2 warns that the choice of a source of counsel is a strategic decision: "Woe to the rebellious children, saith the Lord, that take counsel, but not of me; and that cover with a covering, but not of my spirit, that they may add sin to sin: That walk to go down into Egypt, and have not asked at my mouth; to strengthen themselves in the strength of Pharaoh, and to trust in the shadow of Egypt!"

Preparation for Counseling

Consecration to the Lord is the counselor's first prerequisite. Any human wisdom we might offer a troubled woman is vain, empty. Daily consecration to Jesus Christ will keep our eyes upon

Him, our knees bent before Him, and our lives clean vessels through which His Word may flow to needy hearts and shattered lives.

The woman who counsels must herself go *daily* to her Counselor and the counsel of His Word. Proverbs 19:20 says, "Hear counsel, and receive instruction, that thou mayest be wise in thy latter end." We should be able to say with the psalmist, "Thy testimonies also are my delight and my counsellors" (119:24). If we are not ourselves instructed by the Word of God, our counsel will *blight* rather than *bless.*

Besides being consecrated to the Lord, we need to be dedicated to the task of counseling. This task requires enlarging our stock of wisdom. Colossians 3:16 points to the nature and source of our advising: "Let the word of Christ dwell in you richly in all wisdom; teaching and admonishing one another." First Corinthians 2:12-13 explains its meaning: "Now we have received, not the spirit of the world, but the spirit which is of God; that we might know the things that are freely given to us of God. Which things also we speak, not in the words which man's wisdom teacheth, but which the Holy Ghost teacheth; comparing spiritual things with spiritual." We minister effectively not only through our experience but also, and primarily, through our knowledge of the Word and our moment-by-moment fellowship with the Lord.

We also should be committed to the people God allows us to lead. Our counsel should be motivated and molded by love for those to whom we minister. The Apostle Paul expressed the ideal counselor's spirit: "But we were gentle among you, even as a nurse cherisheth her children: So being affectionately desirous of you, we were willing to have imparted unto you, not the gospel of God only, but also our own souls, because ye were dear unto us" (I Thess. 2:7-8).

Purpose in Counseling

The person of the Lord Jesus Christ Himself is the answer to every human need. We should hold as *few* counseling sessions as possible with those who seek our help. Faith in and dependence upon a human counselor must be discouraged. In effect, the counselor takes the open, extended, grasping hands of the troubled person and places them in the hand of the Savior. *He alone* has the solution to the problem, wisdom for the challenge, strength for victory.

The spirit of our age wants "instant" everything. The burdened, broken Christian, however, must be encouraged to be "labourers together with God." The burden of responsibility lies with the counselee; she must demonstrate active involvement in working out her problems. Such involvement is measurable by the counselor's assigning specific "to-dos." If those are ignored, the counseling sessions should end. It is impossible to help anyone who will not determine to help herself. For example, a woman battling intense bitterness might be told, "Before you come to see me again, study these Scripture passages, write out the personal application, do something kind for _____ (the resented person), and pray for that person every day." If the counselee returns without having carried through on the assignment, discontinue counseling sessions.

Because Satan never tires of using pride against us, a counseling Maidservant may begin to think, "I must be pretty spiritual since these women are coming to me for help." She may increasingly refer to and delight in the number, complexity, and human interest of counseling problems. But the moment pride enters, God's pleasure in us exits, and we become vulnerable to other of the Devil's devices. The Bible makes it clear that God *hates* pride.

Prayer in Counseling

Besides the counselor's personal habit of earnest and persistent private prayer, each counseling session should begin and end with prayer. Prayer invokes the Lord's undertaking during the time spent together and reminds both counselor and counselee that their help must come from Him.

Prayer furnishes and fortifies the Maidservant for a counseling ministry. It overcomes hesitancy. It supports meditation on the Word and absorption of its truths into the life. (Practical scriptural truths built into your life today strengthen the fiber of your Christian character for counseling tomorrow.) Whether or not you are doing personal counseling right now, prayerfully prepare to do it as need and occasion arise. The one-to-one ministry undergirded by prayer can be greatly used of God in the lives of troubled Christian women.

Practicalities for Counseling

Don't overcounsel. It is better to present a few simple truths than to flood the counselee with torrents of advice. Beginning counselors, especially, seem fearful of silence, and so they talk on and on, rambling through unnecessary explanations, questions, opinions, examples, statistics, and so forth. The counselee may instead need *silence* in order to verbalize responses or to digest advice. Also, there is therapeutic value for the counselee in talking. So be a good listener. Often the troubled person begins to see light on her problem just by expressing it.

Don't let tears deceive. When the counselor addresses the matter of sin, the counselee may weep buckets of tears—but they are not necessarily repentant tears. She may cry because of the apparent hopelessness of the situation, its pressures on her, her frustration, her pain over causing someone else pain, or her fear of being caught. Those tears count for little. Effective tears are tears of repentance (facing, hating, confessing, and forsaking the sin). Pray for the ability to discern between the genuine and the false.

Don't be quick to answer. Don't jump to conclusions. It may take a good deal of probing to get all the facts. It is natural for a counselee to withhold detrimental information. She may, consciously or unconsciously, seek the answer or advice she *wants* to hear.

Don't give pat responses. Answers such as "The Lord will take care of it" or "Remember Romans 8:28" leave the counselee frustrated and faltering. Don't apply iodine to deep wounds! There are agonies of living that defy human understanding. It is precisely at that point that the believer must agree to stop struggling and start leaning on her all-wise heavenly Father. Whatever the problem, direct the counselee toward specific instructions, examples, and answers in the *Bible*.

Don't forget the dual nature. We sometimes wonder how a Christian woman could get herself into such a mess. But getting into messes is easy for our old, sinful human nature; it is capable of any depravity. As long as we live on this earth, each of us Christians must endure the struggle between the old and the new natures. If a believer does not maintain a close daily walk with God, feeding the new nature and starving the old, Satan can lure her into moral and spiritual tragedy.

Don't let the counselee think she is unique. A troubled individual may feel that her miseries are worse than anyone else's. That sense of uniqueness predisposes her to feeling helpless. Point the counselee to reassuring passages such as I Corinthians 10:13 and James 5:17. There are few variations on sin's moral, emotional, mental, and spiritual "plots." Only the names change.

Don't show shock. Sometimes a counselee may try to shock you. If she sees that you are shaken by her tale, she gains control of the counseling session. Prevent her dragging you through the mire. Tell her you do not want or need to know sordid details; all you need is a summary of the situation in order to help her. No matter how deep the pit into which the counselee has fallen, assure her that she is never beyond God's reach.

Don't become emotionally involved. Our hearts should reach out to those who have burdens. At the same time, however, there must be a certain emotional detachment in counseling. When emotional involvement enters, objectivity departs. Offer the counselee compassionate listening, prayer, and scriptural advice, but don't step into her emotional quicksand. Two of you floundering make assistance impossible.

Be alert to nonverbals. A counselee may say one thing with her lips while her body says another: avoiding eye contact, turning away, fidgeting. That "body English" may indicate shame, partial revelation, or lying.

Beware of topical hopscotch. If a woman feels guilt or conviction, she may skitter away from the core trouble, trying to distract her own and the counselor's attention. In such cases, persistently bring her back to the point. Don't allow her to control the session's direction and length.

Finally, *don't overlook the importance of a proper setting.* The counselee needs restful quiet in the surroundings. Distractions from people running to and fro, interruptions, or ringing telephones discourage her from unburdening her heart. Tissues should be available but out of sight for the tears that may be shed. If possible, offer the counselee a choice of warm drinks: tea, coffee, spiced tea, for example. Phrase your offer in such a way that she doesn't have the option of refusing: "I have tea, coffee, or herb tea. Which would you prefer?" A warm drink helps begin a counseling session. It gives the counselee something to do with her hands. The warm liquid has a soothing effect. The touch of civility and implied camaraderie contribute to sharing. Keep some kind of breath sweetener on hand. One of the greatest helps you can give a distressed person is physical closeness—holding her hand, giving her a hug—but you don't want to negate the positives with bad breath.

Problems in Counseling

Some specific problem areas are repeatedly encountered in counseling. We will briefly touch upon some of the most common.

Salvation. Troubled unsaved women may seek help from a preacher's wife or other Christian worker. Among these may be an *assumed* Christian who has become aware of her lostness. It is imperative, therefore, that a Maidservant know the plan of salvation and be able to present it clearly. It is also important that she know enough Bible verses on the subject to be flexible in the Holy Spirit's hands. Many will need different or additional Scripture passages. Not everyone responds to the "Romans Road."

Be aware then that human hearts' doors swing on different hinges. Though some few will readily accept Christ, many more will require time to contemplate, to struggle, to observe. Exercise both patience and prayer, remembering that salvation comes as the Holy Spirit applies the Word of God. The harvest is *His,* not ours. A regrettable "rush" emphasis has taken hold in some segments of fundamentalism in the pride-puffing pursuit of numbers in soulwinning.

Satanic oppression. The oppressed Christian may feel bewildered, cold-hearted toward God, depressed, drained of mental, emotional, and physical energy. Before counseling can proceed, she must be made aware of the fact of the oppression. If she has been thoroughly checked by a doctor and no contributive physical condition can be found, then satanic oppression is a valid suspect.

In counseling the oppressed, first urge the counselee to start "bringing into captivity every thought to the obedience of Christ" (II Cor. 10:5). Second, ask her to memorize and meditate upon Psalm 103. Third, recommend *singing.* Point out the many mentions of singing in Scripture. Explain that she will be singing not *because* of the way she feels but *in spite* of it. She should sing as she goes about her daily routine, sing as she feels the urge to sink into depression, sing her prayers, sing the Psalms, and so forth. Satan does not like a singing heart, and he won't stay around one very long.

Depression, whether resulting from satanic activity or arising from a chemical imbalance, is startlingly widespread in American Christianity today. It is a tool our adversary uses with great skill. As a result, many born-again women are listless, pessimistic, and reclusive, hardly the channels of blessing they ought to be. The condition is not untreatable, however, and scriptural remedies must be applied with patience and purpose.

Satanic accusation. Many women feel overwhelmed by guilt and a sense of unworthiness. Often the Devil launches this attack at the moment of some spiritual opportunity. He whispers, "Just who do you think you are teaching that Sunday school class? And teen-age girls, of all things! After what *you* did as a teen-ager!" With that kind of badgering, one may flee opportunities, sidestep obligations, and cringe away from challenges. But, as in all things, God's Word provides the defense for such bombardment. You can point the troubled one to such passages as Micah 7:18-19, Psalm 103:12, Joel 2:25, and I John 1:9.

Physical problems. There are some physical conditions whose complexities or longevity drive a woman to seek counsel. Outstanding among those are illness and fatigue. Sometimes the fact that a woman is a Christian keeps her silent too long about her difficulties in handling her problem. She feels that as a believer she should be able to accept and adjust to whatever enters her life. Thus the intensity of her human struggles gives rise to guilt. And on it goes until desperation drives her to a listening ear.

Counsel, in her case as in others, should be both practical and spiritual. Practicality will dictate that she *make allowances* for her physical debilitation, not drive herself mercilessly as if she had the good health and stamina she would like to possess. Fatigue or illness often signals overload. If she continues to heap stress upon stress, she faces serious consequences. Spiritually she should be encouraged with the thought that God "knoweth our frame; he remembereth that we are dust" (Ps. 103:14). He fully understands our physical limitations (after all, He allows them!), and He empathizes with our mental, emotional, and spiritual struggles.

Rampant emotions. Uncontrolled feelings may bring a woman to seek counsel from one she trusts. Anger, bitterness, hopelessness, fear, worry—all should be confessed, analyzed, and addressed with Scripture. Grief over the death of a loved one will be covered in a later chapter.

Occasionally the counselor may have to deal with a woman who feels that the only solution to her problems is suicide. *Take such threatenings seriously.* Whether they be spoken by a young teen or a great-grandmother, expressing the wish to die indicates desperation. Do not count upon either "common sense" or spiritual restraint to triumph.

The suicidal state does not always indicate a spiritual problem. A chemical imbalance in the body can motivate toward suicide. Urge the counselee to have a thorough medical checkup. Also, suicidal urges run somewhat seasonally. According to statistics, Christmas, other holidays, and spring see more suicides than other times of the year.

With the Word of God, show the counselee that her situation is not without hope; that suicide violates God's commands; that her death would solve nothing, but merely complicate life for those remaining, burdening them with a cruel load of sorrow and guilt. Refer her to Proverbs 29:25, Matthew 10:26-31, Hebrews 2:14-15, and I John 4:18. Make the practical suggestion that the counselee begin a program of physical exercise. Putting stress on the exterior self helps to alleviate stress on the internal self.

Agonizing memories. One of the saddest characteristics of modern days is the revelation of huge numbers of those abused in childhood. Whether physical, mental, emotional, or sexual, those unspeakable realities leave lifelong scars. Prevalent among Christians, unfortunately, has been the naive assumption that such uglies belong to the unsaved world. Not so! They are epidemic among Christians. Surface spirituality—of a preacher, deacon, youth leader, or Sunday school teacher—has long camouflaged cruel depravity. Therefore, *do not be disbelieving or visibly shocked* by the destruction of a facade through a hurting woman's revelations. Second, don't try to give the victim *reasons* for such devastating experiences. There are numberless things in this life we can never understand. Third, when she expresses or implies anger toward God, don't be dismayed. God isn't. But she must be led, step by gentle step, to a willingness to *let God be God;* to believe that in, over, and through all the incomprehensibles, He is *Love;* and that, yes, He can and will fulfill His promise to bring beauty from ashes.

Financial woes. Money problems may bring a woman to a counselor. Perhaps she has been the one responsible through unwise use of credit cards. Perhaps her husband's haphazard spending may be at fault. It may be that medical expenses are crushing the financial life out of her family. Whatever the reason, present realities must be faced, scriptural principles enunciated, and a practical plan yoked to spiritual trust. A brief acrostic may be helpful here:

> **M**—Manage your money wisely (Luke 16:11).
> **O**—Obey God's instructions (Deut. 26:2; I Cor. 16:2; II Cor. 9:7 and 12:14b; Matt. 6:19-24).
> **N**—Nullify Satan's wiles (Prov. 23:5).
> **E**—Employ common sense (Prov. 14:15).
> **Y**—Yield to God the right of ownership (Ps. 4:1; I Chron. 29:9; I Cor. 4:7).

Marital Counseling

Marital counseling may well be the area in which Maidservants will be most active as counselors, both to unmarried and married women. For that reason, we are devoting considerable space to its discussion.

First, a Maidservant may be involved in **premarital counseling.** A single girl may ask, *"Should I marry this young man?"* Respond with questions of your own about his spiritual state. Is he saved? (If not, marriage is not an option; the Bible clearly forbids it.) Is he strong spiritually, strong enough to provide the spiritual leadership so important to a Christian marriage? After she has answered those questions satisfactorily, ask, "Do you genuinely love him?" Though her protestations may sound convincing, discuss the nature of real love. It is safe to assume that a young person's concept of love has been distorted, influenced by the media, constructed from the pooled ignorance of her peer group.

We must base our definition and demonstration of love upon God's Word rather than upon a merely human concept. Otherwise, our hearts, our homes, and our happiness will suffer tragic results identical with the world's. Unlike a frothy or animalistic concept of love, real love is less *emotion* than *devotion*, less *wonder* than *work*, less *getting* than *giving*.

Distilled to its essence, genuine love is *unconditional commitment to an imperfect person.* Analyze this definition with the counselee.

- *Unconditional.* There is no "better luck next time" attitude in real love, no exemptive loopholes. Instead, it reflects God's plan of lifetime dedication.
- *Commitment.* Love is more an act of the *will* than of the heart. For love, what's right is more important than what it wants or doesn't want.
- *Imperfect person.* Many women stick on that snag, accumulating emotional refuse that otherwise would harmlessly sweep past on life's stream. God's marriage book never says or implies, "These instructions apply if your husband is kind, consistent, gentlemanly, supportive." No person is or can be perfect; yet femininity seems bent upon eliminating masculinity's flaws. When the flaws don't fade, we let them become irritants, instigators of our sinful reactions.

As a counselor, you need to urge any prospective bride to analyze carefully and prayerfully herself, her possible future mate, and the "chemistry" of their relationship in light of the following danger signals:

1. *Numerous mixed feelings.* If one of the couple sees consistent problem areas in the partner or in the relationship itself and feels uneasy when thinking of lifelong attachment to that individual, serious reconsideration is imperative.
2. *Lack of peace.* When both young people genuinely desire the Lord's will, He will use unease of heart to warn them against further commitment.
3. *Opposition by relatives or friends.* People who care about the couple do not try to *destroy* their happiness; they seek to promote it. Those outside the highly charged emotional field can exercise unbiased judgment. God gives to parents, in particular, a protective "sixth sense" for the child's good.

Unfortunately, many young people do not seek counsel when they feel themselves to be "in love." They move blithely (and often blindly) into matrimony. Because they do so, a problem increasingly brought to counselors is that of **marred marriages.**

It is heartbreaking to realize the number of Christian homes that could be categorized as "awful." The beautiful unity, warmth, and joy God intended wither and die. Because marriage and home are a woman's primary sphere, the wife most often recognizes trouble spots. Frequently, however, she is unable to discern the real causes.

There are four outstanding problem areas in Christian marriages. The first is *exploded expectations*. A girl expects marriage to be a lifelong thrill. She expects Herkimer Husband to be the ideal man, to dote upon her. She expects "happily ever after" to work its fictional magic. There also are girls entering marriage from Christian homes knowing nothing about the physical aspect of married love. They expect some sort of platonic relationship. They may react to reality with shocked disillusionment. In either case, the basic cause has been unrealistic expectations. The counselee must be made to abandon illusion. Psalm 62:5 directs our expectations to their proper focus: "My soul, wait thou only upon God: for my expectation is from him."

Second, marital problems can result from *appalling approaches* to marriage:

1. Seeing marriage as an idealized cure-all
2. Seeking marriage with a desperate, panicky spirit

Both violate scriptural principles. The first makes marriage an idol; the second demonstrates discontentment and fear. God alone should determine a Christian girl's pathway of life: its destination, its direction, and its dimensions.

Third, a marriage suffers if it has a *faulty foundation*. There are nine outstanding wrong reasons for marrying:

1. *Pregnancy*. Panic over immorality's fruit stampedes some couples into disastrous marriages. Careful, prayerful considerations should be made in the unhappy event of premarital pregnancy. Sometimes marriage is the wisest solution; in other cases it is the worst.
2. *Rebound*. Rejected by a suitor, a girl may grab the first available alternative, attempting to bandage her hurt.
3. *Rebellion*. A girl's sheer bullheadedness can cause her to marry a boy disapproved by family or peers.
4. *Escape*. Flight from an unhappy home sends the escapee toward greater unhappiness.
5. *Loneliness*. Marriage is no automatic, guaranteed cure for loneliness. In fact, the loneliest people in the world are those lonely *within* marriage.
6. *Physical appearance*. Living amid cultish worship of youth and beauty, girls too often say yes to a face or physique—only to find themselves bound to a shrunken, ugly soul.

7. *Social pressure.* Wounded by implications that singleness is freakish, a girl snatches at the golden ring. She finds it sunlight on smoke.

8. *Guilt and pity.* An adoring suitor can fill a girl's heart with benevolent pity or with guilt over feeling no responsive love. These are reasons for bringing home a stray dog, not for marrying.

9. *Infatuation.* A girl "in love with love" becomes blind, deaf, and *dumb.*

Fourth, trouble can plague a marriage that is constructed of *bad building blocks.* Some good building blocks follow:

Personal similarities. "Opposites attract" may be true. Also, in nonessential areas, differences can provide balance and interest. In essential areas, however, the more alike the mates, the better their chances for success. These areas include value systems, moral standards, and ethical attitudes.

Communication. The ability to communicate well—to speak honestly; to share the deepest, most private self with another; to verbalize and settle disagreements—indicates mutual trust and contributes to the bonding of marriage.

Spirituality. Ideally there should be similar spiritual maturity with shared spiritual goals and with the young man demonstrating leadership ability in this vital area.

Sadly, your marriage counseling may also have to deal with **the agony of infidelity.** Should the woman herself be the one involved in sexual immorality, you must be clear but loving in pointing out what God says about her sin. If she has come to you with broken heart and repentant spirit, you can at this time begin helping toward restoration. Sometimes, however, there is neither shame nor sorrow. Don't be shocked that such a one may know all the relevant Scripture passages as well as you do, yet refuse to heed; that is the Devil's hardening. She must be assured that there are no excuses for her infidelity, however she may protest otherwise. Also she needs to be assured of God's love which, while it suffers long and endures all things, also rejoices not in iniquity. God's love will not forever stay His chastening. There is a line beyond which He ceases to strive with the unrepentant, saved as well as lost, and He may end her life rather than allow her to continue profaning His name.

If the wife is the one sinned against, assure her of God's unfailing love in the midst of her shattered world. It is His *goodness* that allows humanity to exercise free will; it is man's sinfulness that makes him choose evil. Gently, too, lead her to understand and acknowledge her own contributions to Satan's triumph (I Cor. 7:1-5). Otherwise she will blame her husband for everything, build walls of bitterness, and carry a twisted spirit throughout succeeding days and years. Finally, she needs to be directed into an ever closer walk with the Lord. Satan's success with her husband doesn't mean he'll call off his attack upon her and the children.

Wherever mental, emotional, and spiritual **healing** needs to take place, lead the counselee toward wholeness through the following four steps. First, however, you must determine that she genuinely desires healing. Some use their wounds as a lifelong crutch or badge of suffering. Besides desire, there must also be a firm commitment to pursue healing.

1. *Recognize and reject cover-ups.* Among the symptoms of a painful past and unconscious reactions to it are distrust of people (and of God), perfectionism, enormous fears, combativeness, inability to be close, and self-denigration. These surface camouflages must be swept away and reality examined. Through probing and by praying for God to reveal what has been hidden, uncover the truth, ugly as it may be. The counselee needs to *verbalize* the painful memories that emerge (James 5:16). The counselor must be both patient and persistent. Women typically deny even to themselves those things that have scarred them most deeply. Removing the blockage of years of silence may be extremely difficult; she may have to force herself to talk. It is critical that you as counselor and confidante demonstrate *trustworthiness* at such a time, becoming a grave for your counselee's secrets.

2. *Remove the guilt and anger.* From life's most hurtful experiences, tremendous anger can build, both against the person who hurt and against God for allowing the pain. Close upon anger's footsteps walks the shadow guilt, whether from the hurtful experience itself or from reactions to it. It is not enough for the wounded woman to remove her anger and guilt; she must *replace* it with forgiveness. She may protest that it is impossible for her to forgive the person who crushed her so badly. If so, she is thinking of forgiveness as a matter of emotion: she does not *feel* she can forgive. Forgiveness, however, is an act of the *will* in obedience to God. It has nothing to do with emotion.

The Bible tells us to let go of our bitterness and to forgive (Eph. 4:30-32). No exceptions are made for feelings.

3. *Rest in the person of Jesus Christ.* Here is the blessed difference between Christianity and human religion. Christianity is a personal relationship. The wounded woman needs to shift her focus—from her hurts and from her hurter—to the lovely Lord Jesus. She needs to do so by studying His characteristics and attributes in the Bible. She must cast her care, and keep casting it, upon Him, praying for victory (Ps. 27:3-5).

4. *Renew the mind with the Word of God.* The victimized woman needs to bathe her wounds and her entire spiritual self in the pure water of the Word—to take in that water daily, letting it permeate her being, washing out all the corruption that may have built up over years. She must learn to bring every thought into Christ's captivity, under His control (II Cor. 10:5). Having done so, she must not remain in the place of self-examination and renewal but move on to ministering to others (II Cor. 1:4).

Final Reminders

Whatever the specific nature of your counseling sessions, make it a practice always to have your Bible with you. Don't feel that you must memorize all the pertinent verses or references. Keep a list of appropriate passages for various questions and problems and don't be timid about referring to the list.

Also, be aware of the need for practical wisdom in counseling. The spirit of this age is such that fury against God and His people is putting ministries at risk in many unsuspected ways. Litigation is one of them. Christian counselors have been and are being taken to court on ridiculous allegations of mental harassment and injurious advice. We who give counsel must know the framework of the law and exercise caution in any counseling session.

In the face of towering human problems, any of us feels inadequate to counsel. Yet as God allows us these opportunities, we can rejoice in them, claiming His wisdom and turning confidently to His Word for answers.

Chapter 17

Shepherdess and Sheep

Since Christian ministry is directed toward and conducted with people, interpersonal relationships are important for the Maidservant. Her effectiveness requires fulfilling her relational responsibilities as the unique individual God made her.

Responsibility to the Group

Within her ministry's circle of influence, the Maidservant must be both a friend and an example.

Friendship

An emphasis on friendship toward those we lead must begin with a caution that may seem contradictory. One of the most difficult burdens borne by Maidservants is the loneliness inherent in ministry. Women have a special yearning for close friends with whom they can share everything. The problem is that leadership imposes restrictions. It limits what we can do even in areas as important as that which we now stress. The sober truth is that a Maidservant must *not have close friends within the group that looks to her for leadership.* By favoring a few of the flock with special friendship, she creates differences—class distinctions that are bound to displease and offend those outside the inner circle.

Some ministry women vow they can have a special friendship or two in the congregation without negative fallout. They are, we fear, bringing serious problems on themselves and on their ministry. The Maidservant's special friendships should be restricted to (a) the Lord, (b) her husband, and (c) other ministry women.

A diagram may clarify the necessity of friendship-with-all and special-friendship-with-none:

For a moment, cover the lead sheep. Imagine her back in the middle of the flock. How many can see what she's doing or where she's going? For the sake of all, leadership demands *distance*. A Maidservant's reaction to this demand is important. She can choose to bemoan her loneliness or to believe God intends it for her good as well as others'. From it may come a sweeter, more intimate relationship with the Lord than would otherwise have been possible.

How, then, does a ministry woman win and maintain the friendship of a group? First, by *approachableness*. Proverbs reminds us that "A man that hath friends must shew himself friendly" (18:24). Your basic personality make-up may not be the outgoing, never-meet-a-stranger type. Also, under the pressure of a tight schedule and jangled nerves, you may not always *feel* friendly. Nevertheless, for the well-being of the flock, you need to appear friendly at all times. Notice that friendly does not mean gushy or sweetie-sweet. Instead, concentrate on learning names, go out of your way to speak to everyone possible, inquire about their families, and so on. Your personal interest will help people feel welcome and important, an integral part of the group.

Another component of approachableness is a sense of humor. A too-serious, too-intent, or too-pious aura repels rather than attracts.

Finally, approachableness is communicated by an attitude of sharing the human state. Don't be loath to confess that you don't have it absolutely "all together" yourself. Acknowledgment of human imperfection will not only endear you to hearts but also encourage them.

Besides approachableness, a Maidservant must convey a *compassionate spirit*. Her heart should be genuinely open toward others. Compassion is not buckets of tears shed at the mention of someone's trouble; it is a heart touched to genuine sympathy, prayer support, and practical helpfulness.

A ministry woman also ought to be *knowledgeable in spiritual things*. Her friendship will then be valued for its solidity. True spiritual knowledge is shown not by the endless spouting of Scripture but by demonstrating—simply and not self-consciously—daily obedience to God's Word.

Example

Beyond showing friendship to the entire group, the Maidservant also needs to be an example. People, like sheep and children, must be *led,* not *driven.* The congregation should be able to see in you how they themselves ought to walk as children of God. Our examples have impact in several distinct areas.

Our first duty is to be exemplary as *believers.* Our spiritual selves never can be flawless here on earth, but they can and should be faithful. Faithfulness is demonstrated in genuine, growing love for the Lord, His Word, and His work; in minds hedged about by and directed into the Bible; in hands busy about His business; in feet obedient to His leading; in lives yielded to Him for whatever service by whatever means He chooses.

Our lives as *wives* ought to be exemplary. If there were ever a day in which live audiovisuals of a woman being a proper Christian wife were needed, it is this day. Everywhere are women with difficult home situations. It is natural for them to watch your life for instruction and inspiration.

You may be sure Satan will be unhappy about exemplary wives. Be warned of at least two attacks he'll make:

1. *Self-advancement.* The naturally retiring heart may occasionally grumble, "Why do I have to be the invisible woman? I'm important in this ministry too. Why should Herk get so much attention?" Or, if yours is an outgoing and vocal personality,

you may find it difficult to maintain the reticence necessary to allow your husband the spotlight.

2. *Self-gratification.* Satan whispers, "You need some building up yourself, don't you? And aren't you lonely?" *Watch out!*

We also need to be examples as *mothers.* Our mothering should faithfully obey God's instructions, not yield to public pressure or seek public impression. The spirit of the age and ungodly child-rearing authorities work against young Christian mothers. Your inspirational example is strategic.

Fourth, we should be exemplary as *church members.* The pastor's desire is for members to be active. How can that be realized if the leader's wife or other ministry women remain uninvolved? Your involvement will be determined and publicly enunciated by your husband or by the leader of your mission/ministry.

Responsibility to Individuals

The Maidservant also has a charge to perform toward individuals within the group. She needs to observe these imperatives.

Be unbiased. There can be no playing of favorites. Some people are naturally more likable than others, but it is a mistake to be warmer toward them than toward those with less attractive personalities. God's Word tells us to be "no respecter of persons." Our kindness and friendliness should be extended to all.

Do not share confidences. As pressures build and as a Maidservant becomes a repository for people's secrets, she sometimes feels as if the bands of her mind will burst without someone she can talk to. Nevertheless, like a doctor or a lawyer she must be faithful to the "client's" best interest and protection. Our motto should be "What comes to me stops with me." That includes talking about ministry matters even with someone as close as your own mother. You must restrict confidences to a triangle: yourself, your husband when necessary, and the Lord.

Do not harbor grudges. Invariably there will be situations and individuals that cause hurt. If you are married, the hurts to your husband will give you even more pain than your personal woundings, and they are harder to forgive. But what good does a grudge do? Does it sweeten your own spirit or quiet your heart? How does it affect onlookers who detect your harsh feelings? What constructive element does it add to the ministry?

Finally, be aware that God ministers to us through our woundings. No one goes through life unscathed. Everyone suffers bruises, cuts, and scrapes. The important thing is not to escape or relieve the hurts but to benefit from them. Life's richest lessons are learned in pain. God does not intend bruisings to destroy us. He desires they make us stronger on the outside, more tender on the inside.

Responsibility to Herself

God intends that we focus proper attention upon the self, the instrument of His service, as well as upon the service itself and those we serve.

We must, of course, hold to proper *priorities*. When the schedule gets pressured, do we let the urgent replace the necessary (personal devotions, housework, or time with family)? Satan knows that if he can puncture our priorities, he can get us off on the shoulder of life's highway. The "impossible" demands of our busy lives prove really impossible only when we confuse their relative importance. If, however, we honor true priorities, God will give the grace, strength, wisdom, and time to do all that we need to do.

But we should never forget that our well-being is a genuine priority. She who ministers must also herself be strengthened. She who serves must herself be served. We would encourage you to read edifying materials, to listen to Christian tapes, to attend seminars and retreats, and to be always open and tender to the Holy Spirit's working in your own life rather than attending exclusively to the lives of others. The sponge that only *gives out* eventually *dries out*.

Be an enjoyment engineer. Build recreational times into your schedule, whether the enjoyments be active things like sports or quieter occupations such as handicrafts. These do not detract from your life and ministry. They expand its dimensions.

Be an ever-more-beautiful woman. We mean from the inside out, of course, but don't neglect the exterior either. No matter where you are in age or locale, you needn't look like life's wreckage. Our appearance should reflect the serenity, the joy, the cleanliness, and the uprightness that only salvation makes possible.

Be a well-read woman. That doesn't mean you snuggle up with a book several hours a day, letting home and ministry slide.

But do determine to read for at least fifteen minutes daily. That may seem a very small snatch of time, but it is enough for an amazing amount of material to be absorbed.

Some will respond, "But why should I read?" First, reading helps you to expand intellectually and spiritually. We have seen married Maidservants vegetate while their husbands advance through reading and study. When one spouse moves forward and the other remains stationary, interpersonal distance is created, making way for marital problems.

Reading is also an excellent source of materials for conversation. For instance, you will not appear ignorant among people discussing political issues and situations if you keep current by means of newspapers or news magazines.

Reading contributes to your store of knowledge for helping others. None of us can have the range of experiences needed to deal knowledgeably with all counseling problems. Reading collaborates with personal experience and spiritual growth to strengthen our ability to help others.

The Maidservant indeed carries a heavy burden of responsibility in interpersonal relationships: to the group as a whole, to individuals within the group, and to herself. Her specific role—its spirit, motivation, manner, and reward—is summarized in I Peter 5:2-4:

> Feed the flock of God which is among you, taking the oversight thereof, not by constraint, but willingly; not for filthy lucre, but of a ready mind; neither as being lords over God's heritage, but being ensamples to the flock. And when the chief Shepherd shall appear, ye shall receive a crown of glory that fadeth not away.

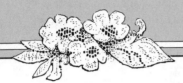

Chapter 18

Pastoring the Porcupines

In whatever particular spot of the world God chooses to place you, you will discover early in your ministry that many of those under your shepherding behave more like porcupines than like sheep. They come with prickly personalities and testy temperaments.

Who Are the Porcupines?

Porcupines can be found in every congregation or group of believers worldwide. Take, for instance, that lovable lady who waylays you at least once a week to give you criticism of your present deportment and advice for your future betterment. She's *Catherine Critic*, finding fault as if there were a reward for it! She has quite a number of cousins.

Nellie Know-It-All can answer any question on any topic. She doesn't just make statements like most people; she issues papal decrees. She considers herself the final authority on every matter.

Anita Arguer loves a fight. Her mental-emotional gear seems to be stuck in "low growl." If an argument doesn't happen naturally, she'll find a way to start one.

Gertrude Grudge-Bearer is a tiresome gal. No matter how long she is around, she holds to one theme: the wrong done her at such-and-such a time by So-and-So. She can (and does) repeat, verbatim, words spoken years earlier.

Tillie Talker is that one, bless her, whose path you try very hard not to intersect, knowing she'll assail you with words until your head rings and your feet ache. Tillie comes with one of two middle names: Busybody or Bore.

Glenda Gloomsayer has a life-or-death hold upon negativism. Despite the best efforts of those around her, she will find (and point out) the shadow under each leaf, the cocklebur on any kitten. Her only joy seems to lie in clouding others' skies.

Samantha Sniper is, as her name suggests, a subtle soul. She's sneaky, attacking from behind hedges of cleverness. She has a limitless stockpile of sarcasm's bullets, and her aim is superb. Remember when, as children, we chanted, "Sticks and stones may break my bones, but words can never hurt me"? It wasn't true then, and it isn't true now. Words can and do hurt us. Samantha knows that, and she pings merrily away at every opportunity.

Connie Complainer was born in the negative, nursed on pickle juice, and teethed on persimmons. Continually she voices her displeasure: sometimes with griping's gruffness; other times with whining. Whatever her choice of tone, she grates on the ears, nerves, and patience of her hearers.

Yolanda Yesser is more subtle than her sisters. She's the one with the "sweet-as-can-be" smile pasted on her face, the "Spiritual Me" tone in her voice; and all the while she has a mindset like that of Shakespeare's Iago when he says, "I'll smile and smile, and murder whilst I smile." When she hugs you, she's locating your fifth rib!

So there they are—porcupine people. They are a problem to themselves and a problem for other people. They can't contain their own character: it comes out in hurtful ways. They hurt you and others personally and hinder the spiritual progress of the flock.

Why do we feel pain from these porcupine folks? It is because of our special relationship with them. If we just passed one of them on the street, her quills would not bother us. But we must deal with them week in and week out. They are a part of the group among whom we move and with whom we commune on a regular basis. The psalmist knew the pain they can inflict: "For it was not an enemy that reproached me; then I could have borne it: neither was it he that hated me that did magnify himself against me; then I would have hid myself from him: But it was thou, a man mine equal, my guide, and mine acquaintance. We took sweet counsel together, and walked into the house of God in company" (Ps. 55:12-14).

When a porcupine whips her quilled tail at us, our natural reaction is to focus on ourselves and our hurt. But the Christian should have a different focus. First, we should look *up,* in obedience to I Thessalonians 5:18, giving thanks for this difficult person and her collision with us. Second, we should look closely *at the offender,* reflecting the spirit enjoined in Philippians 2:3-4: "Let nothing be done through strife or vainglory, but in lowliness of mind let each esteem other better than themselves. Look not every man on his own things, but every man also on the things of others."

It is in scripturally redirecting our attention that we can begin to find an answer to the next question.

Why Are Porcupines Prickly?

The first part of the answer is **family** patterning: the molding done in the home. Children learn by example. Complainers hatch complainers, arguers bring forth after their kind, and so on.

Sometimes the patterning has been established in reaction to something in the home. Perhaps parental attention could be won only by whining. Inconsistent parental living may have made the child disrespectful of all authority.

Negative patterning may be unrecognized by the porcupine herself. It may, however, be a characteristic known and hated. It is not unusual for an offending person, when confronted, to acknowledge the prickliness, recognize its source, and admit a constant struggle against it.

Another pattern besides that of family comes into play in interpersonal relationships: the **personality** pattern. Some personality differences are inborn. Unpleasant traits can derive from the limitations of certain types of personalities. A knowledge of these differences can shed light upon behaviors that might otherwise remain a puzzle.

A simple classification of personalities may help us understand the way in which conflicts can arise from personality differences. While avoiding the dogmatic extremes and simplistic inferences of some personality typing, we can perhaps see from the chart below how natural characteristics may have something to do with problem behavior. To recognize natural factors is not to sanction naturalistic explanations that presume to explain all on the basis of heredity or environment. It is simply to acknowledge what has often been observed: that personalities can be meaningfully grouped and be understood, at least partially, in terms of their groups. Let it not be said of us what Christ lamented as common among His disciples: that "the children of this world are in their generation wiser than the children of light" (Luke 16:8).

With these qualifications in mind, let's look at the following diagram:

The Panels of Personality

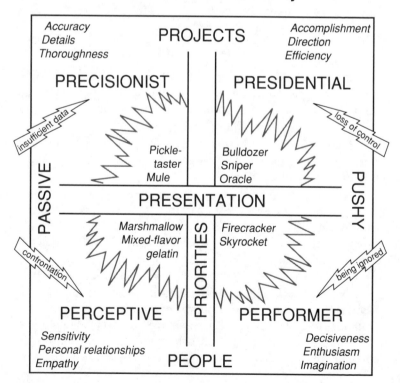

The horizontal *Presentation* bar represents the degree of assertiveness apparent to others. It varies from very strong, or "pushy," to the opposite, "passive." The vertical *Priorities* bar represents the motivation or focus. It ranges from strong "projects" orientation to strong "people" orientation.

The four personality types are defined by their presentation (pushy or passive) and priorities (projects or people). For instance, the presidential type has a strong projects orientation and a pushy mindset.

The chart is not given for the purpose of pigeonholing. Individual personalities should be identified as *primarily*, not absolutely, belonging in one of the personality panels. The degree of the fit varies from person to person. Characteristics of the other three panels join in varying degrees with those of the primary panel to give uniqueness to each individual.

The real purpose of this diagram is, first, *to show that every personality has its genuine strengths.* Consider how each is needed for any well-rounded ministry. We may say in an offhand manner, "She has a terrible personality." We are wrong. We've experienced only a small, negative part of her overall personality. If someone, on the basis of only a casual acquaintance, said the same thing about us, we would resent the unfair judgment.

Second, the Christian needs to realize that *were each one of us under constant control of the Holy Spirit, interpersonal differences would not occur.* But we live in a fallen world; we reflect too much of our Crusher and too little of our Creator.

Third, *each of us has porcupine moments.* Too often in our impatience with other people we forget or deny that fact. Now, looking again at the diagram, let's try to see where our quills originate.

Notice Patricia Precisionist. Imagine that she has been given (wisely!) the job of treasurer for a statewide Christian ladies' retreat. She does an exceptional job of filing every enrollment form, of tracking every penny spent. But as time for the retreat nears and several participating churches lag in mailing their forms, Patricia begins to get jittery. Phyllis President wants final plans now; the campsite needs a head count for meals. *Thwang—* out come Patricia's quills! All of life becomes a dill pickle. She complains about the "overbearing" Phyllis, the unreliability of churches, pastors, and Christians in general. Everyone working on the retreat treads lightly around Patricia. She has become a porcupine. What made her that way? The kind of pressure that most threatens her: insufficient data. Her reactions may become mulelike: she may refuse to make any further entry in what she considers a "disastrously incomplete" financial report.

So it is with the other personality types. Under a certain kind of voltage, each can be instantly transformed into a porcupine. The voltage that destroys one person's equilibrium may not affect another at all. Such differences contribute to our lack of understanding: if something doesn't bother *me*, why should it make you so upset?

Take time to study the personality types: their strengths, the voltage bolt that most threatens them, and the resultant possible porcupine reactions. This knowledge may help you progress in your relationships with the difficult people around you.

When a porcupine person invades your territory, you should respond in a fourfold way:

1. *Seek the Holy Spirit's control.* Stepping toward that porcupine in your own wisdom and strength could leave you a bloody mess!
2. *Seek clues from the porcupine's behavior.* Do not proceed on assumptions. This is an individual you're dealing with, not an item to be labeled in a certain way and dealt with accordingly.
3. *Seek to discover possible contributing causes in yourself.* Ask youself the following questions:
   a. What may my appearance or position motivate her to assume?
   b. What may my voice motivate her to assume?
   c. What may my words motivate her to assume?
   Remember, it may be just as hard for her to figure you out correctly as it is for you to understand her.
4. *Seek flexibility in your responses to and dealings with the porcupine.*

In addition to the quill-producing realities of family and personality patterning, there is also the factor of **pain** to be considered.

We live in a hurting world. While well aware of our own wounds, we tend to be insensitive to the hurts of others. But consider some specific areas of pain that could contribute to a person's prickliness.

A sense of insignificance. In a leader-follower situation such as ministries, those who consider themselves "little people" may simultaneously think of you as a "big" or important person. Hard on the heels of that distinction may come resentment of the "unfairness" of it all and a determination to prove personal importance. Resentment and one-upmanship can produce impressive quills.

Hidden hurts. Each of us has the human tendency to look at other people, as individuals or groups, and make the judgment that they are free from pain. We forget that nobody is free from pain and that the deeper the pain, the greater may be the efforts to hide it. We have known some persons for years before becoming privy to the agonizing hurts they have borne silently throughout those years. Invariably, bruises get bumped, wounds get reopened. And those who themselves hurt *hurt others.*

Frustrated desires and goals. Life seldom if ever turns out as we have pictured it. As dreams fail to materialize, goals are missed, and disappointments accumulate, reality can make our picture of life crash down on our heads. The pain of disillusionment can cause bitter sniping toward those perceived to be successful.

Insignificance, hurts, frustrations—all can become wellsprings of anger. And it is likely that anger stirrings within will cause more than ripples without. "An angry man stirreth up strife, and a furious man aboundeth in transgression" (Prov. 29:22).

What "Sheepdogs" Can Help with Porcupines?

Human porcupines, unlike their animal counterparts, cannot be dealt with by removal from the earth. Difficult people must be endured and even positively integrated into the flock.

There are four "sheepdogs" for the Christian shepherdess to call into active assistance with porcupines. Each one of them must be held on a *double leash,* the strong, interwoven leash described in Proverbs 3:3-4: "Let not *mercy* and *truth* forsake thee. . . . So shalt thou find favour and good understanding in the sight of God and man."

The names of these shepherd's assistants are Compassion, Consideration, Constraint, and Courage.

Compassion. Proverbs 24:29 warns against a spirit of retaliation: "Say not, I will do so to him as he hath done to me: I will render to the man according to his work." The Christian cannot act on his human impulse to repay in kind, to get even. Paul challenges believers obsessed with their rights: "Why do ye not rather *take* wrong? why do ye not rather suffer yourselves to be defrauded?" (I Cor. 6:7).

The poet Rudyard Kipling, though not a professing Christian, understood the need for generosity of spirit when he wrote this prayer:

> Teach us delight in simple things,
> And mirth that hath no bitter springs;
> Forgiveness free of evil done,
> And love to all men 'neath the sun!

How much more fitting is the standard for you and me than for a poet who makes no claim to our belief! Love is, after all, supposed to be the "birthmark" of the person who knows Christ as Savior. Sadly, that distinctive is often hard to find in Christian circles under the best of circumstances, let alone in situations involving difficult people.

But compassion, unconditional as it must be, does not mean condoning hurtful behavior. The second leash, truth, must also be active. By way of illustration, Beneth looks back upon her growing-up years as containing times of very straight talk and honest confrontations by her mother. In fact, *no one* could speak the painful truth more effectively, because unconditional love was so consistently evident in the speaker.

Consideration. Porcupines must be treated in humble consideration of the causes of their spiny natures. Ephesians 4:1-3 reads, "Walk worthy of the vocation wherewith ye are called, With all lowliness and meekness, with longsuffering, forbearing one another in love; Endeavoring to keep the unity of the Spirit in the bond of peace." There must also be consideration of the work of God underway in that person. Spiritual wisdom will keep us reminded that God alone knows the heart of that difficult person and that He alone has the power to change it. This consideration takes a load off our mental and emotional equipment. We can become torn with frustration over some difficult person if we feel compelled to do God's job for Him.

Constraint. Patient self-control is a must in dealing with porcupine people. The persistent porcupine can, at length, make any of us angry. But Scripture clamps on constraint with Ephesians 4:26-27: "Be ye angry, and sin not: let not the sun go down upon your wrath: Neither give place to the devil." Proverbs 12:16 is a convicting passage: "A fool's wrath is presently known: but a prudent man covereth shame." Those knowledgeable in the Hebrew language tell us that *covereth shame* actually means "ignores an insult."

The way will undoubtedly be long with those troublesome people whose porcupine qualities are of years' duration. It may seem at times that progress is nonexistent, that relationships will forever be marred by personality quills. The seemingly endless days can be brightened by recalling the example of Moses, who *"endured,* as seeing him who is invisible" (Heb. 11:27). What did he endure? He had to shepherd *a million-plus porcupines!* God chose His shepherd well, for Moses was "very meek, above all the men which were upon the face of the earth" (Num. 12:3).

Relationships with difficult people are opportunities for applying the Golden Rule. All of us have porcupine times. We know from those experiences that though we make people around us miserable, our own porcupiny selves are even more miserable. We desperately want others to treat us gently and with patience. Do we have the Christian character to step out and do the gentle and patient part toward another porcupine?

Courage. Confrontation sometimes becomes necessary in dealing with porcupines. Confrontation demands courage. It is easier to react to difficult personalities indirectly—mentally telling them off, complaining about them to a third party. Proverbs 25:9 urges us to confrontational courage: "Debate thy cause with thy neighbour himself; and discover not a secret to another."

The spirit of our courage is important. There is a difference between constructive confrontation and *contention.* They are motivated differently. Scripture tells us that "only by pride cometh contention" (Prov. 13:10). We need, then, to examine our spirit to be sure it is not pride masquerading as, for example, righteous indignation. It also must not be one of *fretfulness* (Ps. 37). Our courage must not be born of exploding frustration.

The courage necessary to confrontation must, for the Christian, result in proper speech as well as a proper spirit. God's Word gives us valuable clues about proper speech. Proverbs 15:1 points out that "a soft answer turneth away wrath: but grievous words stir up anger." Ephesians 4:15 tells us we are to be "speaking the truth in love." Colossians 4:6 puts boundaries around our tongue, noting that our speech should be "alway[s] with grace, seasoned with salt."

How Does the Great Shepherd Deal with Porcupines?

The best of us prove to be porcupines when we measure our attitudes and actions against God's standard for us. Yet our loving heavenly Father always remembers that our substance is dust. We can learn how to deal with one another by looking at how He deals with us.

The first principle to practice in dealing with difficult people is **personalization.** When faced with an irritating or intractable person, we tend to distance ourselves from him or her by pigeon-holing or compartmentalizing that one, using labels such as *stubborn, touchy,* and *uncooperative.* The Good Shepherd *individualizes.* "He calleth his own sheep by name" (John 10:3). Though He deals repeatedly with the same problem areas in all of us, He does so in accordance with His intimate knowledge of us as individuals, using different means with different ones.

The personalization principle extends also to the sheep's knowledge of the shepherd. The Great Shepherd knows His sheep, and His sheep know their Shepherd: "I know my sheep, and *am known of mine*" (John 10:14). The sheep's knowledge of the Shepherd is essential to their following of the Shepherd: "The sheep follow him, *for they know his voice*" (10:4).

For our people to know us as we know them, we must allow ourselves to be *transparent*—a difficult demand for leaders, but a strategic one. Earlier we discussed the natural, necessary distance that separates shepherd and sheep. While that distance is proper and necessary, at the same time it is also essential that we allow the sheep to see the real shepherdess. Failing to be transparent feeds the false notion of our being "different" from the sheep, removed from or above their own day-to-day struggles.

If our sheep know us only positionally and not personally, we increase the likelihood of interpersonal problems. God Himself urges us to come closer to Him, to know Him more intimately. "Take my yoke upon you, and learn of me," said the Lord; "for I am meek and lowly in heart" (Matt. 11:29). The more I *know* Him, the less I want to *hurt* Him and the more I want to *harmonize* with Him. If it is easier to hate those you don't know, according to the truism, it is also easier to love those you understand from personal acquaintance.

The second principle of right shepherding is **persistence.** God never gives up on us porcupines. He seeks the wandering sheep, treats her wounds and injured limbs, and returns her to the flock. There He warns, coaxes, chastises, directs, encourages, and gives strength as needed. His longsuffering love is such that He is willing to repeat this cycle many times.

Third, consider the **positives** of the Great Shepherd's responses to us. In Psalm 23 we read, "He restoreth my soul" (Ps. 23:3). Since no occasion is mentioned, we may assume that the restoration is continual. Why should it be so? It is because the Lord knows our constant need for soul refreshment. He refreshes rather than retaliates, and so should we who follow His example. When a difficult member of the flock—a porcupine—is in trouble, we are to "*restore* such an one in the spirit of meekness" (Gal. 6:1).

Finally, in looking at our blessed Good Shepherd, we cannot miss the fact of His **personal sacrifice.** Perhaps the most often overlooked requirement of shepherding is self-denial. In John 10:3-4 we are shown how the Good Shepherd herds the sheep: He "leadeth them out," and He "goeth before them." Every step the Shepherd asks His sheep to take, He takes before them. He goes ahead of them, showing the way. Do we walk similarly? Do we validate the spiritual demands we place on them *by meeting those demands ourselves?* Many of the porcupine quills we feel today are motivated by leaders' betrayals yesterday. Nothing is more destructive to followers than leaders' double standards or defection.

The Good Shepherd is so intent on serving His flock that He "giveth his life for the sheep" (John 10:11). Jesus prophesied, "I lay down my life for the sheep" (John 10:15). Now, was the great, the eternally efficacious sacrifice made for lovable, worthy, obedient sheep? We know that the Lord Jesus experienced every kind of quilling possible to humanity. But despite all, He sacrificed Himself. Are we more deserving of loving, gentle treatment than was the Lord Jesus? Let's take to heart the Savior's reminder: "The disciple is not above his master, nor the servant above his lord" (Matt. 10:24).

Conclusion

Difficult people are in every flock. But the Lord is there too. He assured His disciples, "Where two or three are gathered together in my name, there am I in the midst of them" (Matt. 18:20). Reliance upon His dear presence controlling, enlightening, restraining, leading—that is the secret of rightly pastoring the porcupines.

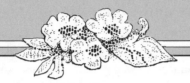

Maidenly Ministries

As Maidservants, our most direct public ministry centers upon women. Fundamentalist churches generally have one or more women's groups, with the names indicating the participants' age or purpose. Such ministries can tremendously benefit the church and its outreach, or they can waste the members' time and be detrimental to the church.

Although simple fellowship is important, women's groups should be motivated by desire to *serve*. Each group should be geared to specific goals. Otherwise it can deteriorate into a gossip circle—the last thing any church needs. In a missions-oriented organization, for example, the goal might be threefold: (1) to work in behalf of missionaries, (2) to maintain up-to-date correspondence with them, and (3) to pray for their ministries. Those goals will in turn determine the choice and length of projects, the priorities assigned to various group functions, and so forth.

Meetings

Women's organizations generally meet once a month. More frequent meetings conflict with members' other responsibilities. Whenever held, meetings should follow a logical, set format including various elements such as prayer time, business details, reading of letters, special reports, and work time. If a refreshment time is included, it should be kept simple and brief so that socializing does not replace service.

Officers and Committees

One of the most important decisions for any organization is its leadership. In women's groups, the pastor's wife usually should not be the president or a main officer, although of course she should actively participate. Church members tend to lean on their pastor and his wife. They need, instead, to be encouraged toward leadership and responsibility themselves.

Care should be taken to see that officeholders for women's groups do not get into competition or one-upmanship. For example, each term's leader might try to outdo her forerunners in personal financial contribution and party-giving. The point of any organization and its leadership should be *service*, not self-exaltation.

Even the smallest group will need a president, vice president, and secretary-treasurer. As the group grows, the following may be needed: hospitality chairman, correspondence secretary, compassion chairman, music chairman, publicity chairman, projects chairman, and chaplain. Each officer then should choose several women to work on her committee. Following are some suggested duties for a few of the divisions just mentioned:

- *Compassion*—notifying the group of a member's illness, sorrow, etc.; arranging for visits, food, notes
- *Publicity*—meeting announcements, bulletin boards, newspaper notices
- *Projects*—choosing work projects, setting up project materials ahead of time to improve production efficiency
- *Chaplain*—arranging for special speakers, giving devotionals, keeping information cards up-to-date

For the spiritual and emotional well-being of a women's group, each lady's name considered for an office *should be checked with the pastor* before it appears on the ballot or is read at a meeting. He will know of any impediments to her serving in a leadership position.

One of the most valuable services the Maidservant can render the church women's groups is investigation: discovering members' interests and then suggesting those women for appropriate activities and committees. Ladies are notoriously reluctant to volunteer; sometimes, in fact, they have no idea their interests, talents, or training could be useful in a ministry undertaking.

Here is a last suggestion for a group's smooth operation: establish a policy that one year's vice president take over the presidency the next year. This will facilitate leadership transitions, since the vice president's work with the president will prepare her for the higher office.

Women's Visitation

It may well be that the women's visitation ministry is headed by the Maidservant. Besides being exemplary in her participation, she must see to it that certain principles are practiced.

- Women going on soulwinning visitation should *go in twos.*
- Women should be cautious when they make house calls, never entering a home when the wife is not present.
- Rather than assigning two extroverted women as visitation partners, pair a ''bold'' with a ''timid'' for the learning and encouragement of both.
- The women should be urged to get quickly to the point of the visit. It is easy to get bogged down in chitchat, wasting everyone's time.
- Once the point of the visit has been made, don't overstay. It is more thoughtful and effective to make repeat visits to a home than to linger past your welcome on one visit.

Women's Bible Class

Women's Bible studies are becoming increasingly popular as Christian ladies feel the pressures of Satan's attack. Women long to know the Word so that they can wield the Sword against the enemy. Bible studies or classes for women hold tremendous potential—for good or for bad.

Leadership

The logical choice as leader for a Bible study might seem to be the pastor's wife. But her holding that position may in some instances be unwise. The Bible says the aged women are to serve as teachers to the younger. Unless there is absolutely no one older to do it, the young Maidservant should not take the teaching position. Ordinarily, every church has a middle-aged or older lady whose walk with the Lord and knowledge of the Word have been proved by the years. She would be the proper one to serve.

Sponsorship

The church itself should sponsor the women's Bible study. Although they are springing up everywhere, Satan is using many study groups as a way to turn women in wrong spiritual directions. Rather than just "happening" into existence, a Bible class is rightly born of the leadership's concern for the women.

Location

We strongly urge using the church itself. The church building is neutral ground; it offers open access rather than the private, "privileged" feel of a home study. Note, please, that this applies to the *main* Bible study of the church. Outside of that, the congregation women may be engaged in informal, small coffees or teas in their homes with the purpose of winning unsaved neighbors to Christ; the new believers then should be channeled into the main Bible class and church ministry.

Attendance

Your church's Bible study will be composed mostly of your own church women. If you intend to use the study as a means of outreach, however, advertise so that women of other churches, or even the unchurched, have opportunity to come under the sound of God's Word. For this purpose to be achieved, the church women must feel a burden, extending invitations and welcome to those who inquire or come. Should Bible class members begin to feel exclusive, the group is losing its spiritual health.

Scheduling

The time set for the Bible study should reflect the individuality of your group. If most of the women hold jobs outside the home, an evening class may be preferable. The usual frequency for studies is once a week. Many Bible studies recess during Christmas and the summer holidays, since family duties during those times make attendance difficult for young mothers.

Maintenance

Beginning a Bible study or class is not difficult. Maintaining it is a greater challenge. The spirit of the study must remain sound. The emphasis, therefore, should be fundamental, inspirational, and consistent in its presentation of the gospel. It should not emphasize denominational doctrines. Those are the nonessentials upon which mature Christians simply "agree to disagree." The basic structural elements of the Faith and the practical application of the Word to everyday living are the great need of the day. The Person and work of Christ should be central to the class: He promised that if He were lifted up He would draw people unto Himself. There should be genuine enthusiasm in the class for what the Lord has done and is doing—not a long-faced, mournful, "deeper" spirit masking spiritual pride. There should be constant stress on personal spiritual responsibilities. If the atmosphere of the class is relaxed and informal, members will feel free to ask questions, and the teacher can more easily direct attention to problem areas.

In order to keep the Bible study sound, *the pastor should know what is being taught and how it is being taught.* A hands-off policy on his part can prove disastrous. Bobbie even makes an audiotape of each Bible-class session. If a question is raised or a claim made about the teaching, there is an unarguable means of settlement.

Focus

The core emphasis, of course, must be the Bible itself. It should be the *only* book taught. Getting off on side trails (other books) poses complications and dangers. The teacher will necessarily spend a great deal of time studying relevant sources. As she does, she needs to check with her husband or the pastor about the soundness of her sources, lest error inadvertently creep into her teaching.

Benefits

Several benefits can be derived from a women's Bible study. First, special fellowship and unity come from group in-depth study of God's Word. Personal growth is also encouraged. As unsaved women are brought into the group, the saved become aware of their needs, of their hungry response. They awake to the fact that they have neighbors and acquaintances who need to be reached for the Lord, and their personal outreach is stimulated. Nonmembers have an unpressured opportunity to hear the Word and to see the Truth lived out in other Christian women. For those whose membership in dead churches has prevented their spiritual birth or growth, there is opportunity for both.

Invitations for Salvation

Should a salvation invitation be given at women's Bible studies? Such an invitation definitely should be extended, but in a quiet, nonpressuring way. Not every session of the class will necessitate an invitation. Much can be said in favor of the Holy Spirit's cumulative pressuring as a lady attends the class several times in a row, getting her ready to respond. When given, the invitation should avoid causing embarrassment. Perhaps any who feel a need could be asked to raise their heads and look at the speaker while everyone else prays, or just quietly to raise a hand. Then a member of the group can take that person aside afterward to explain the plan of salvation person to person.

Refreshments

The inclusion of light refreshment at the close of each Bible study gives an opportunity for church women and outsiders to get together in a casual social setting. It enhances the sense of unity and welcome. It can also awaken a compelling desire for such fellowship in those who attend apostate churches. Bobbie has had the joy of seeing a number of women renounce their dead churches after attending her Bible studies.

Physical Considerations

What materials and equipment are needed for a Bible study? If your church has either a chalkboard or an overhead projector, it can be used to clarify and illustrate. The women may want to keep a notebook for class use. Occasionally, charts and handouts for specific studies may be effective.

A Final Analysis

A women's Bible study—do you need to have one? In the final analysis, only the Lord should determine that. Any study group, at any point in its existence, must be considered only a spiritual tool. If it becomes anything else, or if it threatens harm, the tool should be swiftly laid aside.

Other Women's Ministry Opportunities

Organized groups are not the only service opportunities available to women. Some women may prefer to participate in behind-the-scenes activities. In order to give everyone the opportunity to become involved, Bobbie each year circulates an information sign-up sheet. By reproducing it here, we hope to give you impetus and ideas for your own women's ministries.

Hampton Park Baptist Church
Greenville, South Carolina
Opportunities for Women

Please find listed below some of the various opportunities that you as a lady can take part in. We have many ministries here at Hampton Park Baptist Church in our effort to further the gospel and win others to Christ. Please prayerfully consider one or more of these privileges in which you can be of great help.

Baby and Bridal Showers
    Host a shower
    Assist with refreshments
Bus Ministry
    Bus captain (chaperone) Sunday A.M.
    Teach/assist in class
    Help with bus visitation
Children's Bible Clubs
    Teach
    Assist
Compassion
    Help prepare a meal for someone
    Give child care for someone
    Sit with ill person
Day School Ministry
    Volunteer teacher aid
    Volunteer clerical help
Elementary Department
    Teach
    Assist
    Substitute

Kitchen Assistant
    Help with churchwide functions (picnics, etc.)
    Help clean up after functions
    Help wash dishes after a wedding
    Serve on team for Wednesday evening dinner (once per
        month)
Ladies' Bible Study
    Provide transportation in my community
    Teach children's class during study
    Work in nursery during study (once a month)
Ladies' Visitation
    Visit shut-ins
    Visit unsaved people
    Visit newcomers
    Make hospital calls
    Make "sunshine baskets" for patients
Nursery
    Work one service per month
    Teach short Bible lesson to toddlers
Preschool Department
    Teach
    Assist
    Substitute
Publicity and Artwork
    Prepare a banner or poster
    Make phone calls
Welcome Program
    Assist with refreshments for new members' reception
    Serve on Welcome Committee
Women for Missions
    Clerical work for WFM
    Clerical work for MFM
    Provide refreshments for meeting
    Serve on phone committee
    Keep a visiting missionary in home
    Work on projects at home

Special Events Committees:

Ladies' Christmas Fellowship
    Decorating Committee
    Food Committee
    Kitchen Committee
    Program Committee
    Publicity Committee

Ladies' Seminar Committee
    Food Committee
    Program Committee
Mother-Daughter Activity
    Decorating Committee
    Food Committee
    Kitchen Committee
    Program Committee
    Publicity Committee
Overnight Retreat Committee
    Planning Committee

Skills/talents I am willing to use in the Ladies' Ministries:
    Art
    Calligraphy
    Floral Arranging
    Sewing/Needlework
    Catering/Serving Meals
    Ventriloquy
    Photography
    Decorating
    Other: _____

Maidservants often ask how to get women involved in ministries. Our response to that query would be to be *prayerful* about the situation and at the same time to be *practical*. That is, if you try fruitlessly for a long period of time to get your ladies active in a ministry, or you find fewer and fewer showing up or less and less enthusiasm, *drop the effort!* It is frustrating and useless to persist in (a) trying to get them involved or (b) being the only active member of a "group" effort. Before you discontinue a women's ministry, however, try changing the approach. For instance, in hospital visitation, assure the women that you will *train* each one of them how to do what needs to be done. Women do not like to attempt something in which they feel awkward and uncomfortable.

Church women individually and in groups represent tremendous potential for God's service. They are also the object of Satan's particularly strenuous attack. Therefore, the formation, the leadership, the direction, and the maintenance of women's ministries need to be hedged by sensitive watchfulness and persistent prayer.

Chapter 20

Attending to Adolescents

Runaways denotes adolescents and teen-agers who leave home for parts unknown. In the latter part of the twentieth century another term has been coined: *throwaways*. It refers to children whose parents refuse responsibility for them and force them out of the home. Such parental callousness seems unbelievable to those who know that the Bible declares children to be gifts from God.

The world sees children as troublesome, expendable—hence the ever-rising tide of abortions. Even if a child is allowed to be born and remain in his home, he may be poorly cared for, resented, disliked, and/or abused. Indicative of prevailing American attitude was the study done by a national women's magazine. When asked, "If you had it to do over again, would you have children?" the overwhelming majority (70%) responded no!

Christian homes are not exempt from teen problems, nor are they free from parental irresponsibility or responsibility shifting. Bewildered, frustrated parents and teachers look to the church, pleading, "Help!"

Those whom God loves, we should love. Jesus evidenced a special regard for and tenderness toward children during His earthly ministry. Teen-agers are children in transition to adulthood.

Difficulties of Teens

True to their reputation, teens are difficult creatures, both to themselves and to adults around them. Modernity's plethora of broken homes adds tremendously to the normal insecurity of teen years. Christian young people often are as discouraged and disillusioned as the world's young because they don't know where to look for good examples of the adulthood toward which they are speeding. Too often those they hold in high esteem betray their trust: parents live contrary to the precepts they proclaim; youth leaders and pastors fall into immorality.

Teen years are a time of turmoil. The bridge to maturity is not easily crossed; its planks are shaky and irregularly spaced. Young people themselves are uncertain about their passage, and watching adults often adds to those uncertainties rather than allays them. The internal metamorphosis is not alone at fault for unease during the teens; the external upheaval of our times adds to a youngster's difficulties. He sees ethical standards changed, sexual standards flung aside, and divine standards ignored.

The teen-age years also are a time of great temptation. The rapid chemical and physical changes of adolescence bewilder through their strength and strangeness. While desperately searching for a sense of belonging, the teen faces rejection by peers unless he conforms to their standards. Often the anxieties of physical change and peer pressure are too strong to withstand, and he succumbs to the allurement of drink, drugs, and immorality. The fact that he or she is a Christian does not lessen the pressures, nor does attendance at a good church and/or Christian school guarantee his escape. Those very safeguards themselves may result in a *language* rather than a *life, hardness* rather than *tenderness, rebellion* rather than *obedience.*

Delights of Teens

All is not dark on the teen scene. Often, so much focus is put on the negatives that we despair of or overlook the positives. There is, first of all, *character crystallization.* We who are parents of teen-agers have experienced the thrill of seeing our children become *people,* fascinating individuals whose personalities have solidified and whose character takes shape before our eyes. What an opportune time to influence them for God!

Teen years also are characterized by *vision focusing*. It sometimes surprises us adults to see the vitality of the teen-age view of life in contrast to our own rather jaded perceptions. This is the time to direct their spiritual gaze. Biographies of great Christians can inspire; fine examples and worthwhile goals can challenge idealistic hearts; the plight of lost souls can become a personal, lifelong burden. *But* these positive developments require adult attention and effort. Too often we let our teens become ensnared by materialism, self-centeredness, and pursuit of pleasure.

We become exasperated by teen-age enthusiasm, letting the very thought of it wear us out. Instead, we should be *challenged* by that enthusiasm, challenged to use their soon-passing energetic era for the Lord and His people, challenged to channel teens' boundless bounce into worthwhile Christian service.

The Substance of Youth Work

Rather than technique, successful ministry to youth springs from the ability to be positive toward and concerned for young people. Youth workers and their wives should have the unshakable conviction that God can and will meet the youngsters' needs, as well as the determination to work and pray fervently to that end.

Proper example is of utmost importance to this age group. Many Christians have abdicated parental responsibility, saying to their teen-agers, in effect, "Do what I say, not what I do." Teens are aware of the inconsistencies; they yearn to see someone whose walk coincides with his or her talk. Youth workers need not be perfect, but they must be faithful and consistent in their Christian lives. Setting the proper example should not convey "I'm up here on a pedestal; now stand back and take notes on how I do things." Instead, there should be unpretentious, joyful, and dedicated daily living as the worker moves among the teens with ready ear and open heart.

The System of Youth Work

The primary component of an effective youth work is respect for the teen-agers: respect for their individualities, for their characteristics of personality and age, for the *potential* they represent. In this regard, beware of simply categorizing young people as teen-agers. There is a vast difference between thirteen and nine-teen; yet both are teens.

A second necessary cog in the youth-ministry mechanism is the desire and ability to listen to the teen-agers—even if their ideas are half-baked, impractical, super-idealistic, questioning, or argumentative. Responses to their observations must be honest, thoughtful, and *consistent with Scripture as it is*, not just as you'd like Scripture to be. Many adults tell of being embittered during their teens by leaders who demanded behavior or appearance set by personal preference rather than biblical mandate. As already noted, it is vital when working with youth to differentiate between standards according to source and rationale: biblical, cultural, practical, or preferential (see Chapter 11). On moral and spiritual issues, God's Word speaks directly and absolutely. In other areas it allows latitude. Claiming that all required standards are bibli-cally absolute and harping on externals produces young people whose outward conformity disguises inward rebellion or spiritual pride.

Youth workers need to believe in the teens they lead. Each youngster's potential should be cherished and nurtured, regardless of the difficulties he or she represents at the moment. Don't react to failures with discouragement or disgust. Make allowances for immaturity and inexperience. There was a time when you, too, had to try your wings—with a good many crashes marking the flight path.

Youth leaders should consistently, diligently pray for their young people, as individuals and as a group. Let the teens know they're being prayed for. The knowledge of supportive, loving prayer can have tremendous impact in their lives.

Leadership of teen-agers should be companionable and bal-anced. While not making all decisions for the group, the leader cannot realistically expect the group to come up with all the ideas. Don't be afraid to set high standards. If leaders clearly explain the bases of the standards and live up to the requirements them-selves, teens will respond positively. Those most effective in youth work entertain young people in their homes. An open home bespeaks an open heart, which these tadpole humans desperately need.

Boredom is a great enemy of happiness in the between-child-hood-and-adult years. Teens want to be doing things. Keeping them busy keeps a youth leader busy, but the effort is worthwhile. Imagination and innovation are hallmarks of good youth leadership. Meetings do not have to be nonstop entertainment and fun, fun, fun. A wise mixture of fun, relaxation, and spiritual challenge predisposes young people to receptiveness. Teens should also have organized, regular witnessing times. Take them on mission trips, not just to look but to help. Use them in jail services, rescue mission programs, and the like; let them see sin's skeleton stripped of the Devil's glamorizing.

Finally, teens need to be challenged. Introduce them to great literature, art, and music. Create projects to help build confidence in the group and in individuals. Be generous with genuine praise. Allow honest expression of feelings. Don't argue when emotions are out of control, but rather wait for teachable moments and "bootleg" scriptural principles to them. Make much of their special times—the end of exams, high-school graduation, ballgames. Involve parents in the teen activities as much as possible. Work to build happy memories. Avoid playing favorites: work equally with the problem teen and with the presidential type. Help the introverted get involved in activities. Encourage all the teens to recognize and enunciate present blessings and the working of God in their lives.

It is important that the youth leader's wife be actively involved in the work as well as the husband, whether he be pastor, assistant pastor, youth pastor, or layman. Her involvement will not only make the ministry a unified one from their standpoint but also present a healthy example for the teens and guard against problematic emotional attachments. Her degree of participation will of course be influenced by the ages and needs of her own children.

Leadership largely determines whether a youth group thrives or withers. Leader attitudes which kill a youth program are

- a critical spirit toward the young people.
- negativism.
- lack of enthusiasm.

The thriving youth group is characterized by love, reasonableness, patience, prayer, and zest. Leaders and church members in general need to be reminded that today's youth group is tomorrow's church.

Chapter 21

Criers and Crawlers

Just as today's youth are tomorrow's church members and leaders, so today's Criers, Creepers, and Toddlers are day-after-tomorrow's congregation. Even before babies become conscious of their surroundings, their nursery care can set the stage for future spiritual receptiveness. The Lord Jesus said, "Suffer little children to come unto me, and forbid them not; for of such is the kingdom of heaven." The "coming" of little ones to Christ begins long before the age of spiritual accountability.

Reasons for a Church Nursery

A nursery exists, first, to ensure *cared-for children*. Childhood's characteristics and limitations should be recognized at whatever age: babies are not ready to attend church services. A nursery allows the little one freedom of movement and care for his physical comfort.

Second, a nursery makes possible *care-free parents*. Any of us who have struggled with a baby through a church service can attest to the difficulty of concentrating on the sermon. Young parents need to be fed spiritually while feeling confident Junior is getting loving care.

Third, a nursery proclaims a *care-taking pastor*. Maintaining a nursery demonstrates his concern for the entire congregation. The Devil will use anything to disrupt the revelation of Christ, including otherwise adorable babies. Many a sermon's force or invitation's impact has been demolished by a baby's scream or coo. A nursery removes the baby from the Devil's pinch. It shows the pastor's burden for the needs of his congregation: for the effectiveness of the preached Word, that central concern of fundamentalist churches.

When to Start a Church Nursery

A church nursery should be established when the first baby arrives. So even a brand-new church may need a nursery. At the start, the Maidservant probably will be the entire nursery staff.

Nursery Environment

A nursery's outstanding physical requisite is *cleanliness*. Responsibility for other people's children is a solemn one indeed.

Crib sheets must be changed after each use, however briefly a baby may have been in the crib before another replaces him.

The entire nursery needs an antiseptic wash after each day's use. Cleaning should include carpet, woodwork, walls, furniture, and toys. Babies don't just look at things; they *taste* them too.

The nursery should be *colorful*. Although clean, it needn't look like a hospital, with everything painted white. When selecting colors, prefer crisp, cheerful shades. Avoid much use of red: it is an irritant. Wisely chosen color helps create pleasant surroundings for children, workers, and parents.

Third, the nursery environment should be *comfortable*. A warm, cozy feeling as conveyed, for instance, by ruffles and cushions is ideal.

Nursery Personnel

Although a large church may have a hired nursery supervisor, most nursery workers are volunteers. Each person allowed to work in the nursery should meet certain qualifications.

First, and most important of all, a nursery worker must love children. There are people who do not like children and to whom children do not respond well. Such persons do not belong on a nursery staff roster. Loving workers benefit the emotional well-being of their small charges, and their involvement in nursery functions means more to them than just a job. Ability to work with children is a gift not bestowed upon everyone. Emphasizing that fact can help recruit personnel for the nursery.

Second, nursery workers must respect the children's parents. Parental directions should be followed, not set aside in favor of what the worker feels would be better. The proper attitude for nursery staffers is that they and the parents are working together for the child's good.

Finally, nursery personnel must be trustworthy. Dr. Bob Jones, Sr., coined the saying, "The greatest ability is *dependability.*" Parents, pastor, and staff all need to know that a nursery worker will be where she's supposed to be when she's supposed to be there.

Practical Suggestions for the Nursery

Check-in. This should be as efficient as possible. A routine needs to be established and maintained so that workers and parents feel comfortable with the handling of details.

Parents should not be allowed into the room when leaving a child; it gives the little one opportunity to cling, wail, and fuss. Equip the entrance with a counter or with a Dutch door whose lower half can be kept closed.

Supplies and furnishings. Cribs should be sturdy, easy to clean, and free of features that might endanger children. A nursery needs one or more rocking chairs, several baby walkers and swings, and *walled* changing tables (even tiny babies can twist or flip off a surface that has no sides).

Premoistened towelettes, baby powder, disposable diapers, and other supplies can be kept in a cabinet close to the changing table so that the workers do not have to step away to reach them.

Choose sturdily constructed, washable toys that have no potentially dangerous features.

Outfitting the nursery need not bankrupt even the tiniest, newest church. Nursery furniture and supplies can be purchased secondhand or may be donated by members or friends of the congregation.

Nursery Rules

Though the term may seem incongruous when speaking of babies, nursery rules are necessary for the sake of the *adults* using the facility. Put rules into writing and distribute them to parents and workers. In that way, there is no chance for the excuse, "But I didn't know . . ." Some especially helpful rules are the following:

1. No child will be allowed to cry endlessly. The mother will be called from the service if workers cannot quiet him.
2. No medicine will be given (including baby aspirin) without specific written instruction from the parents.
3. No sick children will be allowed in the nursery. [It would be wise to add a description of what is considered sick: runny nose, cough, fever, etc.] There is a responsibility to protect the health of the healthy and curb the spread of even mild illnesses.
4. No meals will be served in the nursery. [Some parents would gladly turn Baby's feeding over to nursery personnel so that they don't have to do it.]
5. Children must be picked up immediately following the service. [Parents have been known to leave a baby in the church nursery while they went to a restaurant for lunch!]

Identification and Care

Some system must be established to make the nursery efficient. What works well for one church may be cumbersome for another. Find what is effective for your group. You might choose a card system in which a file card listing pertinent information is kept for each child. Members' children would have permanent cards on file, pulled at check-in; visitors would fill out a new card. Preprinted cards save time. It might also be helpful to have visitors' cards a different color from members' cards.

Rather than cards, you might use a chart system with a line of information following each child's name. Write the information in large print for easy reading.

Whether cards or charts are used, information for each child should be updated regularly.

Nursery staffers need to know where parents sit in the church auditorium so that they can be contacted easily. This information could be noted on the cards or charts, or there might be a parents' section reserved near the rear of the auditorium. In some churches, as in Hampton Park Baptist, a special code light in an easily visible but nondistracting place signals when a mother, who has been assigned a number, is needed.

Since workers and children in a church nursery vary from week to week, identification must be carefully handled. A picture of each child could be placed with the written information. Or a name tag may be placed on each baby as he or she is checked in. For name tags, small strips of paper, cloth, or masking tape work well. The name tag should be placed somewhere on the child's *back* so that he or she can't remove it.

Parents who use the nursery should take turns *staffing* it. Husband-wife teams are excellent for the nursery. Masculine presence enhances control.

The question about having teens work in the nursery is often asked. Those with genuine interest in child care may be used, but always under adequate adult supervision and so scheduled that they can't use nursery work as an excuse for repeatedly missing church services.

In order that a nursery not be overpopulated with children and understaffed by adults, an effective weekly calling or notifying system is needed. For times when the nursery may be expecially crowded, such as Christmas, Easter, and evangelistic services, enlist additional workers well in advance.

A Final Word About the Nursery

Inevitably, there will be some parents who cling to the theory that babies should be in church services with them. Be patient, but work to convince them otherwise—for the good of everyone. Rather than dealing with the problem yourself, you might wisely defer to the pastor. There would be more authority and less awkwardness in his handling the matter—mentioning it from the platform occasionally without calling names—than in your confronting the parents.

An attractive, clean, well-run nursery is not only an asset to the church but also a ministry in itself—to day-after-tomorrow's church.

Chapter 22

Feasts of Fellowship

Church banquets are occasions for fellowship of church members and guests—for widening and enriching acquaintance in a festive setting. Their success reflects the special thought and effort that go into them.

The Occasion

Although a banquet may be held at any time and for any number of reasons, consider a few possibilities.

Seasonal banquets
> Mother-Daughter
> Father-Daughter
> Mother-Son
> Father-Son
> Thanksgiving
> Christmas
> Valentine
> Harvest, etc.

Honorary banquets
> Church anniversaries
> Charter members' recognition
> Junior-Senior
> Pastoral appreciation

Farewell to field-bound missionaries, etc.

Institutional banquets
 Christian school students
 Traveling musical ensembles
 A rescue mission
 Awana
 Sunday school workers
 Stewardship, etc.

Organization

A banquet becomes reality through concentrated effort by many people. There are four main areas of emphasis and endeavor: place, price, planning, and program.

With regard to the *place* for a banquet, the church facility itself may be the logical choice. If the church is small and lacks a fellowship hall or gym, you might instead use an available vacant house, Sunday school room(s), or even a hallway. You may prefer to contract for a community center, a restaurant banquet room, a school gymnasium, or the like. Or a banquet may take the form of a progressive dinner.

Wherever the banquet is to be held, its proposed date and time must be checked early against the church and school calendars to avoid conflicts, and the banquet entered on the various calendars. If a rental facility is chosen, reservations may be required as much as a year ahead of the desired date.

The *price* for the banquet must be determined. It will necessarily reflect the place, menu, and number of people expected to attend. Also to be figured into the cost are decorations and the speaker's honorarium. In some cases, people in the church may want to underwrite a portion of the expense in order to lower ticket prices and put the banquet within financial reach of a greater number. Food costs will differ according to the type of preparation and service. Those choices include the following:

- by restaurant personnel
- by catering service
- by church women (or men!) preparing and serving
- by attenders: a covered-dish meal with everyone providing a requested food item.

Planning for a banquet must begin well in advance of the chosen date. Don't be discouraged by limitations that may immediately leap to view. Imagination can counteract apparent disadvantages.

As soon as time, date, and place are established, get committees working. Committee assignments, operating under a general chairman, should include the following:

- Food
- Decorations
- Program
- Invitations/Publicity
- Cleanup

Contact the special speaker for the banquet about one year ahead. For an out-of-town speaker, a host or hostess should be assigned to be in charge of lodging, food, and transportation arrangements before and after the banquet.

Although this chapter is not intended to be a complete banquet guide, a few suggestions concerning some matters of detail may be helpful.

1. Unify decorations around a theme, carrying it out in centerpieces, background scenery, name tags, and printed programs.
2. Arrange buffet tables carefully, considering convenience and logic in the layout. For instance, here is a layout listed from its beginning point on the first table:
   Plates (have flatware and napkins at place settings)
   Salad(s)
   Vegetables
   Meats
   Beverage table(s) (if serving only one drink, have it at place settings)
   Dessert table
   Note: Remember to include some foods suitable for restricted diets.
3. Set up the food tables so as to have as many serving lines as possible. Have people find their seats first and then go through buffet lines a table or section at a time. Provide juice and nibble foods for those who have to wait.
4. Have the speaker go through the buffet line first so that he or she can finish eating before having to speak.
5. Plan food quantities carefully. Listed below are quantities adequate for twenty-five people. Simply multiply according to the size of your group.

Chicken or turkey	13 lb.
Bone-in ham	14 lb.
Boneless ham	9-10 lb.
Hot dogs	6 $\frac{1}{2}$ lb.
Hamburger	9 lb.
Potato salad	4 $\frac{1}{2}$ qt.
Baked beans	$\frac{3}{4}$ gal.
Watermelon	38 lb.
Sandwiches (1 each)	3 1-lb. loaves
Mayonnaise	1 cup
Lettuce	1 $\frac{1}{2}$ heads
Coffee	$\frac{1}{2}$ lb. to 1 $\frac{1}{2}$ gal. water

Note: There are differences in consumption. Teens eat most, with girls eating less when boys are present. Men enjoy hearty fare and generous helpings. Women like food that is attractive and to some extent "light."

The *program* for a banquet should grow out of the theme. Remember, however, that a few well-chosen things are better than too many. Work for a balance between light and serious, but *don't over-program.* The speaker should be featured. A lengthy program followed by a speaker is exhausting rather than exhilarating. Do not feel that a special speaker is always needed. At times a well-planned program is sufficient.

Special Speakers

Special evenings are enhanced by bringing in outside speakers. A well-chosen special speaker generates excitement among those planning to attend.

The first contact with a prospective speaker may be made by telephone. Be sure, however, to confirm all that has been said *in writing* so that both sponsor and speaker have details in black and white. Let the speaker know the purpose and theme of the banquet, the formality of dress expected, and the length of talk desired. When bringing in someone special to speak, the sponsoring group pays expenses and gives an honorarium above expenses.

Banqueting Benefits

Both social and spiritual benefits can be reaped from banquets. Jesus Himself set an example for the fellowship enjoyed at such occasions by His eating with others. Many people crave social occasions that offer their lives something special. Such occasions also are excellent opportunities to integrate less gregarious or timid members into the group. In a day when there are so many things Christians must avoid in the way of entertainment and recreation, church banquets can fill a real social need.

Spiritually, a ministry banquet can be a time of accomplishment for all who attend. It can appeal to those with special needs within and without your own group. Unsaved people feel less threatened by and more attracted to such "nonchurch" occasions. Believers resisting the Holy Spirit in some area of their lives also can be challenged in social settings such as banquets when their mental guard is down.

Supplies

If in-house banquets are going to be frequent, it is wise to collect permanent banquet paraphernalia, thus reducing the expense of purchase or rental of items and the hassle of borrowing. For instance, many department stores give away or sell their seasonal decorations at extremely low prices. Watch, too, for sales of tablecloths, flatware, glass plates (they double for salad and dessert), and so forth. Have your ladies keep an eye on local yard sales for needed items as well.

Ideas

Keep a file of banquet-theme decoration possibilities. Include as many details for each theme as possible.

Make a practice of having a "rehash" meeting of all committee chairmen within a day or two after each banquet; have them evaluate, discuss problems, and make suggestions for improvement. Note these things for your idea files.

Variations

Banquet does not automatically mean an evening meal; a luncheon often works well. Nor does a banquet meal have to be heavy; consider an all-salad buffet that includes a variety of meat, pasta, vegetable, and congealed types.

Themes

Following is a brief listing of banquet themes we personally have seen beautifully produced:

Patterns (for Motherhood, Christian Living, etc.)
When I Look into the Mirror
Old Woman in the Shoe
Daisies Do Tell
Letters from Mother
Sugar 'n' Spice
Pilgrim's Progress
Notes of Praise
Transformed
Precious Jewels

Decorations

Here are a few imagination stimulators:

Spray-painted chicken wire background with flowers and greenery attached
Miniature trees decorated with gingham bows or gumdrops
Painted tree branches, potted and decorated according to theme
Miniature mailboxes filled with flowers
Jewel-box treasure chests
Clear goblets containing candles floating in colored water

A Final Encouragement

Banquets are special. They provide fellowship for believers and can also be a means of reaching the unsaved. They are challenging to produce; approach them with enthusiasm and imagination. Get your women working together, and you'll be delighted at how much can be done without great expense.

Should the time come when banquets become *drudgery*, stop having them. Perhaps a few banquetless years will give your group opportunity to renew enthusiasm. After all, the very word *banquet* should suggest a happy occasion, not a joyless chore!

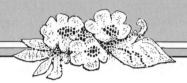

Chapter 23

Retreat Realities

Because of her leadership position, a Maidservant probably will not be so much involved with attending women's retreats as with organizing them.

Although the word *retreat* seems to be the most commonly used among fundamentalists, alternate terms are *conference, seminar,* and (for women's retreats) *feminar.* The purpose for such occasions is physical and mental relaxation plus spiritual refreshment. Whatever they are called, getaway times are proliferating as churches recognize the need for and positive results from ladies' retreats.

Retreats can be uniquely effective for several reasons:

1. Respite from routine and responsibility frees a woman for special spiritual receptiveness.
2. A woman talking to women about women's problems can be used of God to dig into areas long hidden or overlooked because of their intimate or gender-related nature and the difficulty of dealing with them in mixed groups.
3. Recognizing that she's not alone or unique in her battles encourages a woman to continue the struggle against her soul's enemy.

An effective women's retreat, however, doesn't happen spontaneously. Myriad factors can make or break the occasion. *Positive spiritual results come in direct proportion to the time, effort, organization, and prayer that go into constructing the retreat.* With these essentials in mind, we will present a step-by-step retreat-building plan.

Initial Planning

The initial planning is a "rough-in" period in which the most basic determinations are made. Several heads, at this time as well as later, are better than one. The leader, however, should come with definite suggestions and a list of choices in each area rather than starting with nothing in mind. The initial meeting sets the tone for the entire undertaking. If time is wasted and little accomplished, the road of preparation will likely prove long and rough.

The broad divisions for consideration and effort in retreat construction are time, place, budget, and participants.

Time

The most popular seasons for women's retreats are spring and fall. In determining your choice, don't ask "What worked for Such-and-Such a group?" Rather, consider which season is best for your group. The best time of year is not so much a matter of present preference—what the women might say they want—as it is of past demonstration. Historically, have the members of your group been more actively involved during one season than during another? Check attendance at regular meetings and participation in special activities to determine this.

After choosing the season, decide upon a specific weekend. (A retreat generally runs twenty-four hours, more or less, beginning late afternoon or early evening on Friday and running until early or midafternoon on Saturday.) But which weekend should it be? Choose as wisely as possible, avoiding obvious conflicts that affect your group: special church services, school opening, major vacation periods, school closing, and so forth. But while looking for a time of minimal conflict, realize that no weekend can prove perfect from everyone's standpoint. Life just isn't like that anymore.

Location

Basically, you will have three choices for location: a church, a camp, a motel-resort. In making your decision, consider the accommodations offered by each. Which would enable you best to host the probable number of women you'll have? Which would give the greatest comfort? What type accommodations does the majority of your group prefer? Would your ladies be willing to open their homes to overnight guests coming from a distance if you choose to use the church? What about the opportunities each facility offers for physical activity between sessions? What about available food service? Also consider accessibility. Distance is an important factor for women driving without their menfolk. They dislike great distances and complicated directions.

Finances

Preliminary plans also should focus on expenses. You can estimate total expense by figuring rental of the facility; food purchase, preparation, and service; transportation costs; and speaker travel, entertainment, and honorarium. How, then, do you meet the estimated budget? Perhaps the church would consider underwriting part of the total, viewing the retreat as a ministry. Realistically, how many women can be expected to attend? With these basic factors in mind, figure attendance fees *at the lowest rate for the highest benefits*.

Participants

Will retreat attendance be limited to your own church women? Will it be open to several local churches? Or would you like to undertake a statewide retreat for churches within your circle of fellowship?

When you have all of these initial considerations taken care of, you're ready to get underway with the actual plans.

Site

Finalize site choice; if you will be using church facilities, *enter the retreat in the church calendar*. Trying to hold a ladies' seminar in the church school's gymnasium will be disastrous if a basketball game is planned for that same Friday evening!

If you've chosen a camp or motel-resort, although you may make the reservation by telephone, *be sure to confirm it in detailed written form.* Give the management an estimated number of rooms needed, with an understanding about adjustments that may be required as the retreat date nears.

Transportation

Participants must be able to reach whatever location you choose: if considerable distance is involved, you may decide to use church buses, vans, or individual cars.

Schedule

Construct a rough schedule for the retreat, aiming for *balance* in the overall program. Balance is achieved by alternating different types of activities:

- Main speaking sessions
- Smaller workshops
- Skits
- Games
- Programs
- Activity and rest (Mealtimes count here.)
- Question/answer periods

The ideal is to keep the women *busy* but not *buried* throughout the retreat. Hour after hour of similar, structured activities becomes monotonous. Attendees grow numb on both ends!

Speaker

Contact the speaker of your choice about twelve months ahead.

Publicity

Having dealt with the preliminary behind-the-scenes work, begin handling those things that are more tangible. Announce the retreat to your immediate group and to whatever others you wish to include, making the first announcement about six months in advance. Send frequent reminders.

Workshops

Choose workshop topics and assign their leaders. A workshop is a mini-session by a woman from among your own participants.

Topics may range from "how-to" demonstrations (e.g., crafts) to age-interest areas such as rearing teens, music in the home, and parenting toddlers. *Be sure not to duplicate or overlap topic areas handled by the main speaker.*

Schedule several workshops to run simultaneously and allow the women to choose which they will attend. (In order to assign rooms with adequate seating, you may need to have workshop sign-ups ahead of time.) Be sure to include workshop topics of interest to various categories of *single women.* Singles often feel discouraged about attending retreats because so much emphasis is placed on marriage and child rearing.

Choose workshop topics and leaders early so that time-pressure excuses by prospective leaders won't be valid.

The coordinator's efforts concerning workshops must continue right up to the retreat's opening. She must stay in contact with each workshop leader, emphasizing the workshop planning.

1. Is the plan practical? Does the outline cover the subject in such a way that the attendees will be able to comprehend and apply the material? Is information balanced with inspiration?
2. Is progress being made on the plan? Has it taken clearer shape each time it's been reviewed? Is the subject development going in the right direction? What about its overall emphasis? (Check to be sure the leader is not counting on emotionalism or sentimentality to replace the hard digging, strong material, and solid preparation that benefit hearers.)
3. Is the outline approved? Set a deadline, telling leaders when you will collect the outlines. Review them yourself. If they deal with a biblical theme, have the pastor review them. Pastoral review can be strategic in preventing any (even inadvertent) doctrinal error from creeping into a workshop presentation.
4. Is there performance on outline development? The outline must come into existence; it must make progress. Do not accept haphazard, last-minute work. If, after several proddings, any workshop leader fails to produce something concrete, *change leaders.* Remember, the retreat's purpose is to minister to women's needs. It is distressing to sit through a session whose leader has not prepared sufficiently and tries to compensate by "cuteness," impromptu generalities, a book report, or a string of sentimental stories. Such sessions waste attendees' time. They also indicate the organizer's failure to supervise.

Handling Details

Advancing weeks will demand your checking repeatedly on food, transportation, cabin or room assignments, individual responsibilities, and the program. Although you will have put committees or individuals in charge, you nevertheless must keep in close touch.

With regard to *food,* ask yourself these questions. Have you rightly calculated the number of meals to be served during the weekend? Are the menus varied, reflective of women's likes, and manageable from a serving standpoint? Are there adequate facilities and eating space? There must be a place for each woman to sit for meals. If your own group is providing the food (rather than camp or resort personnel or a caterer), have you arranged for the preparation, equipment, and personnel? Have you planned for getting the food to the site?

Check on *transportation* for the women. Having generally decided whether you will use church vehicles, private cars, or both, you must know exactly who is going in each vehicle. You cannot safely depend upon everyone to find her own ride. In every group there are those too timid to ask someone to take them. Check to be sure everyone has a ride, whether by choice or by assignment.

Rooming arrangements are important. Whether accommodations are to be individual homes, motel rooms, or campground cabins or rooms, there must be a bed for each body. When homes are used, the lodging may be handled by a combination of assignment and choice. There may be out-of-towners coming who are friends of some in your group as well as those who do not know anyone personally.

If using a camp facility, you might decide to let the women choose where they want to sleep, or you may prefer to assign beds or rooms. However you handle the distribution, it is wise to separate "chickens" and "night owls." If some attendees are nursing mothers with their babies, *put them all in one room or area.*

Curfew

Do set a curfew. Not even the bounciest night owl is at her spiritually receptive best if she doesn't get to sleep until 5:00 A.M.

Individual Responsibilities

List things each attendee should plan to bring. Women like to feel secure. Give them a "needs" list including Bible, notebook and pen, sleeping gear as necessary, money (for book table and snacks), bath linens, soap, toothbrush and toothpaste, and appropriate clothing (according to season, place, and planned activities).

Program

Produce the best-looking paper program your group can afford. Women enjoy having something to keep as a reminder of special times.

Programs range from a single sheet of paper listing the schedule to more extensive booklet types. If possible, have appropriate thematic artwork on the program. A printed program may include the following:

- A directed devotional (*Many* Christian women are unsure of how to have personal devotions.)
- A schedule of sessions (with time and place)
- "Ground rules" (promptness, cleanup, curfew, no smoking, etc.)
- A biographical sketch of the speaker
- Poetry or prose reflecting the theme
- Songs and hymns to be used

Speaker

Don't let the speaker's acceptance letter be your last correspondence before her arrival. Keep her informed, telling her specifics that apply to her. These should include the following:

1. Retreat theme
2. Number of times she's to speak
3. Specific topic requests
4. Length of sessions (It also would be helpful to let her know workshop topics so that she can avoid overlapping.)
5. Place the retreat will be held
6. Expected weather
7. Planned physical activities
8. Anything about your group's needs and personality that might be helpful

Send the speaker not only early schedule plans but also all subsequent changes in it.

Make arrangements about her transportation. Will you get her ticket, or should she? If the latter, how will you handle payment? If she is to get the ticket herself, she will need to know such things as opening and closing time for the retreat and ground-travel time between airport and retreat site, all of which will have a bearing upon the arrival and departure times she arranges.

Let your speaker know what her lodging will be before, during, and after the retreat. If yours is a campground retreat and the speaker is coming from some distance, arrange for one of your group to bring the bed and bath items she will need. If at all possible, arrange for the speaker to have a separate room at the retreat site. Though organizational work ends when the retreat begins, the speaker's work moves into high gear. She needs an "apart" place in which she can rest, pray, and prepare.

If there necessarily are "on her own" eating arrangements, how should she handle them? For example, if she's spending the night preceding the retreat in a motel, what should she do about breakfast?

Just in Case

The wise retreat organizer will have alternate plans and equipment ready. You can never tell when something won't go as planned. The weather may turn rainy, making outdoor activities impossible. A workshop leader may come down with the flu. Electricity can fail. Be prepared for any such situations.

A Plus

A nice extra touch is *name tags* on hostesses and counselors.

Finally

We wish to stress that the technicalities just discussed will come to nothing if over, under, around, and through all the work and details each worker neglects to concentrate on the true goal of the retreat: *spiritual advancement for each lady who attends.* It is vital that the entire seminar-retreat project, from conception to completion, be bathed in consistent, solid prayer.

Chapter 24

Times of Tears

Christians are told to "weep with them that weep" (Rom. 12:15). Grieving is as much a reality in the believer's life as is laughing. Sympathizing with another's sorrow is a tangible way to bear one another's burdens.

The Maidservant's part in carrying others' sorrow burdens is great. Her role in such times is fourfold. She may act as comforter, guide, encourager, and helper.

The ministry of comfort often begins before death, as a family waits helplessly in the hospital while their loved one suffers and drifts further from earthly life. Hurting ones are best helped by visits that are brief, words that are few, and compassion that is genuine. Do not withhold the comfort of human touch—for the well and for the sick. However, realizing that hospitals are a prime breeding ground for germs, make a habit of washing your hands thoroughly before leaving the building.

When death comes, the first reaction of a Maidservant may be the question, "But what can I say to comfort someone who has lost a loved one?" The best answer may be "Nothing." Sympathetic silence holds more soothing power than a week's worth of words.

Immediate practical assistance is also needed. The Maidservant can play a key role by arranging for meals to be brought in to the family, taking and making telephone calls, receiving visitors, finding a house sitter for the funeral and burial time span, and handling other practical necessities.

It is important that the Maidservant recognize and properly respond to varying human manifestations of sorrow.

The Nature of Sorrow

God's Word talks to us about sorrow in Job, the classic picture of godly suffering, as well as in I Peter 2:21 and 4:1, I Thessalonians 4:13-18, and II Corinthians 5. In none of these passages does the Lord deny or denounce sorrow's agony. He does, however, point to the *hope* that makes the Christian's sorrow differ from that of the unsaved.

Just as there are various reactions to loss, there may be various phases in the grieving process. These are akin to the physical healing process. Intensity and duration vary according to the manner of death, personalities involved, and their spiritual states.

One grieving reaction is *denial.* Some people throughout their loved one's final illness and even past the death itself steadfastly deny reality to themselves and others. This reaction seems incomprehensible to those looking on from the outside, but it may be the only way the sufferer can handle the situation emotionally.

Perhaps the reaction that most shocks Christians is *anger.* Nevertheless, it is normal, human. Shaming the person who feels anger shows lack of wisdom and compassion. God says, "Be ye angry and sin not." Evidently, then, our wrong use of anger is sin, not the anger itself. Job expressed anger over his deprivations, and he was no spiritual pygmy. The Lord recognizes death as mankind's last great enemy. Why then should Christians gasp in shock when one among them expresses angry helplessness against so cruel a foe? It is better that anger be acknowledged than to deny and cover it with pretended piety. Repression may let it fester, eventually erupting in another area or manner.

Inertia—the numbed inability to feel, to think, or to act—is a common characteristic of grief. Also common is its opposite, *panic.* The panic response is typical of a widow whose husband's death leaves her ignorant of practical matters such as insurance, bank accounts, and mortgages. When reactions to grief affect decision making, the ministry woman may have to step in—to help the sorrowing person think rationally.

There is no way to predict how sorrow will take its toll upon an individual. That realization is itself the key: we are working with *individual people,* not with patterns.

In the topsy-turvy world of grief, there is another area in which the Maidservant can be particularly helpful: guarding the bereaved during her time of vulnerability. A sorrowing heart is vulnerable to wounding words and deeds. Christians most often inflict hurt to the sorrowing by speaking words which, under other circumstances, would be harmless. The glib quoting of Romans 8:28, for instance, can wound one whose loss is so fresh that it cannot be comprehended as ultimately bringing good.

A sorrowing person is also vulnerable to shysters. Unfortunately, there are individuals and institutions eager to prey upon those who grieve. They may solicit estate money to "memorialize" the dead loved one or insurance funds to reinvest. Urging the sorrower *not to make any major decisions* for several months (preferably a full year) after the death helps protect her from human vultures.

The Longevity of Sorrow

How long does grieving continue? The length of time varies; there is a recognizable pattern of healing, however. First is the initial shock period, which lasts from one to six weeks. Even though the loved one's last illness may have been of years' duration, the actual fact and finality of death comes as a numbing blow. This numbness acts as insulation during the difficult period of funeral arrangements and service. Following numbness comes the adjustment period, in which searching and yearning predominate, while the sorrow itself becomes manageable for longer and longer periods. This phase lasts, generally, into the fourth month. From the fourth to the sixth month disorientation and disorganization may set in. Basic survival needs may be ignored. Grief's wound loses its cutting edge, except at special holiday or anniversary times. Finally, usually between the eighteenth month and the twenty-fourth month, the grieving person makes the decision to pick up life's pieces and move on. The specific times will vary according to individuals involved, the manner of death, and the quality of relationship between the dead person and the survivor.

Those who have never personally experienced grieving tend to become impatient with the bereft person when she can't "snap out of it" within a few months' time. You as a Maidservant can help all concerned by identifying grief's realities, its variables, and the patient adaptation demanded by it. In particular, *children* of Christian homes need to be assured that grieving is not unspiritual. Great harm and hampered healing can result if a child is shamed about crying over the loss of someone beloved.

Funerals

Funeral arrangements ordinarily are handled by the immediate family. For every phase of it, however, your objective assistance may be sought.

The specific arrangements for a funeral include the following:

1. choice of funeral home
2. choice of burial plot
3. choice of casket
4. decisions about the service itself

The decision about date, time, and place for the funeral may be influenced by your locale. In some areas the funeral and burial occur within one day of the death, while in others they are delayed for as much as a week. Time requirements for relatives coming from distant places must be considered.

Also to be chosen are the organist, soloist, musical selections, minister, pallbearers, and any additional participants to pray, read Scripture, or otherwise contribute.

The family may ask help with the obituary. An obituary notice for a newspaper should contain at least the following essentials: biographical information, surviving relatives, church and civic memberships of the deceased; date, time, and place for the funeral service; indication if flowers are not desired by the family (a typical notice might read, "In lieu of flowers, the family requests that memorial donations be made to _____.").

If you are asked to advise or to accompany the family member handling arrangements, ask the funeral director for a breakdown of expenses as well as the overall price quotation. There are variables in pricing:

1. *Burial.* Plots vary widely in purchase price, not only from cemetery to cemetery but also according to "aesthetics"—such

as shaded spots and so forth. There also are so-called "after-hours" burials that may include late afternoon or evening hours and weekends, for which additional fees will be charged.

2. *Casket.* The cost range is tremendous. The funeral director will be interested in selling the most costly casket. He may talk about "a fitting tribute" and so on. Don't let the sorrowing person be pressured into unnecessary expense by such subtleties. Point out that simplicity is always in good taste; that the dead loved one would not want to create financial burdens for the sake of appearances.

3. *Transportation.* There is a fee for using mortuary vehicles. Expenses are lowered with each unit deleted. The hearse alone can be used, with family and other mourners following in private cars.

4. *Flowers.* Customarily, the largest expense in this category is the flower "blanket" given by the family and placed atop the casket. If expenses are a factor, consider less costly alternatives. A veteran's casket can be draped with an American flag; any believer's, with the Christian flag. In Beneth's mother's funeral, the closed casket lid displayed the deceased's well-worn Bible. It lay open to her personally marked passage of II Corinthians 5. Across it lay a single long-stemmed red rose.

5. *Printed programs.* Because these contain biographical details such as date and place of birth, they are a nice memento for those attending the funeral. They are not a *necessity,* however.

In each of the above considerations, you can steer the bereft person toward sensible choices by asking the question, "Why is _____ important to you?"

Collect and store information about funeral-expense variables for that time when it can help someone whose grief makes decision making difficult. Etiquette sources can be consulted for further details, and reputable mortuaries themselves are good sources of information and assistance.

After the Funeral

Acts of kindness need to continue following the funeral. Too often a grief-stricken individual is inundated with home-baked goodies, flowers, and offers of assistance the week of the funeral but then suddenly forgotten. The timing could not be more cruel. She is abandoned just as numbness begins to wear off and intense pain floods in upon her. Emotional wounds, like physical ones, need continuing medication as they heal. It is in this extended-care ministry that a Maidservant can be particularly strategic. Schedule a follow-up ministry, arranging for help in her small but nagging duties: housework, errands, note writing, grocery shopping, cooking, and the like. Spread the project out among several women. Chart a gradual cessation of such helps so that the recipient does not feel left suddenly to herself. It might be wise to ask one or two ladies to maintain special contact for several months. Older, retired widows can be especially effective in this important ministry. Their help for a sorrowing sister will in turn be therapeutic for them.

A Unique Spirit

Although she probably will not have a direct part in the funeral service, the Maidservant can positively affect the occasion through her advice and example.

The centrality of Jesus Christ in the service is essential. A funeral is difficult for the survivors, regardless of their spiritual maturity. To have the preacher or preachers go into eulogistic rhapsodies only brings fresh tears and new soreness to sorrow's wounds. Urge the family to ask that the focus be on Christ: His victory over the grave, the loved one's delighted presence now with Him, heaven's joys after earth's pain and illness. That heavenly focus allows grieving hearts to know the Holy Spirit's balming touch.

When advising about a funeral for someone who was unsaved, do not suggest a message that comforts on the basis of a false hope of secret, last-minute conversion. The thrust of the message should be to challenge the living to increased faithfulness and greater witnessing efforts toward those yet living.

Death, grieving, and funerals are inescapable realities of our mortality. A Maidservant's wise and compassionate ministry can help the sorrowing to see hope's rainbow through their tears.

Chapter 25

Nuptial Notes

Modern weddings too often reflect the low esteem in which marriage is held by the unsaved world. Exhibitionist, corny, gaudy—anything goes. By contrast, the tasteful wedding of born-again young people presents a wonderful opportunity for testimony by its very contrast to the norm.

For Christians, a wedding is more than mere ceremony; it is a joyful picture of Jesus Christ our Savior taking to Himself the Church as His bride. It is important, therefore, that a Christian wedding be conceived and conducted in a manner befitting that picture.

The Maidservant may be called upon to contribute to these joyous occasions in practical ways through her guidance and counsel. Suggestions we feel are most helpful for a Maidservant's possible involvement with wedding ceremonies follow.

The Principals

Director

Beautiful, smoothly run weddings have an overseer. This person may come from within the church family itself—the preacher's wife or another woman assigned the duty—or from outside the church (with, of course, pastoral approval).

Bride

The central "player" in the wedding drama is the bride. Her wishes are primary in all decisions. Ideally, the director will confer with the bride and her mother a number of times prior to the wedding date. If the bride tends toward extravagant or unorthodox details, the director should urge her toward conservatism and tastefulness.

Families

The families of the bride and groom are a wedding's "production staff." As wedding plans take shape, the question arises: which family does what? The answer is that the bride's family does almost everything in producing the wedding itself; the groom's parents traditionally host the rehearsal dinner, pay for certain of the flowers, and give an honorarium to the minister.

The couple's families may cause problems in wedding plans. For instance, parental divorce and remarriage may cause nasty tempers to flare over who will sit where during the ceremony. The seating of family members should be determined by the bride and groom and conformity to standard practice. If warring erupts between factions, the wedding director may have to handle the matter firmly—without running to the bride (and dimming her joy). As an extreme example, Bobbie once had to tell a tantrum-throwing bride's (divorced and remarried) mother, "You may have ruined *your* marriage and life. Surely you can at least have the decency not to ruin your *daughter's!*" Explosive situations must be handled firmly but tactfully, keeping an eye toward future family relationships.

Wedding Party

The wedding party is the "supporting cast," chosen by the bride (maid or matron of honor, bridesmaids, flower girl) and groom (best man, groomsmen, ushers, ring bearer). The director of course needs to note everyone who takes part in the wedding.

Using children—a little boy as ring bearer and a little girl as flower girl—can wreak havoc in the wedding's "stage picture." In order to reduce possibility of a child's distracting miscues, suggest using children *no younger than five years old.*

The Principles

The church itself is the "stage" for a wedding ceremony. It is of prime importance in a Christian wedding. The specific date and time for the rehearsal, the wedding ceremony, and the reception should be discussed and written into the church calendar as soon as the couple's plans are set. Premarital counseling may also be scheduled at this early stage.

No doubt the church will have some policies about weddings. As questions and problems arise, those may need to be extended. It is better to have rules such as "Rice throwing is not permitted within ten feet of the front door," "Wedding photographs must be taken prior to the ceremony," "Music must be checked beforehand for acceptability" than to have irritating, embarrassing incidents. It is a good idea for the church to have its wedding policies in written form to ensure everyone's understanding them ahead of time.

Church policy also may affect the choice of officiant for the wedding. For instance, some pastors refuse to marry divorced persons. Others prefer not to have an outside preacher perform a wedding ceremony in their church.

If the reception also is planned for the church site, the bride needs to know what facilities and supplies are available. Don't overlook janitorial arrangements.

Planning Ahead

A workable timetable for wedding preparations follows:

One year to four months before the wedding
>Set wedding date and time.
>Plan the wedding budget with families.
>Determine formality of the ceremony.
>Reserve the wedding site. Get the ceremony on the minister's schedule.
>Reserve the reception site.
>Determine the type of food service. Contact a caterer.
>Select and contact attendants.
>Begin compiling the guest list.
>Send the engagement announcement to the newspaper.
>Shop for the wedding wear.

Three months before the wedding
> Order the wedding gown, attendants' gowns, and mothers' gowns.
> Schedule the wedding director, photographer, florist, and musicians.
> Order wedding invitations and personal stationery.
> Select and purchase wedding rings.
> Select and register dinnerware, flatware, and glassware patterns.
> Shop for attendants' gifts, trousseau, and wedding accessories.
> Plan the honeymoon.

Two months before the wedding
> Plan the ceremony, being sure to consult with the minister.
> Check on marriage-license requirements.
> Write thank-you notes for any shower gifts received.
> Select and order formal wear for men in wedding party.
> Address invitations.

One month before the wedding
> Mail invitations.
> Have wedding gown and attendants' gowns fitted.
> Shop for groom's wedding gift.
> Arrange lodging for out-of-town attendants.
> Handle address and name changes on business, legal, and financial forms.
> Plan rehearsal with wedding director and minister.
> Begin packing for honeymoon and moving to new home.
> Get plenty of rest.

Appropriateness

The wedding of a born-again couple is a sacred ceremony. Formality is an important ingredient for such a ceremony, and the bride should be encouraged in that direction. The entire ceremony should be a means of honoring the Lord. That criterion will help weed out details that are maudlin, upbeat, or otherwise in poor taste. Dignity is the hallmark of a beautiful Christian wedding ceremony. Because of their youth, bride and groom may lean toward flashiness or sentimentality, as, for instance, in the choice of wedding invitations. Although the final choice is the bride's, it is proper to urge her toward good taste: *restraint* and *traditionalism* are two prime characteristics. The same principles should apply to gowns and music. Unlike a worldly ceremony, the Christian wedding should be characterized by lovely, modest clothing, a traditional atmosphere, and refined music. It is also important to point out to the bride early in the planning process that the audience never should be made uncomfortable by something in the wedding ceremony. For instance, if bride and groom stand holding hands and gazing longingly into one another's eyes during a seemingly endless musical number, or if the wedding kiss is unduly prolonged, people become uneasy; they are embarrassed. Interestingly, etiquette books state that the public kiss is not considered proper for formal weddings; it detracts from the restraint and dignity of the occasion.

Rehearsal

A smooth wedding ceremony depends a great deal upon an efficient rehearsal. To that end, ceremony details should be thought out ahead of time. Certainly there may be changes at the rehearsal after the bride, her mother, and the director actually see the wedding party on the platform. But at least there will be a starting point. It is a good idea to have the plans in typed form, with copies distributed to all who need to know details of the service.

The rehearsal is the appropriate time for instruction in matters sometimes left to chance. The ushers, for instance, should practice escorting and seating. The groomsmen should be reminded not to lock their knees while standing during the ceremony—unless they want to faint amid candlelight and solemnities! The female attendants can well do with some instruction, demonstration, and practice in getting into position gracefully despite bulky or long skirts and hands full of flowers.

If the wedding party are dressed well, the rehearsal goes more smoothly than if they dress too casually.

A rehearsal should have two complete walk-throughs for the confidence of all involved. It is a good idea, if possible, to have the pastor open the rehearsal, lead in prayer, and then turn the proceedings over to the director. That voice and presence of authority can encourage a productive atmosphere. In the first walk-through, have three stand-ins: for the bride, groom, and mother of the bride. It gives them the chance to judge placement, timing, and so on.

Expense and Extensiveness

The loveliness of a wedding does not depend on quantity—whether in financial expenditures, flowers, or attendants. In fact, too many or too much of anything can look ostentatious and cluttered.

Candles and flowers are costly. A bride need not feel bound to the customary décor if finances are tight. There have been elegant, lovely weddings performed amid banks of evergreen boughs, magnolia leaves, and the like. Assure the bride that her going to a new home does not mean that she must send her mother and father to the poorhouse!

Platform Arrangement

Arranging wedding participants on the platform may take some ingenuity. Of course, much will depend upon the physical make-up of the church building and the platform. The three basic arrangements of attendants follow:

1. Women on one side, men on the other
2. Attendants standing as couples
3. Alternating men and women on each side

Seating of Guests

The left side (facing the platform) is considered the bride's side; the right, the groom's. Ushers inquire of arriving guests, "Friends of the bride or groom?" and seat them on the respective side. The first row on either side should be empty. The second row is for the parents, the third for grandparents. Other rows "within the ribbon" are for other family members, special friends, and guests of honor.

Photographs

Suggest that most or all wedding photographs be taken before the ceremony. In order to get fine-quality pictures, a photographer spends a good deal of time posing, focusing, and lighting. Wedding guests attend as a courtesy; each has sacrificed time that could have been used for something else. There are few people in the world who have hours free to stand around waiting for a wedding party to arrive at the reception. Taking pictures ahead of time also eases the tensions of the participants so that they can fully enjoy the ceremony.

Just in Case

On the wedding day, be prepared for something to go awry. Most of us have heard of grooms detained by traffic, flowers sent to the wrong church, a bridesmaid's shoes being three sizes too small, and other horror stories. If possible, avoid telling the bride of things that don't go according to plan; she has enough tension to deal with already. It's a good idea to keep some emergency supplies handy: matches, candles, smelling salts, sewing kit. They could prove to be lifesavers.

A Final Word

"Everybody loves a wedding" may or may not be true. Almost anyone would admit, however, that a lovely wedding is a sweet, happy occasion. Solemn vows of love, obedience, and dedicated oneness of life are admirably set in a ceremony of candlelight and organ music. All come together into a worshipful masterpiece by careful, prayerful preparation.

Chapter 26

Blooms for Blessing

One of the "extra" opportunities or duties that may come to Maidservants is flower arranging—not just for her home but also for the church and special occasions as well.

Most flower arrangements may be categorized as one of three types: Oriental, mass, or line.

The *Oriental flower* arrangement stresses simplicity. It has three classic parts. The tallest piece, with its tip over the center of the arrangement and pointing upward, represents heaven. The middle-sized flower, approximately two-thirds the size of the tallest and placed close to it, represents man. The third and shortest piece, one-third the size of "man," represents earth.

Mass arrangements include all full bouquets. They are typical of Victorian, English eighteenth-century, French, and Flemish tastes.

Line arrangements stress pattern or design as in the Oriental, but with less starkness. An example is the crescent-shaped arrangement.

Whatever the arrangement used, the stems should all come from one point.

Elements of Arrangement

The elements of flower arranging are much the same as those considered by an artist working on canvas.

Pattern or design. The form may be oval, triangular, rectangular, crescent, fan, or any other established design. Among these is the Hogarth curve (an S curve)—a simple and beautiful form. Church arrangements, because of their location and size, usually will follow the form of oval, triangle, or fan.

Line. A form in motion, line will create the artistic shape.

Focal point. A point where all the lines come together to create a center of interest is necessary in every arrangement.

Proportion. The way the elements work together should be considered. An arrangement should not look as if it might tip over.

Scale. The container and the materials it holds need to have a proper and pleasing relationship.

Color. The colors in an arrangement and in its surroundings should harmonize. When seen from a distance, blues and purples give a "black hole" effect; they are better used in a small room than in a large one.

Texture and form. There should be a strong relationship of texture in flowers and container. The forms should contrast.

Preparing the Flowers

Good flower arranging actually begins before the blooms are placed in a container: conditioning the flowers when picked will extend their life. Plants should be cut in the early morning or late afternoon. Make a slanting cut with sharp shears and put the plants in sugar water immediately. Plants having milky sap (poinsettias, poppies, and tulips) should have cut ends burned or dipped in boiling water before being placed in water. Heavy stems (such as lilacs) should have the stems split and then hammered so that they can absorb water easily. Bulb flowers (like daffodils and tulips) should have any moisture at the stem end wiped away to keep it from sealing out water.

Equipment

Certain items are needed by those who frequently do flower arranging:

1. Shears (one for cutting flowers, another for cutting branches and wires)
2. Pin holders
3. Oases and metal oasis holders (Soak oases for at least two hours before inserting flowers.)
4. Florist picks and water picks
5. Adhesive and florist clay
6. Stones and florist moss to cover "mechanics"
7. Pill bottles and long sticks
8. Wire, cellophane tape (for fixing broken flowers), and florist tape
9. Chicken wire
10. Containers (Clear containers are good; the stems are then considered part of the arrangements. If you are using a silver container in church, it needs to be somewhat *tarnished* so that it does not reflect too brightly.)

In Conclusion

Why does a flower arrangement make such a pleasing addition to a church auditorium or to a home? First, flowers are a bit of God's own creation brought indoors. Second, they assist us in applying the principle of Philippians 4:8—thinking on things that are lovely. Acquiring some basic skills in flower arranging will encourage not only your own heart but also the hearts of others.

Chapter 27

Typewriters, Telephones, and Technicalities

With more fundamentalist ministries "starting from scratch," it may fall a Maidservant's lot to organize and staff an office. If that be the case, her efforts will focus upon five needs: reception, records, correspondence, telephone, and travel.

Reception

As a place of welcome, an office needs to be not only adequate for its practical functions but also attractive.

Some furnishings are basic to office operation: desk, chairs, typewriter, storage space, duplicating equipment. These need not be expensive or new; they may be donated or purchased inexpensively from auctions, warehouses, or private owners. Whatever their source, they should *look as good as possible*. That may mean refinishing, repainting, reupholstering, and so on. The extra effort is worthwhile: *impressions of the reception area influence response to the entire ministry*.

Office seating is of two types: for visitors and for office personnel. Two comfortable chairs or a small couch is standard for visitors. Chairs with lumbar support and adjustable height are necessary for office workers. More expense should be incurred for staff furniture than for visitors'. The comfort of those who spend their days in the office is more important to the well-being and efficiency of the ministry than that of those who spend only minutes or even hours, though neither should be neglected.

A ministry office should have pleasant décor. Choose restful, attractive colors for paint or wallpaper. Pictures and bric-a-brac should show restraint and taste.

Ideally, there should be an inner and an outer office. If the size or newness of the ministry makes two offices impossible, at least erect some sort of screening divider to protect the pastor or administrator from constant interruptions.

Office upkeep is as important as its design. Furniture with chipped surfaces or broken parts, pictures hanging crooked on the walls, coffee-stained rugs, books and papers strewn haphazardly over surfaces—all of these leave negative impressions in a visitor's mind. They also reflect *and contribute to* slovenly work habits.

Even more important than the physical office setting is the atmosphere created by the receptionist/secretary. Although there will always be paperwork demanding attention, she must keep in mind that *people* take first priority. They should be greeted with warmth and kindness (although they will not always demonstrate those characteristics themselves!). Even when a request must be denied, it should be done tactfully with consideration for sensitivities. If people are kept waiting in the outer office to see the pastor, the secretary need not keep up a running conversation with them. After explaining the delay, she may excuse herself and get back to her desk work, perhaps offering a magazine to those waiting.

Records

Efficiency in office work does not come automatically; it develops as effective systems are established.

As soon as an office is opened, the secretary should analyze, record, and organize her various duties. She can start by simply jotting down a running tally of what she does throughout the day. After several weeks she will see a pattern emerge. This pattern can then be translated into a scheduling plan. It is wise for her to *write out* the procedures necessary for each of her various office jobs. She may put this in the form of a chart, breaking each job into its component parts in their chronological order and with indications of priority. By recording even the simple routine procedures, she solidifies procedures in her own mind while providing a guide for training a replacement or helpers.

Accurate records are essential to an effective ministry. That means keeping files—many different files. Below is a suggested filing guide:

Activities
> Banquets
> Receptions and dinners
> Retreats
> Weddings

Addresses
> Audio-visual suppliers
> Book companies
> Craft suppliers
> Curriculum and general bookstores
>> Children's materials
>> General suppliers
>> Government agencies (for free materials)
>> Specialized materials
>> Vacation Bible school suppliers
>> Youth materials
> Equipment suppliers (furniture, etc.)
> Individuals
>> Church members
>> Business people
>> Evangelists
>> Friends
>> Pastors
> Organizations
> Periodical publishers (magazines)
> Public-relations materials (church bulletins/signs/ advertising)
> Tract suppliers

Adult education
> Characteristics and needs (age groups)
> Curriculum
> Groups with special needs (handicapped/widowed/ singles/shut-ins, etc.)

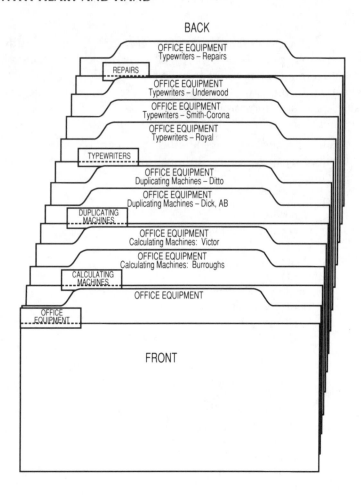

BACK

OFFICE EQUIPMENT
Typewriters – Repairs

REPAIRS

OFFICE EQUIPMENT
Typewriters – Underwood

OFFICE EQUIPMENT
Typewriters – Smith-Corona

OFFICE EQUIPMENT
Typewriters – Royal

TYPEWRITERS

OFFICE EQUIPMENT
Duplicating Machines – Ditto

OFFICE EQUIPMENT
Duplicating Machines – Dick, AB

DUPLICATING
MACHINES

OFFICE EQUIPMENT
Calculating Machines: Victor

OFFICE EQUIPMENT
Calculating Machines: Burroughs

CALCULATING
MACHINES

OFFICE EQUIPMENT

OFFICE
EQUIPMENT

FRONT

Programs and organizations
Women's work
Audio-visual aids
Bulletin-board ideas
Bulletins and programs (samples)
Charts and graphs
Films
Filmstrips
Flannelgraph
Maps
Models
Object lessons
Overhead projector and transparencies

Patterns and clip art
Pictures
Record of cassette tapes
Slides (list by topics)
Bibliography
Camps and conferences
Activities
Curriculum
Equipment
Personnel (staff, director, counselors)
Programs (activities, schedules)
Publicity
Children's work
Activities
Characteristics and needs
Curriculum
Nursery
Programs and organizations (children's church, dedications, etc.)
Toddlers
Christian day school
Curriculum
Day care
Elementary
High school
Kindergarten
Organizations
Philosophy
Christian living
Devotional life
Duties of the Christian
Stewardship
Counseling
Bible, use of
Marriage and family
Premarital
Special problems (age groups, developmental, crisis)
Craft ideas (for all ages)
Discipline (home and church)
Equipment
Calculating machines
Duplicating machines
Typewriters
Family life

>   Dating
>   Husband-wife relationship
>   Seminars
> Missions
>   Agencies
>   Missionaries
>   Programs
> Records
>   Agreements, deeds
>   Bank statements
>   Contracts
>   Insurance
>   Membership
>   Minutes

For an idea of how the filing system might look, note the segment illustrated above.

One of the most important files in the office is the "tickler" or follow-up file. This file enables the secretary to remember numberless details. To set up a tickler file, you need 44 folders labeled as follows:

- 31 folders numbered 1-31 for days of the month
- 12 folders labeled for months of the year
- 1 folder labeled for future years

To operate the file, you put into it a reminder for *each matter requiring future attention*. The following are examples:

1. Correspondence for which a reply must await further information, a decision, etc.
2. Reports requested for future dates
3. Matters referred to other people or departments for advice or information
4. Matters requiring attention at regular intervals: salary considerations, annual reports, contract renewals, etc.
5. Miscellaneous promises made that must be followed up either by you or your boss

Mark a follow-up date on each paper you place in the file, putting it in the appropriate folder. (Some secretaries prefer not to place originals in this file, but use copies instead. It may be wise to put a letter's photocopy in the tickler file if an original is needed for action.) If the follow-up date is more than one month away, the item would be placed in the folder for the month in which the follow-up date falls or into the Future Years folder.

The key to the effectiveness of a tickler file is *daily* use. Each morning take out the material from the folder for that day and place the empty folder in order behind the last one. In this way the daily folders gradually shift, keeping the current date in front. Folders representing nonworking days may be left in the same order, but each month turn those dates to face backwards. This reduces the chance of misfiling.

Sometimes you will find that items in the file have already been handled. If such is the case, destroy or file the paper as necessary. If a matter has an indefinite follow-up date or if you cannot handle it on the day you had planned to do so, mark it with a new date and file it in the appropriate folder.

On the first day of each month, remove the materials from that month's folder and file them in their proper daily folders. Place the newly emptied folder behind the other monthly folders.

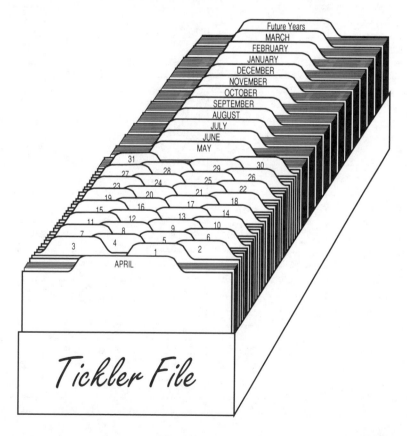

Tickler File

When a new year begins, pull the year's materials from the Future Years folder and distribute them by month, and then file the first month's by days, according to the method.

Perhaps two of the most frequently used records in the office will be Transportation and Hospital Visitation. It is essential for tax purposes to keep careful track of official local travel. A vehicle mileage log might look like this one.

Vehicle Mileage Log

Dating from _____ to _____

Date	Beginning mileage	Ending mileage	Total miles	Destination	Purpose	Driver

A good pastor is careful to visit those who need him. To insure that he won't miss seeing a sick person, hospital visitation records should be kept. Rather than simply jotting down the names of sick people on various bits of paper, list the needed visits systematically. The card which the pastor or church member will take with him on visits might look like this one.

Hospital Visitation

Week Beginning _____

Name _____

Hospital _____ Room _____

Date Entered _____

Book Taken _____ by _____

Visitation Check List

| SUN | MON | TUES | WED | THURS | FRI | SAT |

Comments

The secretary, on the other hand, should keep a tally sheet that she checks against the card before and after the visit.

Illness / Hospital Information Sheet

Date	Member	Nature of illness	Location	Call requested by	Date call made	Follow-up needed Yes No

Correspondence

Efficient handling of mail is essential, not only for smoothness of office operation and sanity of employees but also for the ministry's consistent testimony.

Before opening mail, assemble supplies: letter opener, date stamp, pencils, stapler, transparent tape, paper clips, and your Mail Received/To-Do list. There are logical steps to follow in handling incoming mail:

1. Classify and sort
2. Open
3. Remove and inspect contents
4. Stamp with date and time
5. Read and annotate
6. Paper-clip envelope to its own opened letter
7. Present mail to boss
8. Distribute and route mail to proper places and people

You may wonder about two items in particular on the above listing: numbers 4 and 6. All mail should be stamped with date and time received; *the arrival time of certain correspondence has legal significance; the date/time stamp is a safeguard.* Envelopes kept loose from their letters are notorious for getting lost. Although you think you will remember what letter came in which envelope, that's not always the case, and you may thereby lose the writer's return address.

There will be times when the boss is away from the office, and the secretary will have to handle the mail. The efficient way to do so is to use a digest-summary of daily mail. This summary serves two purposes: it provides a control for keeping up with the manner in which mail is handled, and it provides the boss with a digest of incoming mail for quick review upon his return.

As soon as you finish reading the mail, type in information for the first three columns. Pencil in the action taken for each piece of correspondence *as you do it.* The form for this digest might look like this one.

Digest of Daily Mail			
Date	From	Content	Action taken
11/3	Dr. Dewayne Felber	Would like you to speak at the Missions Conference 6/8/85 – Indianapolis, Indiana	*Replied – stating you would send a definite answer on your return.*

If the boss is away for only a day or two, you probably will just set aside all the mail you cannot answer. However, never put away correspondence that should be handled immediately. Call your boss (or have the mail ready when he calls in) to determine how an urgent matter should be handled. Number the items you want to mention. Stack them in that order. During the telephone conversation, mention the most important correspondence first.

Answer first-class letters by saying your boss will be back at a certain time and will then reply. Avoid giving out confidential information about his whereabouts. You should observe several principles when answering letters:

1. *Answer promptly.* Correspondence left for weeks and months frustrates the writer and leaves a sour taste in his mouth about the entire ministry you represent.
2. *Answer neatly.*
   a. Use proper letter forms. Secretarial manuals are commonly available.
   b. Do not send out a letter with strikeovers, erasures, and white-outs.
   c. Do not send out a letter typed with dirty typewriter keys.
3. *Answer carefully.*
   a. Check spelling.
   b. Use proper English construction.
   c. Use proper signature form:
      > Sincerely yours,
      > (*Handwritten signature*)
      > Harold Smith

> *Note:* he does not sign himself "Pastor _____"
> or "Dr. _____."

    d. Avoid listing "credentials"—both in typing and in signature:

> Harold Smith *Ll.D., Th.D., Founder-President, Chairman of the Board . . . etc.*

Appropriate Stationery

Whatever ministry you are a part of, there will be many whose only impression of the ministry is through its correspondence. Use your influence to see that the ministry's stationery makes the best impression possible. Specifically, consider the following:

1. High-quality letter stock (weight and weave of paper)
2. Tasteful letterhead (*Simplicity* is the hallmark of quality.)
   a. Avoidance of pictures (Pictures detract from high-quality appearance.)
   b. Minimal information (Detailed information detracts from tasteful appearance.)

Telephone

Every time an office worker picks up the telephone receiver, she makes a public relations impression—positive or negative. Telephone manner will reveal two things: attitude about self and others; attitude about work. Use good telephoning principles:

1. Answer promptly. An immediate answer communicates efficiency and courtesy.
2. Use proper identification. For instance, "Good morning. Oak Lawn Baptist Church. This is Kim. May I help you?"
3. Speak distinctly and pleasantly. A friendly voice makes friends.
4. Listen attentively.
5. Use the caller's name. If necessary, jot down the name as soon as the caller gives it so that you can use it often.
6. Screen calls tactfully: "May I tell Pastor Smith who is calling?"
7. Help the caller when the person called is unavailable. "Pastor Smith will not be back until later. Perhaps I can help with some information or materials."
8. Be discreet in discussing your boss's whereabouts. "The pastor is out of the office right now, but I will be happy to give him a message when he returns."
9. Transfer calls carefully. No one likes to get the "run-around." Tell where and why you are transferring the call.
10. Take messages accurately.

Typewriters, Telephones, and Technicalities

    a. Keep message forms handy; record details completely.
    b. Request information: "May I have your name, please?"
    c. Always speak or spell back the name and verify any number(s) given.
    d. Include on your message form spaces for complete information.
       (1) Whom the message is for
       (2) Who took the message
       (3) The day and time

11. Never leave a caller wondering. If you must put someone on hold, explain the wait. Give a report after thirty seconds.
12. When placing a call, be sure of the number.
13. Allow enough time for the person to answer (10 rings).
14. Identify yourself immediately. Identify your organization.
15. Plan your call. Have all necessary information ready before placing the call.
16. Speak directly into the mouthpiece. Do not place your hand over the phone or put it under your chin.
17. Hang up gently. Slamming the receiver is as discourteous as slamming the door.
18. Have necessary "tools" at your desk:
    a. Note pad
    b. Pen or pencil
    c. Calendar
    d. Frequently called numbers

It is wise to keep a telephone log. The one for local calls might look like this one.

Telephone Log

Date	Time	Caller	Nature of call	Referred to	Additional information

A long-distance telephone log could be set up this way.

								Direct dial	Collect	Person to person	Connecting time	
Date	Time	Person placing / receiving call	Person / organization called	Name of person talked with (if different)	City / State	Area Code	Telephone number					Charge to

Long-distance Telephone Call Log

Telephone logs can be valuable not only for keeping current in the office but also for checking against telephone bills.

Travel

A final function that may be handled by your office, albeit sporadically, is travel. It is a good idea to use a travel agency. Travel agencies do not charge (except for train reservations). Find an agency you like and work with the same person in that agency each time you have to book a trip. The agency can furnish guidebooks and information about baggage, currency, and other concerns.

In order to make smooth travel arrangements, you need to have certain information:

1. Destination
2. Intermediate stops
3. Dates of departure and return
4. Date and time of the first appointment; overall time requirement for the visit
5. Preferred time of day for travel
6. Method of travel—air, rail, bus, auto
7. Kind of service—first class or coach
8. Hotel preference or desired location within city

9. Need for transportation at the destination and at intermediate stops
10. If car rental is involved, the make of car preferred

You will need to consider the time-zone factor. Crossing time zones demands built-in time for rest.

If the trip is overseas (e.g., to the Holy Land), you will want to be familiar with how to obtain passports and visas and with what is involved in meeting immunization requirements.

Airline reservations must be reconfirmed on international flights. Place a reconfirmation reminder in the traveler's folder. Be sure you are clear on when, where, and how the tickets will be available. Will they be delivered by the travel agent, or must they be picked up? Will they be picked up at the agent's office or at the airline counter?

Make a list of supplies the traveler may need on the trip. Include dried or canned foods, nuts, crackers, and other such items if he is going to a remote area where the food may be unsafe or undesirable.

One good source for travel information is the *Official Airline Guide and Hotel/Motel Guide.*

Conclusion

An office, for whatever type of organization, is a place of business. Efficiency and neatness count for much. But personableness and considerateness add an invaluable "plus." All should characterize every ministry office.

The
Maidservant's
Hazards

Chapter 28

Doors to Destruction

Within the Church Visible, the blood-purchased Bride of Christ is hardly recognizable. Rather than pure and radiant in spotless white, she stands today disheveled, her eyes dull and her gown tattered. The unsaved world looks at, laughs at, and scorns the Bride besmirched. Impurity marks the pew. Worse, it mars the pulpit. In speaking of fallen Israel, Scripture graphically depicts the church today: *"Her priests* have violated my law, and have profaned mine holy things: they have put no difference between the holy and profane, neither have they shewed difference between the unclean and the clean, and have hid their eyes from my sabbaths, and *I am profaned among them"* (Ezek. 22:26).

Contrary to our fond illusions, ministry does not mean immunity. Fundamentalism is no freer of moral tragedies than liberalism. During these years bridging the twentieth and twenty-first centuries, the Enemy has swept away many who were considered stalwarts of the Faith. The writer of Proverbs perfectly stated the threat within the stronghold when he said, "I was almost in all evil in the midst of the congregation and assembly" (Prov. 5:14). Within the "sanctuary" of Christian service, moral and spiritual defeat taints every theological stripe, every type and size of ministry, every age and personality of Christian servant. Almost daily, shameful blots are put upon the name of our lovely Lord Jesus Christ by leaders' shattered testimonies. In this chapter we will focus upon the moral dangers threatening the ministry man and the right response of the married ministry woman to these dangers.

Each of us, man or woman, needs to be reminded that *God's standards for leaders are very high.* That fact is unmistakable both in the Old Testament and in the New. Despite God's clear speaking in the matter, however, His people allow sin to continue and even to flourish in parsonage and pulpit. Three words of the Apostle Paul describe proper leadership living. To the Thessalonians he wrote, recalling his example before them, "Ye are witnesses, and God also, how holily and justly and unblameably we behaved ourselves among you that believe" (I Thess. 2:10). Holy, just, unblameable—Paul not only cited these characteristics as a ministry standard but also *demonstrated* them. How foreign these are to today's scene! Almost daily we witness five specific disasters claiming ministry men.

Imperialism

In direct contradiction of Scripture's spirit and instruction, self-exaltation characterizes a large segment of fundamentalism. At home and abroad, preachers build works and win followers through the magnetism of personality. The "preacher-king" has risen in all his ugliness, displaying an empire mentality that belies the definition of the word *minister—to serve.* In such personality-cult "ministries," God's glory is usurped; His Word is replaced by personal pronouncements; His people are spiritually starved and intimidated into submission to the self-proclaimed guru.

Capitulation

Rather than step onto and over the pulpit in self-exaltation, some flee the ministry's pressures. They do so in several different ways. Many play pulpit hopscotch, jumping into a new "calling" whenever faced with a difficulty. Others capitulate by leaving the *work* of the ministry. They use their domestic or foreign pulpit to camouflage laziness and fat-cat living. Still others leave the ministry entirely. Nearly every profession can point to ex-preacher employees who left the Lord's work through discouragement or sold out for big paychecks and "success" by human standards.

Imbalance

For those who have not watched the ministerial scene closely, imbalance may seem an unlikely item to introduce into a listing of ministerial disasters. Actually, it is *central*: it lies at the root of many other types of defection. All Satan has to do to begin a man's fall is to *get him off balance*. He can then push in any direction to cause the fall.

Ministerial imbalance is "hobbyhorse riding." For whatever reason, a preacher begins to focus upon one tiny item on the great canvas of "the whole counsel of God." He may feel that he has discovered something new or that he alone knows this thing in depth or that he is superior to others because of his emphasis. As a consequence, he narrows his study, concentrating as if with a magnifying glass on that one brush stroke. His vision for and interest in other aspects of the ministry dim. Ultimately, he twists Scripture to fit his pet theory or emphasis. Inevitably, imbalance produces bitterness and mean-spiritedness. Reasonableness and Christian charity fly out the window. Anyone who does not see things *his way* is not only shunned; he is kicked.

A notable hobbyhorse of fundamentalist preachers today is an obsession with the issue of women's dress. Paradoxically it often accompanies in the preacher moral failures of the very sort it condemns. Whether the obsession with immodesty comes first or whether it is adopted afterward hypocritically is hard to say. But repeatedly it happens that the one who sounds most strict and most puristic in his incessant declaiming on behalf of "modesty" and "plainness" in women *is or becomes morally defiled*.

Crookedness

Dishonesty in ministry has become so commonplace that we rarely recognize it in some of its forms: for example, exaggeration of numbers in attendance, conversions, and the like. Rather than hating what God calls lying, those in ministry laugh off their inflated reports as true "evangelistically speaking."

Crookedness often goes along with the imperialistic approach to ministry. Bigger and bigger buildings must be put up, for instance, at the expense of putting the congregation under a killing load of debt, which is smiled away as the "visionary" leader promises Christ's return to rescue them from pay back!

Among ministerial crooks are those who engage in outright thievery. They see to it that they alone handle the ministry finances. They thus are able to juggle accounts, divert funds, and even withdraw all the ministry's money and abscond.

Sexual Immorality

This is probably the disaster that first comes to our minds when we think of moral failures in today's ministry. Sexual immorality is racing like wildfire through fundamentalist circles. There is every imaginable degree of involvement: from a single incident to keeping a harem-sized stable of women to visiting prostitutes all over the world. Its duration runs from a one-night experience to an involvement of many years. Its extent varies from an unintentional fall to thirty years of double identity.

Suddenness

Whatever disaster overtakes the Christian leader, we who see and shudder at the blemish on God's holy name are prone to exclaim, "What happened? So-and-so was such a fine man, such a strong preacher. How could his fall have come about so *suddenly?*" It is imperative to realize that *it did not happen suddenly.* All along the path leading to the pit were signposts that might have been recognized and heeded. There were symptoms of spiritual malaise before sin's sickness revealed itself as cancer.

Men and women in intermittent contact with the fallen leader could conceivably remain unaware of the warning signs. *But where was his wife?* Where were the godly women (secretaries, Sunday school teachers, etc.) whose daily intake of Scripture and control by the Holy Spirit should have activated the "radar" of intuition and motivated their intense, specific prayer?

The histories of ministerial disasters show eight outstanding danger signals. They appear in various combinations and degrees but with remarkable consistency.

Deflection

Probably the most incomprehensible fact about preachers, missionaries, and other Christian leaders who have experienced moral disaster is that these are men who have handled the Word of God on a daily basis. But let's remember that each of us chooses *how* we handle and respond to Scripture. It's possible that a person might memorize the entire Bible without its affecting his life. He could do so by, and only by, his ability to *deflect* its message. Bible study can become study for study's sake. Scripture can be appropriated as a club for battering others. Bible-toting, Bible-quoting Christians can be spiritual pygmies. Head knowledge does not necessarily imply heart knowledge.

An outstanding example of Scripture deflection occurred in the spring and summer of 1988, when an influential expounder of biblical detail proclaimed that Jesus Christ would return in September of that year. Understandably, some infant and fringe Christians fell for the ballyhoo. Tragically, there were also preachers—*fundamentalist* preachers—who did likewise! Obviously, they had not been heeding the Word they had been preaching, which states plainly that it is not for Christ's disciples "to know the times or the seasons" of His return in power and glory (Acts 1:7).

Rigidity

Each of us has opinions and viewpoints. Some statements in the Word of God allow for no variation of interpretation—for instance, the fact of Jesus Christ's virgin birth. But there also are a great many matters of sincere belief wherein the Lord allows room for different viewpoints. He does not intend that all believers *walk lock step.* Here is where some preachers part company with God. They demand that their hearers hew to the line of *their* opinion or doctrinal slant to the minutest detail.

The rigid person is humorless. He acts as if smiling is a minor sin and laughter unforgivable. All of life is serious, serious, serious. Every molehill becomes a mountain. He does not enjoy the blessings of life, and he resents those who do. He, above all, takes *himself* seriously. As a consequence, he is unreasonable in his relationships. Dr. Bob Jones, Sr., used to say, "A good man is always a *reasonable* man." Experience confirms that chronically unreasonable men are men whose rigidity disguises deep character flaws.

Private discourtesy

The necessary distance a leader maintains between himself and his flock might allow the congregation to perceive a midget as a giant in the spiritual sense. But his wife and children know his true stature. Blessed indeed is the woman married to a man whose walk matches his words. Tragically, many pulpits are occupied by men holy in public but cruelly harsh in private. Those men are actors playing a role. God's Word demands that leadership positions be accredited by consistent living.

Imitation and ambition

Some men in ministry are not willing to be themselves. They consciously or unconsciously mimic the voice, gesture, and personal style of someone else. Unwillingness to be an individual bespeaks insecurity. It also may indicate ambition: the mimic takes on the trappings of someone he considers successful. There are segments of fundamentalism in which all the preachers look and sound the same: in vocal inflection, pronunciation, volume usage, even stance and mannerisms. It is interesting that the Apostle Paul admonished the young preacher Timothy to "stir up the gift of God, *which is in thee*" (II Tim. 1:6).

Questionable ethics

Christian leadership rightly challenges followers to live honestly, even in the smallest things. Unhappily, almost anyone over the age of ten can recall disappointment because of unethical leaders. The leader's shortcomings may be in what are generally considered "small" things: making up excuses, asking a son or daughter to tell a caller he's not in, ignoring speed limits, cheating on income tax. A friend of the Joneses tells of his awakening to ministerial realities when he established his own business. Time after time when he tried to collect money from a preacher he was assured, "The check's in the mail!" When the payment very belatedly arrived, the date on the check was days, weeks, even months beyond the time it was said to have been sent.

Beneth personally witnessed a heartbreaking example of ministerial lack of ethics. In the course of an out-of-town seminar for pastors and their wives, she took a rest room break, walking past the bank of pay telephones. Standing talking on one of those phones, with his back to her, was a well-known preacher. As she passed, the preacher was saying into the telephone, "I'm really sorry I won't be able to keep that 2:00 appointment with you. I didn't realize this seminar would run all afternoon. I'm going to be tied up here in the meeting until evening.'' On the way back to Greenville, Beneth happened to mention the incident to her husband. He responded with shock and disappointment: ''He was *breaking* his two o'clock appointment? He told me he'd have to slip out and miss the rest of the afternoon meetings with us *because he had to keep a 2:00 appointment!*''

Weariness

The Christian life is a battle, and the Christian ministry is the hottest part of it. Any one of us can court physical exhaustion by overcommitment. Because we are such marvelously integrated beings, damage to or weakness in one part of our nature can affect the rest. So it is that the body's weariness can impair the mind's clarity and the spirit's strength.

There is also weariness from the battle itself. As we move closer to Christ's return, the intensifying spiritual warfare can so wear upon a leader that he yearns to forsake the hot spot of leadership. Sometimes the most spiritual advice a preacher's or missionary's wife can give her husband is to urge that he rest.

Conceit

Satan never tires of using the weapon of pride. A man whose church grows quickly may lose sight of the fact that the growth— whatever is substantial about it—is God's doing. And so he talks more and more of the ''I'' he credits for it all. Added to that is the heady stuff of publicity and the admiration of ''underlings.''

Careless counseling

Personal counseling probably has been the single most successful stage for the Devil's triumphs in sexual immorality. The danger lies not in counseling *per se,* but in its manner, setting, and frequency.

Wives need to recognize their husbands' sexual vulnerability. The time is long gone, if it ever existed, when we could naively assume our husband's automatic, unfaltering, exclusive attraction to us alone. Recognition in turn demands responsive and responsible wifing: keeping his emotional-need tank full at home and hedging him about with consistent, specific prayer when he's away from home.

Ideally, older women should counsel younger women—the plan given in the Bible (Tit. 2:3-4). When it becomes necessary for a preacher to counsel a woman, there need to be *definite safeguards* in place:

- The preacher's wife should be present whenever possible.
- When she is not available, the counseling should take place within the ministry building, and only when another person is present and clearly visible.
- The office door *should not be shut* during a counseling session unless a window allows the office interior to be seen at all times.
- Man-woman counseling should be a once-or-twice-only thing. If the counselee seeks more sessions, she should be referred to the preacher's wife or another woman counselor.

Response to Danger Signals

While she is not ultimately responsible for her husband's moral and spiritual safety, a wife nevertheless is *his first line of defense humanly speaking*. Three *R*'s should come into play when and if a wife becomes convinced the Devil is making headway against her husband:

Realism. When evidence of her husband's moral decline starts to accumulate, a ministry wife must cast aside naiveté and wishful thinking. Scripture repeatedly urges us to vigilance and discernment.

Restraint. The spiritual devastation taking place throughout the ranks of professing Christians demands awareness. Awareness, however, must not become panic. When dealing with the subject in seminars, Beneth always urges her listeners, "Now don't sit in the car on the way home from the seminar and snap at your husband, 'Okay, you'd better be mighty careful from now on, 'cause I'm gonna be watching you!' " We need a godly balance between watchfulness and trust.

Righteousness. It is not our own "righteousness" that sits in judgment upon an erring husband, but the righteousness of God. We must accept and apply the viewpoint of Scripture. One of the many passages dealing with profane priests ends with these words: "So shalt thou put the evil away from the midst of thee" (Deut. 13:5). Irrefutable evidence of a man's disqualification for ministry should be met by the following of the biblical procedure of Matthew 18:15-17. We must not conceal, and thereby abet, a husband's unrepented sin.

Not long ago a missionary family was removed from their field of service; the wife had discovered—and revealed to their mission board—her husband's adultery with a native woman. When he stood before his commissioning church, the man told the congregation that his wife had done exactly the right thing; her silence would have betrayed the people and churches supporting them, extended the disgracing of God's name, and abetted his sin.

Finally, a wife must also be sure that she is herself genuinely spiritual in her motivations and responses, demonstrating the combination of serpent's wisdom and dove's harmlessness. She must respond prayerfully, taking the whole matter to the Lord at every point and stage, considering her obligations to her husband, to the situation, to the other people involved, to herself, and preeminently to God.

Doors to destruction—they yawn open on every side for the ministry man. But let us take heart, turning minds and hearts from the darkness of that dismal region to the light of God's Word: "Greater is he that is in you, than he that is in the world" (I John 4:4).

Chapter 29

Vulnerability—Vanquished or Victorious?

Having dealt with the dangers threatening men in ministry, let us move on now to consider those that loom over women in full-time Christian service. Neither of these problem areas is a subject we would choose to deal with. But because of our Arch-enemy's intense, determined attack, we cannot hesitate to sound a warning. We must warn with clarity and emphasis, "For if the trumpet give an uncertain sound, who shall prepare himself to the battle?" (I Cor. 14:8). It is the hearer's part not to generalize the warning or divert it to others but rather to personalize each part, realizing that *not one of us is invulnerable*.

Our Entity

Against what is the satanic assault directed? Against the self of each of us—the entire being. We have already noted the good creation God has wrought in making us tripartite beings, with each part intertwined with and closely affecting the others. Honesty compels us to admit that we fall short of what God would have us do and be in body, mind, and soul. How accurate the cry of the psalmist in Psalm 73:26: "My flesh and my heart faileth; but God is the strength of my heart, and my portion for ever."

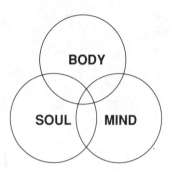

Knowing our frailty, the Devil pressures each part of our being. Our Body he attacks with the *lust of the flesh;* our Mind he batters with the *lust of the eyes;* our Soul he bombards with the *pride of life*. His intention is to wreak destruction in one or every human function, and no part of this self is off bounds, no weapon in his arsenal reserved by pity. Whatever the age, experience, location, personality, or type of ministry, *we are each vulnerable*. Any sense of sufficiency or invulnerability is sharply rebuked by I Corinthians 10:12: "Wherefore let him that thinketh he standeth take heed lest he fall."

Our Enterprise

The Maidservant has a clearly defined enterprise: service for the God of glory. We're aware that this is a special task, a privilege. We are taking the light of the gospel into sin's darkness. But is the Devil impressed with this pygmy self involved in service? Is he scared off by my ministry endeavor, preferring to attack someone who is less strongly fortified? Not for a moment. In fact, just the opposite is true: we who serve the Lord in a full-time capacity are objects of special satanic hatred. He particularly delights to lure the ministry woman—married or single—into sexual immorality. Yes—you, me. It seems easier for us women to recognize the susceptibility of *men* to such an attack than to realize or admit that we ourselves also are frighteningly vulnerable.

Our Enemy

We know that our enemy is Satan. We know that he sends against us "fiery darts." But what are these arrows? Exactly how does the Devil attack when he tries to tip or trip us into sexual impurity? There are four arrows he uses regularly.

Arrow #1—*Playboy philosophy.* The bold, gross, constant, glamorized exaltation of sex is all-pervasive in modern American society. Sex is a constant focal point in the media. It is used to sell almost everything. Its discussion appears in the most unlikely places. It is included gratuitously in anything and everything.

The problem is that we Christians are being more strongly affected by the bombardment than we care to admit. Some time ago a letter was sent out by a preacher appealing to other preachers to send financial help toward righting a certain minister's "mistake." The "mistake" referred to was a thirty-year history of persistent whoremongering! This is the *leadership*—Christian leadership—that is supposed to be resistant to such temptation! Christian teen-age girls will say without a qualm, "Oh, I'm not a virgin. . . ." Christian mothers allow their daughters to begin dating at a ridiculously early age. They push them to be "popular," assuming to themselves and implying to the girls that the cost may be virginity. On and on the sad examples go—indications of decay within the body of Christ's bride. How it must reek in the nostrils of our holy God!

Arrow #2—*Professional pressures.* We in Christian ministry need to recognize that the calling has facets which, if allowed to do so, can open the way to sexual immorality. As mentioned earlier, there is a certain degree of isolation in ministry, especially on the foreign mission field. Women are particularly sensitive to that isolation, whether it be underlined by singleness, by locale, or by the husband's need to be available day or night to members of the flock.

Dashed expectations may be used of Satan to weaken a woman's defenses. Dreams of the ministry seldom resemble actuality. The missionary, for instance, may be jolted and disappointed by the contrast between the commissioning service's thrills and the mission service's *toils.* A depressing type and location of ministry may be an irritant. Or the always-tight finances of ministry life may grind a woman's resistance to powder.

Arrow #3—*Paraded pleasures.* God's Word makes it clear that there are worldly pleasures that can draw us from God (Luke 8:14; II Tim. 3:4). The Devil sees to it that they are dangled before the eyes of each person in Christian ministry: expensive boats, cars, clothes; exotic vacations; gorgeous homes, and so on.

There is also the constant, nagging awareness that the great majority of Christians are almost totally self-indulgent. Satan directs our eyes to them and queries, "Why are you knocking yourself out in full-time service while everybody else just sits back and enjoys life's good things?"

Arrow #4—*Personal perturbations.* Besides the general means of attack against all ministry women as mentioned above, Satan also zeroes in upon the weaknesses inherent in our individual personalities. Each personality has its specific frailties as well as strengths, which the Devil well knows and gleefully uses to trip us.

Background may be a chink in the armor. Painful *dones* or aching *undones* from the past provide our enemy with a tender target.

Legitimate feminine needs are yet another place favored for attack: the innate longing for security, affirmation, attention, sexual fulfillment.

What is it, exactly, that the Devil wants to destroy in my life and yours, Maidservant? The answer is simple: everything. *What better way to do it than to plunge us into sexual immorality?* Tirelessly, analytically, the Devil chooses his arrows, tips them with the poison of his God-hatred, aims carefully, watches closely, listens intently—then lets fly.

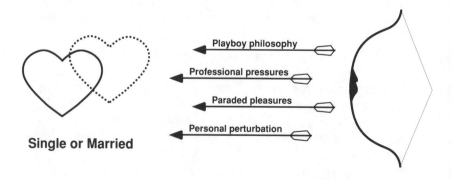

Single or Married

Playboy philosophy

Professional pressures

Paraded pleasures

Personal perturbation

Our Engagement

What should be our response to satanic attack upon us? We are to stand, shielded. To stand is to hold fast our position, to bring our own best efforts to bear at the same time we rely upon God's presence and power. To do so is to activate the scriptural principle of being workers together with God. To be *shielded* is to be protected by that shield of faith urged upon us in Ephesians 5. The shield obviously does not float, cloudlike, before us. It must be gripped firmly in wisdom's hand. Note that the shield has four strong props necessary to its effectiveness.

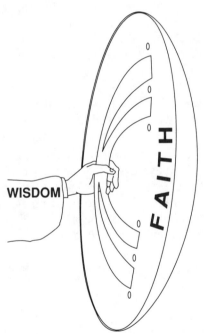

Prop #1—*My will in daily commitment.* Each day we must individually determine to obey God. Obedience to God requires knowing the Word of God. Joshua recognized this necessity when he commanded Israel: "This book of the law shall not depart out of thy mouth; but thou shalt meditate therein day and night, that thou mayest observe to do according to all that is written therein: for then thou shalt make thy way prosperous, and then thou shalt have good success'' (Josh. 1:8). Only by consistent, persistent obedience can we successfully live and lead. Our daily commitment must be to serve our all-holy God *acceptably.* There actually are Christian women who have been lured into adultery on the premise that their sexual favors ''minister'' to the preacher-enticer!

Prop #2—*My heart in daily communication.* We have already noted the ease with which a Maidservant can skip or skimp on her personal devotions. But again we must emphasize the centrality of that personal relationship with God. Each day we must *listen* to the Lord—read and study His Word, allowing it to probe and speak to our every weakness. We must, too, daily *lean* upon Him, like the Apostle John, drawing as close to Jesus Christ as we can (John 13:33). Memorization of and meditation upon Scripture is a wonderful means of leaning on His breast. And, finally, each day we must *live* in ongoing communication: that is, performing all of our outward service with our inward self on its knees. That humble, loving, petitioning position of heart will result in genuine reverence and worship. It will reveal itself in the quality both of our ministry and of our music.

Prop #3—*My mind in daily caution.* We who are mothers know how repeatedly we caution and instruct our children with protective advice. God expresses the same concern for us in the words of Paul: ''But I fear, lest by any means, as the serpent beguiled Eve through his subtilty, so your minds should be corrupted from the simplicity that is in Christ'' (II Cor. 11:3). There is much of Eve within each of us women, and her better part is weaker now than it was in the Garden. Our minds must be constantly analyzing people and situations for possible danger. As in our childhood, we need to

> stop . . .
> look . . .
>   listen . . .

before committing ourselves to any direction or action.

An admission that may be abhorrent to the Maidservant is that there *are men around her who are attractive.* That is true whether she is married or single. It is true whether she is in New York City or New Guinea. Furthermore, it is true that any of those men could become a growing attraction if she allowed it. The consequence is that every extramarital man-woman relationship needs to be bound with impenetrable thorn hedging *from the outset.* The extent and type of hedging must be carefully, prayerfully chosen.

Beneth has a lovely friend who, after moving to a new town, entered a bank to open an account. When ushered into the office of the vice president, she found him to be one of the most handsome men she had ever seen, and she was shocked by the strong surge of emotion she—a happily married Christian woman—felt. Moreover, the man's demeanor and voice betrayed the fact that the attraction was mutual. Because her mind was exercising daily spiritual caution, *she walked out of the bank, deciding against placing an account there, and further, determining never to enter the building again.*

Extreme, you say? Not at all. This incident represents the kind of prudence God desires in each of us. Prudence will also recognize that man-woman attractions are of different types. Like that bank executive, one man may be magnetic through sheer physical beauty, another in charm of personality, yet another by his compassionate spirit. Satan will see to it that the *type of attraction coincides with the specific need of the moment.*

Prop #4—*My body in daily construction.* The Apostle Paul wrote, "I keep under my body" (I Cor. 9:27). He meant that he disciplined his physical self for the sake of enhancing his mental, emotional, and spiritual discipline. We need to do the same—in four specific areas.

First, we need to endure the discipline of exercise. The activity of housework doesn't count. Calisthenics, aerobics, and flexibility exercises should be part of our daily routine.

Second, we need to undertake the discipline of temperance: control of our food intake and sensible attention to our physical appearance.

Third, we must allow the discipline of rest. The tired woman is a *vulnerable* woman. It was His closest, busiest disciples that Jesus several times took "aside" to rest.

Fourth, we must accept the discipline of obedience in the sexual realm. This discipline applies to the Maidservant whether she is married or single. The married woman must obey God's command against defrauding her husband or herself sexually. Husband and wife should enjoy the God-designed fulfillment of one another's bodies regularly and frequently. The single Christian worker must put this desire on the altar, making it a part of her "living sacrifice," *trusting* her heavenly Father to be doing all things well. She needs resolutely to redirect the energies ordinarily expended in sexual fulfillment by avoiding romantic stories, by engaging in strenuous physical activities, by cultivating warm Christian friendships with other women and families, by giving of herself to nurture the growth of spiritual babes.

The bowshots of Satan's attack against our moral purity, frightening and unrelenting though they may be, nevertheless do not automatically spell our defeat. Even in this extremely vulnerable area of our frail selves, we can, through Jesus Christ, be *more* than conquerors. As it is said of Joseph, so too one day may it be said of us: "Joseph is a fruitful bough, even a fruitful bough by a well; whose branches run over the wall: The archers have sorely grieved him, and shot at him, and hated him: But his bow abode in strength, *and the arms of his hands were made strong by the hands of the mighty God of Jacob*" (Gen. 49:22-24).

Indeed our success is assured if we lean upon Christ and allow Him to share with us His triumph over sin. Paul reminds us of the source of our strength: "For though we walk in the flesh, we do not war after the flesh" (II Cor. 10:3). He promises victory in the struggle:

> But thanks be to God, which giveth us the victory through our Lord Jesus Christ. Therefore, my beloved brethren, be ye stedfast, unmoveable, always abounding in the work of the Lord, forasmuch as ye know that your labour is not in vain in the Lord (I Cor. 15:57-58).

A Final Word

We women who have been entrusted with full-time Christian service are exceedingly rich: rich in opportunity, rich in privilege. May we always be excited about and grateful for God's entrusting ministry to us! May we lean upon those blessed Everlasting Arms each moment for the strength that demonstrates itself in our weakness. May we faithfully maintain a service wherein all that is outward springs from a heart clean before God, empty of self, and loving toward others. May the precepts we teach to others be lived out in ourselves. May we focus eyes and hearts upon those things that lie beyond any present pressures. May we draw strength and purpose from that wonderful benediction that closes the First Epistle of Peter:

> But the God of all grace, who hath called us unto his eternal glory by Christ Jesus, after that ye have suffered a while, make you perfect, stablish, strengthen, settle you. To him be glory and dominion for ever and ever.
>
> Amen.